First published by Carlton Books Ltd 2012

Copyright © Carlton Books Ltd 2012

Carlton Books Ltd
20 Mortimer Street
London W1T 3JW
www.carltonbooks.co.uk

Contributing writer: Chris Hatherall

Senior Editor: Conor Kilgallon
Design direction: Darren Jordan
Designer: Ben Ruocco
Picture research: Paul Langan
Production Manager: Maria Petalidou

A CIP catalogue record for this book is available from the British
Library.

10 9 8 7 6 5 4 3 2 1

ISBN 978-1-78097-095-0

Printed and bound in Dubai

THE RYDER CUP

THE COMPLETE HISTORY OF
GOLF'S GREATEST COMPETITION

FOREWORD BY **TONY JACKLIN** CBE

NICK CALLOW

CARLTON

Contents

OPPOSITE: *The Ryder Cup is one of the most iconic trophies in world sport. It stands 17 inches (43 cm) high and weighs 4 lbs (1.8 kg). The golfer on the lid is Abe Mitchell, Samuel Ryder's coach and golfing mentor, who played for Great Britain in 1929, 1931 and 1933.*

Foreword

Golf has been my passion since I can remember and turning professional in 1962 was a very proud moment for me. It was the culmination of years of dedication, laced with a lot of fun along the way. The game has taken me all over the world and I have been lucky to play in all the great tournaments against some of the finest golfers of all time.

I took part in my first Major – The Open – in 1963. Just standing on the first tee was such a thrill – with over a century of history behind it, being involved in that kind of competition was exactly what I had always dreamed of. That dream then turned into beautiful reality in 1969 when I had the pleasure of lifting the Claret Jug myself. The following year was just as special when I had the honour of winning the US Open.

As well as the competitive side of golf, the game has a set of principles that have always meant a lot to me. Its good grace, sportsmanship and integrity have made it a beacon among sports. Nowhere is this epitomized more than in the Ryder Cup, as I personally experienced in 1969 when Jack Nicklaus famously conceded my final putt, which resulted in the tournament being tied. Samuel Ryder, the Englishman who started this unique competition back in 1927, was very keen that the Cup that bears his name should be contested in the right spirit. That moment in 1969 would have made him proud.

But this does not mean that the Ryder Cup is a friendly exhibition match – far from it. It has always been played with an intense competitiveness that has captured the imagination of players and fans alike, who turn up in their tens of thousands to see the best players from both sides of the Atlantic go head-to-head. But at the end of the competition, win or lose, the players should always be able to raise a glass or two together.

I'm proud to say that I've been a player on what is now the European Ryder Cup team on seven occasions. The tension, drama and atmosphere of each of those Cups will live with me forever but my time as captain stands out. It was my great privilege to be the four-time captain who broke the American stranglehold on the competition in the mid-1980s. As if the European win in 1985 – its first since 1957 – wasn't momentous enough, the 1987 event was even more special as Europe won the Cup on US soil for the first time ever. I'm delighted to say that those wins, plus retaining the Cup in 1989, contributed to reigniting the Ryder Cup as a hotly contested event, one that is obviously still fiercely fought over today.

So I hope you enjoy reading about all the Ryder Cups in this book – the stories, titanic tussles and endless talking points make this a fascinating read.

Tony Jacklin CBE

OPPOSITE: *Tony Jacklin, captain of the European team, celebrates winning the 27th Ryder Cup in September 1987 at Muirfield Village, Ohio, USA.*

There's something unique about the Ryder Cup, something that lifts it above other sporting occasions, that almost defies explanation. Maybe it's the unique team-play format. Or maybe it's the "us-versus-them" aspect of a game more usually associated with individual play that resonates so loudly over three tense, action-packed days. But whatever the reason, the end result is something truly special.

IT'S NOT EASY TO SUM UP what the Ryder Cup means to those who follow it avidly or to explain why the competition resonates so profoundly with the players themselves but over the next seven chapters, in which the story of golf's greatest team competition from its earliest beginnings in England to the high-octane drama of the current era will be recounted, the essence of one of the world's most remarkable sporting battles will surely start to embrace anyone who comes into contact with it, too.

Of course, every golf fan has his or her own theory about what makes the Ryder Cup so unique. Perhaps it's the fact that in this modern, materialistic world, the competition generates such immense passion and drama, even though there is nothing more than a golden trophy at stake - the players, teams and PGAs receive no revenue whatsoever for lifting it. Maybe it's because it combines individual head-to-head battles so easily with team play and team spirit or could it be the interaction of the crowd, who get closer to both the action and their heroes than in almost any other sporting event? But whatever the reason the Ryder Cup can justly claim to be right up there with the most iconic sporting trophies in the world.

When the world's greatest golfers step out onto the 1st tee on the first day of each Ryder Cup, chills run down the spines of each and every one of them – even superstars such as Tiger Woods or Sergio García, who have been there and done it many times before. Those involved in future Ryder Cups will be following in the footsteps of some of the finest golfers ever seen, men like Arnold Palmer, Nick Faldo, Jack Nicklaus, Seve Ballesteros, Tom Watson, Colin Montgomerie, Tiger Woods, Tony Jacklin... the list reads like a Who's Who of golfing legends.

But the modern superstars already have an aura of their own: players like Graeme McDowell, who hit the winning putt for Europe at Celtic Manor in 2010, or his fellow Northern Irishman Rory McIlroy, who many see as the new Tiger Woods; even the USA's own young contender, Rickie Fowler, who was just 21 when he performed so well in the 2010 event. These young players have much to live up to because as the years go by, the Ryder Cup has generated so many memorable moments and simply grows in popularity and intensity.

There was a time in the post-war period that the US was so dominant against Great Britain (almost always winning the trophy, often by large margins) that the future of the event as a properly competitive match was in jeopardy, but this is no longer the case. Since the Great Britain team first opened up to include players from the Irish Republic, then players from all over continental Europe in 1979, matches have become increasingly competitive and passionate. That newfound competitiveness has its roots in a pulsating history that includes so many iconic tussles – for example, the "War on the Shore" at Kiawah Island in 1991, when controversy reigned on the back of Gulf War symbolism; the Battle of Brookline in 1999 when the US came from 16-10 down to win on the final day in controversial but dramatic fashion. But the true spirit of the Ryder Cup is still the cornerstone of the whole event, shown most clearly of all by "The Concession" of 1969, when Jack Nicklaus conceded a putt to Tony Jacklin that saw the Cup tied.

These are just some of the moments that have built the Ryder Cup and today it ranks among the greatest, and most eagerly anticipated, sporting contests in the world. Not bad for a tournament that began in the mid-1920s with a round of golf and sandwiches at the Wentworth course in England. This book tells the whole story of every Ryder Cup – a story that gets richer and more compelling with every tournament.

BELOW (l to r): *Ryder Cup legends: Abe Mitchell and Samuel Ryder; Jack Nicklaus and Tom Watson (crouching); José María Olazábal and Severiano Ballesteros; Phil Mickelson and Tiger Woods.*

The Great Britain and USA teams pose with the Ryder Cup in 1929. Samuel Ryder (front centre, with moustache) is flanked by Britain's George Duncan (left, with the Cup) and the USA's Walter Hagen (right, arms folded).

The Ryder Cup is one of the most highly anticipated and intensely hyped sporting events on earth, but it hasn't always been this way. The story begins more than 90 years ago with a gentle exhibition match, the brainchild of an English businessman who was determined to see his idea take root.

A New Competition

The two key facts that any fan of the Ryder Cup often knows are that English merchant Samuel Ryder founded the competition and the very first one was staged in 1927. But what if both those assumptions were wrong or told only half the story? For golf historians, the debate surrounding the origins of one of sport's most iconic competitions still lives on.

ENGLISH BUSINESSMAN, BENEFACTOR and social riser Samuel Ryder, who donated the trophy and worked tirelessly to see the competition introduced, has become synonymous with the most prestigious team tournament in golf and one of the world's biggest sporting occasions. Indeed, his name still adorns the trophy and is recognized by golf fans across the globe – even though he himself was never a professional golfer and only came to the game late in life at the age of 50 at the suggestion of his church minister, after giving up cricket.

It's down to Ryder that the competition still exists in largely the same format as it began and maybe this too generates the kind of friendly rivalry and bonhomie between players that makes golf so different from other sports. In fact, to this day you'll hear players and commentators talk about "honouring the spirit of Sam Ryder" whenever putts are conceded or fair play is adhered to. In short, there's no doubt that Ryder is the Cup's founding father and without his investment, enthusiasm and support, this celebrated event would never have taken off. But was it necessarily his vision that created the competition in the first place? After all, for several years there had been talk of a Great Britain v USA tournament before Samuel Ryder took up his new interest and at least two other characters can claim to have played a part in the origins of the format.

In America, Ohio businessman Sylvanus P. Jermain encouraged English professionals Harry Vardon and Edward Ray to compete in the 1920 US Open at his home course of Inverness, and many regard him as the man who sparked the competition to life. Jermain believed in the worldwide appeal of golf and in an annual play-off between British and American professionals; reports suggest Walter Ross, president of the Nickel Plate Railroad Company in Cleveland, offered to pay for a trophy to kick-start the competition. So, if events had turned out differently, we might have been looking forward to the Ross Cup or the Jermain Trophy at the Medinah Country Club in Illinois, 2012.

ABOVE: *A map outlining the design of the newly opened King's Course at Gleneagles, designed by James Braid, that staged the first Great Britain v USA match in 1921.*

It could just as easily have been the Harnett Cup, too, because the circulation manager of *Golf Illustrated* magazine, James Harnett, played a major role in making the Ryder Cup what it is today. Encouraged by support from Walter Hagen, possibly the greatest American golfer of his time and a player who would later win the British Open, Harnett began raising the finance to send a representative team of US golfers across the Atlantic to compete in a challenge match. In the end he couldn't quite achieve his goal, but the resulting publicity generated by the venture was crucial in opening up future possibilities for the expansion of the game. It proved there was an appetite for the venture among the golfing public and when the Professional Golfers' Association discussed the prospect, it proposed to advance Harnett enough money to finally make it happen.

At this stage, the only barrier was the opposition of PGA president John Mackie who, rightly with hindsight, disapproved of plans to fill the team with British professionals working in America in a bid to make the tournament more competitive (the suggestion being at this early stage in the game's history, US professionals were unlikely to make an impact). Mackie approved the motion only after a rule change was agreed, requiring players to have lived in the USA for at least five years before they could qualify for the American team. An important decision in the history of the Ryder Cup, it underlined an intention to create not just an exhibition match but also a serious and passionate competition between rival countries. And anyone lucky enough to have attended a Ryder Cup in the modern era – there were 35,000 fans on course at Celtic Manor in 2010 to witness Europe's narrow victory – will testify patriotic fervour only adds to the spectacle and importance of the occasion.

The first Britain v USA match was scheduled for June 6, 1921 on the King's Course at Gleneagles, Scotland. Suddenly the early seeds of the Ryder Cup were being sown, even though it would be another six years before the event really came to fruition. At this stage no one could have predicted the format would become so successful, so important, nor indeed, so loved, but on both sides of the Atlantic, a vision was now in place and was about to be realized.

RIGHT: *Sylvanus P. Jermain (right) was first to promote a Great Britain v USA match. Left is US golfer Bobby Jones.*

THE GLORY GAME

It may be some 86 years since its inception but the Ryder Cup has stayed true to its early values and one feature makes the competition stand out from almost every other major sporting event in the twenty-first century: no financial reward is offered. Indeed, profits from the tournament are split between the relevant PGAs, with much of it spent on development or charity projects. But the match itself is for glory only and there is no prize fund.

Crossing the Atlantic

When a team of American golfers – you could even call them the first Ryder Cup combatants, even if at this stage there was still no Cup to play for – arrived in Southampton, in 1921, there must have been a real sense of expectation and excitement. They would have little idea just what pioneers they would prove to be, especially when not everything went to plan. Having crossed the Atlantic by boat, America's top golfers faced the long trek to Scotland by sleeper train and one can only imagine just how tired they must have been after finally ending up in Perthshire. These days, of course, the Ryder Cup is regarded as glamorous and prestigious – the very pinnacle of sport. But the Americans arrived in Scotland to find that they were to sleep in five converted train carriages shunted into the sidings of a local train station. The sight of the US golfing greats fetching and carrying their own water would no doubt leave some of today's professionals wincing, but this is where it all began: six years before the first Ryder Cup officially took place.

The British team that day was filled with talent, including six-time Open champion Harry Vardon, James Braid, Ted Ray and Abe Mitchell. With Josh Taylor, James Ockendon, James Sherlock, Arthur Havers and George Duncan also selected, the home side were strong favourites for a match that strangely seemed to generate little enthusiasm, just weeks after Britain had lost 9-3 to the USA in an amateur competition at Royal Liverpool. It was also played 24 hours after the end of the prestigious *Glasgow Herald* 1000 Guineas, won by George Duncan, and therefore took place in front of a sparse crowd, who would have had no idea they were watching history in the making. Compare this to the scenes at Celtic Manor in Wales (2010), when a weekly total of 244,000 enthusiastic fans paid to watch Europe's memorable victory over a US team that included some of the legends of modern golf, among them Tiger Woods and Phil Mickelson.

POOR SHOW

American golfer Walter Hagen may have played a major role in the birth of the Ryder Cup, but professional golfers were not always treated so well in England. At the British Open of 1920, Hagen was forced to hire a Pierce-Arrow motor car to serve as his personal dressing room after being refused entry to the clubhouse dressing room.

LEFT: *Stylish American golfer Walter Hagen, a big character and a big influence on the growth of the Ryder Cup.*

RIGHT: *The British team that faced the USA at Gleneagles in 1921.*

The Americans of 1921 were not quite so well known and certainly not in Britain, where even two-times US Open winner Hagen was not yet a household name, although the crowd would have at least recognized Scottish exiles, Jock Hutchinson and Fred McLeod. Captained by Emmett French, the team also included virtual unknowns Clarence Hackney and Bill Mehlhorn – a real character who wore cowboy hats on course and was naturally nicknamed "Wild Bill". Wild Bill went on to play in the first Ryder Cup in 1927 and became a real favourite with the galleries long before Thomas Brent "Boo" Weekley famously "rode" down the fairway using his golf club as a horse during the 2008 Ryder Cup. At this stage he was hardly a legend with fans in Scotland and it came as no surprise to see the British trounce their visitors 9-3 in what proved to be a somewhat unheralded sideshow.

The players were presented with gold medals, courtesy of the *Herald*, but the match turned out to be such a walkover that even the home newspaper was scarcely filled with pieces calling for the competition to become a regular event. Stories of the US Ambassador driving up from London for the presentations only to make a hasty exit after learning his team had been trounced suggest no political will for the format, either. To their frustration, Harnett and Hagen's great vision of a regular Britain v USA tournament appeared doomed for hardly anyone had turned up to watch, the players barely socialized together and the British press seemed to have taken an instant dislike to the notion. But looking back, it's almost as if the Ryder Cup was destined to survive for over the next few years the competition between British and American golfers increased steadily, while the debate over which country's players were the stronger grew ever more intense.

Hagen certainly played a part, returning to Britain to win The Open in 1922 and 1924, with Britain's Arthur Havers securing the title in between after George Duncan won in 1920. Suddenly golf's greatest prize was being shared between two nations and all the fans wanted to know was: who would win in a play-off?

Ryder Cup legends
Samuel **RYDER**

In early twentieth-century England, Samuel Ryder was an enormously successful businessman. He was well thought of in civic circles and a generous benefactor in his local community, but his life – and the lives of so many others – was changed from the moment a friend suggested he should take up golf.

OPPOSITE: *Samuel Ryder and his daughter Joan wave off the British team that travelled to America for the first ever Ryder Cup in 1927.*

Most people have heard of the Ryder Cup, but how many of them would be able to tell you who it was that the competition is named after? In fact, the man whose name graces the coveted trophy was an English entrepreneur and businessman, who made his fortune selling packets of "penny" seeds. Generous though he undoubtedly was, and successful as he became, the memory of Samuel would surely not have endured until today, had a friend not handed him a piece of casual advice in 1908.

Having gone through a period of illness and injury, Ryder had given up his favourite sport of cricket and therefore needed an alternative pastime. His friend Frank Wheeler, preacher at Trinity Congregational Church in St Albans, suggested that he should try golf as a way to get more fresh air. Ryder duly hired a local golfer to give him personal lessons at his Hertfordshire mansion and practised relentlessly until he was good enough to join his local club, Verulam. Within two years, he had risen to the role of captain and national golfing promoter in three. Of course, the rest is history.

An incredible turn of events was set in place the day Wheeler made his suggestion. Maybe he knew Ryder would take his words to heart, because whether it was supporting city charities for the poor or helping the elderly, or even staging high-profile fund-raising events at his home, Marlborough House (including garden fêtes and concerts), Ryder was always involved in some kind of project. Very soon, golf – and in particular, promoting golfing events – became his all-consuming project. By June 1924, he had already placed an article in the *Herts Advertiser* stating his firm, Heath & Heather, "were contemplating challenging the Americans to a match".

Born in Walton-le-Dale (a village outside Preston in Lancashire, England) on March 24, 1858, Samuel Ryder was one of eight children of Samuel (a professional gardener) and Elizabeth (a dressmaker), and his early experience of poverty in northern England made him all the more determined to provide employment for others in the future. Having started work in his father's business, he eventually made his fortune as a seed merchant, selling penny packets of seed via mail order just as the British homemaker's interest in gardening took off. After moving to St Albans, where he set up a new company with his brother James, selling herbal remedies, Samuel's life really took off.

Whether at church (Samuel was a Methodist), in business, working for charities or carrying out civic duties (later, he became mayor of St Albans, as well as a magistrate and alderman), it

seems Ryder threw himself into these roles with equal vigour – just as he did in golf. Within two years of starting lessons, he was a big name at Verulam and his love affair with golf was to have huge knock-on benefits for the sport, enriching the lives of so many for almost 100 years. Samuel made large donations to the club, where he was appointed captain in 1911, 1926 and 1927. He swiftly brought his handicap down to single figures, too, which gives an insight into the determination of the man.

As a promoter he first tinkered with the prospect of staging team matches in 1923 when Heath & Heather attracted the cream of British golf (including six Open champions) to play a challenge match. It was the first time that every player who turned up for such a match was paid expenses for appearing – and so the world of golf sat up and took notice. Ryder's growing friendship with British star Abe Mitchell also had a major impact on his status, especially when he took on his newfound partner as a personal coach, paying him an annual salary. The plan was to give Mitchell the time to practise and progress his own career. Sadly, he didn't achieve his great dream of winning the British Open, but it is Mitchell's likeness that graces the golden Ryder Cup trophy, earning him a place in history all the same.

It was Ryder who made the greatest contribution towards the moulding of the solid gold trophy produced by London jeweller Mappin & Webb and presented for the first time at Worcester Country Club, Massachusetts in 1927. Two years later, he himself presented the Cup in the first home match at Moortown, handing it to British captain George Duncan. In that moment a personal dream came true and a golfing phenomenon began.

Samuel Ryder died, aged 77, in 1936 and was fittingly buried at Hatfield Road Cemetery in St Albans with his favourite five-iron.

> **" We must do this again. "**
>
> *Samuel Ryder addresses players after a Great Britain vs. USA challenge match in 1926*

12 U.S. GOLF PROS TO INVADE ENGLAND

Hagen Will Captain Team That Will Meet Force Headed by George Duncan.

CONTINGENT SAILS MAY 26

Matches Between American and British Stars Will Be Played at Wentworth, Near London.

PINEHURST, N. C., April 4.—The strongest golf team ever to represent the United States, composed of twelve American professionals, will meet the British pros at team play in Great Britain this coming Summer, according to Walter Hagen.

Hagen has been working on plans for the matches during the past month and has decided to ask more pros than the original four for whom he was allowed $1,000. The professionals, eager to play, have waived all rights to a guarantee of $250 each and are willing to split the $1,000 among the whole team.

Hagen will name a committee of four or five leading players to pick the team. It is up to the British, according to Hagen, to name as many players as they like. If more than twelve are named it is likely the British will call on some of their famous old-timers, including Harry Vardon, J. H. Taylor, James Braid, and Sandy Herd

George Duncan is captain of the British team and some of his team-mates are Abe Mitchell, Archie Compston, Arthur Havers, the Whitcomb brothers, Jimmy Ockenden, Ted Ray, Sid Wingate, George Gadd, Len Holland and Jimmy Ellis. Several younger players who may be added include Jolly, Boomer and Murray.

The First Competition

The seeds of the Ryder Cup had clearly been sown by this stage, not just by merchant Sam Ryder, but by others, too, and so the next question to look at is when was the very first competition played? The history books all state 1927, no questions asked and no arguments. In fact, a competition played a year earlier in England might have been the starting point, even if the PGA doesn't recognize the fact.

With interest in the rivalry between British and American golfers growing by the day, the public's appetite for a team competition to compare and contrast the great stars of the game had become increasingly obvious by 1926. And the first chance to test the depth of interest came at Wentworth that very year in what some have described as the "lost Ryder Cup". Certainly, it was here that the name Samuel Ryder first became important, and his part in turning the dream into a reality is unquestionable.

Over the last few years, the successful merchant – who came up with the concept of selling seeds to amateur gardeners in "penny packets" and lived in St Albans, Hertfordshire (just north of London) – had become the main talking point of many a fairway after ploughing funds into his new love. However, he only took up golf at the age of 50 because he could no longer play cricket and was advised by his local Methodist minister to try something new. Following this, he spent a fortune on lessons – first from his local club pro, John Hill, and then English legend, Abe Mitchell. Within a year, Ryder had joined his local club – Verulam – and 12 months later, had already been elected club captain. By 1923, his interest in the sport was all-consuming and so he began, along with his brother James and their new company, Heath & Heather (herbal remedies), to sponsor professional tournaments at Verulam. All competitors were paid an appearance fee of £5 (approximately $25 at the time), while the winner was awarded £50 ($250). These were astronomical sums (that year, the winner of The Open received just £75 ($375)) and so Ryder's event attracted some of

THE BIRTH OF AN IDEA

The "Eureka" moment that put the Ryder Cup in motion took place, according to Ryder's daughter, Marjorie (who produced a booklet about her father in 1979), at Came Down Golf Club in Dorset during a holiday game with club professional Ernest Whitcombe. Ernest casually remarked to his opponent: "The Americans come over here smartly dressed and backed by wealthy supporters, the Britisher has a poor chance compared to that." His comment clearly struck a nerve and in that moment Ryder vowed to do something about it.

LEFT: A local newspaper reports the birth of the Ryder Cup as a team of American golfers heads to England in 1926 in a forerunner of the competition.

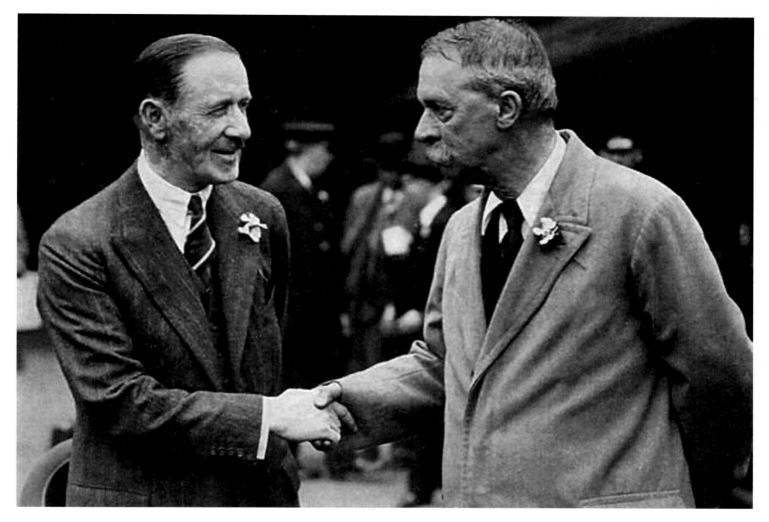

ABOVE: *Samuel Ryder (right) greets friend and inspiration Abe Mitchell, the golfer whose likeness would adorn the Ryder Cup trophy.*

British golf's biggest names, from Harry Vardon to James Braid, George Duncan to Open champion, Arthur Havers.

Ryder's subsequent friendship with Abe Mitchell saw him pay the Englishman £500 ($2,500) a year to be his personal coach. Reportedly, his primary concern was not his own tuition, but to give Mitchell the time and funds to further his own career and achieve his dream of winning the British Open. Sadly, Mitchell was never able to do this but it wasn't long before golf's newest benefactor made his own considerable impact as he woke up to the excitement of team golf. In 1926, he pitted Harry Vardon and J.H. Taylor against James Braid and Alex Herd in an England v Scotland match at Verulam, noting the enthusiasm with which the event was received. Then, a few months later, came the beginnings of the Ryder Cup.

On April 26, 1926, Samuel Ryder announced in the Press that he had presented a trophy for an annual competition between British and American golfers to be played at Wentworth prior to The Open. His decision was perhaps sparked by the news that The Open – to be played at Royal Lytham & St Annes – was oversubscribed and the Royal and Ancient had therefore opted to stage three regional pre-qualifying tournaments. Naturally, the Americans arriving by boat in Southampton were allocated to the southern event at Sunningdale, giving Ryder the perfect excuse: everything, including a squad of 12 US golfers, was already in place.

> **❝** *I trust that the effect of this match will be to influence a cordial, friendly and peaceful feeling throughout the whole civilized world. I look upon the Royal and Ancient game as being a powerful force that influences the best things in humanity.* **❞**

Samuel Ryder's vision for the Ryder Cup

RIGHT: *US captain Walter Hagen tees off at Wentworth in 1926, when Great Britain beat a much-weakened American team, 13.5-1.5.*

The First Cup

With Ted Ray captaining the British team and Walter Hagen leading the American challenge, Wentworth hosted a moment in history on June 4 and June 5, 1926, when Samuel Ryder's vision became reality. As a contest it was destined to be scrubbed from the record books but its importance should never be overlooked.

Like its predecessor of 1921, the "lost" Ryder Cup match proved something of a walkover, with a strong British team trouncing their rivals, 13.5 to 1.5, but this time the interest was far greater as an enthusiastic crowd followed the players around the West Course. The British team, which included former Open champions Ted Ray, George Duncan and Arthur Havers, as well as Abe Mitchell, Archie Compston, Fred Robson, Ernest Whitcombe, Herbert Jolly, Aubrey Bloomer and George Gadd, was far too good to suffer serious setbacks, winning all five Foursomes on the opening Friday.

In the nine singles matches scheduled for the next day, highlights included a remarkable 6 and 5 victory for Duncan against Hagen - who had all-too readily accepted an invitation to play in his second Britain v USA clash. Mitchell, watched by his friend Ryder, thrashed Jim Barnes, 8 and 7 - although this time the match and the post-match presentations were much more convivial than in Scotland five years earlier, with Ryder in particular revelling in the camaraderie.

In fairness to the Americans, they were unable to field their strongest side after the Great Strike of May that year complicated travel arrangements - meaning the US team included guests such as Scotland's Fred McLeod and Tommy Armour, England's Jim Barnes and Joe Stain, plus Australian Joe Kirkwood. Players of the calibre of Gene Sarazen, who would go on to become a Ryder Cup legend, were unable to make it - and the United States PGA was understandably reluctant to recognize it as an official result. Even so, in many ways, this was the first Ryder Cup and the main reason why it is not included in the record books is because the trophy itself was never presented.

A report from Harnett's *Golf Illustrated* of June 11, 1926 provides the ultimate explanation, which even appeared under the headline "Ryder Cup".

BELOW: *US captain Walter Hagen (left) greets opposite number Ted Ray prior to playing Great Britain at Wentworth in 1926.*

RIGHT: *Scottish professional Tommy Armour lines up a shot at Wentworth in 1926 – but he was playing for the USA, not Great Britain.*

COMMISSIONING THE TROPHY

Much debate reigns over the sequence of events that led to the Ryder Cup trophy being commissioned. An alternative view may be found on the Cup's official website, where it is suggested Samuel Ryder took tea with British team members, George Duncan and Abe Mitchell, and the American Emmett French, after the match in 1926. It was Duncan who ventured the suggestion that Ryder might provide a trophy, to which he immediately agreed. Of course, we may never know for certain which version of events is true.

It read:

> **Owing to the uncertainty of the situation following the Strike in which it was not known until a few days ago how many American professionals would be visiting Great Britain, Mr J Ryder decided to withhold the cup, which he has offered for annual competition between the professionals of Great Britain and America. Under these circumstances the Wentworth Club provided the British players with gold medals to mark the inauguration of this great international match.**

The success of the event, although never made official, further encouraged Samuel Ryder in his belief that the idea of an annual challenge match was now feasible and his trophy would not be wasted. In fact, he had already paid £100 ($500) towards its making, with *Golf Illustrated* adding another £100 ($500) and the Royal and Ancient Golf Club of St Andrews £50 ($250). It was initially unveiled a year later when the first true Ryder Cup took place in Worcester, Massachusetts.

By that time the trophy, which included a likeness of Ryder's great friend, Abe Mitchell, had been hallmarked 1927, so one must wonder whether it had ever been ready to present at Wentworth at all, even if the Americans had arrived at Southampton with a full team on board. Whatever the reasons for the "lost" Ryder Cup of 1926, a year later the most famous trophy in team golf was about to be presented. It would create a dynasty even its founding father could never have imagined.

> **❝** *I will give £5 ($25) to each of the winning players, and give a party afterwards, with champagne and chicken sandwiches.* **❞**

Samuel Ryder introduces his new competition

Great Britain's George Duncan on his way to victory over US captain Walter Hagen at Moortown Golf Club in 1929, the first official Ryder Cup staged in England.

CHAPTER TWO
THE DRAMA BEGINS

With the idea of a transatlantic competition already in place, a trophy commissioned and public interest stirred, the Ryder Cup was finally ready to make its formal entrance onto the global sporting stage with its first event in 1927. It didn't take long to make its mark as the matches quickly grew in stature and popularity.

1927

USA 9.5
Great Britain 2.5

Worcester CC, Massachusetts

June 3-4

THE COURSE

Worcester Country Club
Location: Worcester, Massachusetts, USA
Par: 72
Yards: 6,422

Designed by Donald Ross in 1913, Worcester Country Club had just staged the US Open in 1925 and is the only course to have staged the US Open, Ryder Cup and the US Women's Open. US captain Walter Hagen already had happy memories – two years earlier, he had scored his first hole-in-one there.

Worcester Country Club in Massachusetts holds a special place in Ryder Cup history because it was here, on June 3, 1927, that Samuel Ryder's great dream finally came to fruition. Unfortunately Ryder himself wasn't able to be there to see it, and the United States put down a marker for the future by scoring an emphatic victory against their rivals from across the Atlantic.

THE SIGHT OF US CAPTAIN Walter Hagen lifting the golden trophy for the first time must have sent a shiver down the spines of the men who had worked so hard to make it happen. But it would be wrong to give the impression that the event had been all plain sailing and had not taken a huge amount of effort – and money – to get it off the ground. Just getting the British team to America was no mean feat, given the distances and costs of the travel involved, and it took time and effort for the necessary finance to be raised. In fact, an appeal launched by George Philpot, editor of *Golf Weekly* for £3,000 ($15,000 at mid-1920s prices), fell on deaf ears, much to the chagrin of the magazine as it ran an editorial criticizing the "indifferences or selfishness" of golfers and golf clubs who opted not to pay.

Only 216 out of the 1,750 clubs that were contacted replied with a donation and even after a £500 ($2,500) contribution from Sam Ryder himself, there was a significant shortfall. It was eventually made up by Philpot, who contributed £500 ($2,500) of his own money to the project and was subsequently named team manager. His problems were then exacerbated by the news that Abe Mitchell, Ryder's friend, confidant and inspiration, had been struck down with appendicitis just as the team was due to leave London. It was a major blow for this was the man earmarked as captain for the first Ryder Cup, whose very likeness adorned the trophy.

Herbert Jolly was added to the squad and the experienced Ted Ray chosen as new captain. The Jersey-born golfer had learned his trade at the same course as the legendary Harry Vardon and

LEFT: *Samuel Ryder joins the British Ryder Cup team as they prepare to leave London en route to Massachusetts.*

OPPOSITE: *Late call-up Herbert Jolly practises his swing on the deck of a ship as he rushes to join the British team in America.*

was beloved by fans for his daring play and genial character. He was, by any stretch of the imagination, past his prime at 50, but considering he had won the US Open aged 43, it was decided his vast experience would serve the team well.

The next hurdle to clear was simply making it to America. After a particularly rough six-day crossing on the RMS *Aquitania*, the team arrived, tired and ill. And once they landed in New York, they were rushed to a glitzy reception organized by American captain Hagen. Limousines flanked by police officers whisked them off on a hectic schedule of sightseeing that included a gala at the Westchester Biltmore Country Club and an evening spent watching the New York Yankees.

By the time Ray's team got to practise they were in a whirl, but alert enough to turn down a last-minute request from their hosts to change the format to include Fourballs instead of Foursomes (known as "Scotch Foursomes" in the USA and rarely played); for two points instead of one to be awarded for a Fourballs' victory; and for matches level after 36 holes to be continued until there was a clear winner. Indeed, the only concession made by British team manager Philpot was to allow both teams to substitute a player in the second day's singles, if required, and he was secretly furious at having to make any late changes at all.

It was clear gamesmanship from the Americans, but they were to prove pretty adept at "Scotch Foursomes" as they won the opening session 3-1, with a side much changed from the one beaten so easily a year earlier at Wentworth. Having chosen a team of native-born Americans (with the exception of Eastern European immigrant Jimmy Golden), only Walter Hagen, Bill Mehlhorn and Al Watrous were retained. But Hagen teamed up with Golden to win the first match of the day, 2 and 1 against Ray and Fred Robson, before Johnny Farrell and Joe Turnesa completely demolished George Duncan and Archie Compston, 8 and 6, to put the USA two points ahead. The only British win came from Aubrey Boomer and Charles Whitcombe – a face-saving 7 and 5 win that prevented a whitewash. But with Gene Sarazen and Al Watrous comfortable winners against Arthur Havers and Jolly, clearly the British team were not adapting to new conditions as well as they hoped.

> **" *Let us hope our team can win, but it is the play without the Prince of Denmark.* "**
>
> *Samuel Ryder on Abe Mitchell's withdrawal from the British Ryder Cup team*

DAY ONE

CAPTAINS

USA: Walter Hagen   **Great Britain:** Ted Ray

FRIDAY FOURSOMES

Hagen/Golden *beat* **Ray/Robson,** *2 and 1*

Farrell/Turnesa *beat* **Duncan/Compston,** *8 and 6*

Sarazen/Watrous *beat* **Havers/Jolly,** *3 and 2*

Diegel/Mehlhorn *lost to* **Boomer/C. Whitcombe,** *7 and 5*

Session Score: 3-1

Overall Score: USA 3, Great Britain 1

> *The Ryder Cup has done so much to foster that great spirit of international rivalry that makes the present-day sport the great thing that it is.*
>
> *Golf Illustrated magazine*

By the time the singles arrived, it was clear that the British team were mentally and physically washed out. By contrast, the Americans were vibrant and confident. Backed by surprisingly large crowds, they were in no mood to make allowances either. The victories rolled in one after the other and although the opening match was tight, with "Wild Bill" Mehlhorn beating Archie Compston by just one hole, most were not. Golden lived up to his name with an 8 and 7 victory over Jolly, while veteran Ray succumbed to Leo Diegel, 7 and 5. Hagen led by example with a 2 and 1 win against Arthur Havers.

For Great Britain, the only bright spots were Whitcombe's hard-earned half against Gene Sarazen and a welcome win for George Duncan in the last match, sneaking past Joe Turnesa at the last. But with Al Watrous also adding a point for the USA against Fred Robson, the singles were won 6.5-1.5 and the match 9.5-2.5 – a hugely convincing victory. As early as the first day, British captain Ray identified the problem, noting his side were competitive to the greens but regularly beaten once they arrived there, saying: "One of the chief reasons for our failure was the superior putting of the American team – they holed out much better than we did." However, if there was a feeling of huge disappointment and weariness for Britain as the first Ryder Cup matches came to a close, it was soon replaced by a pride in what had been achieved to set up the competition in the first place.

The final day's play received little coverage back home, no doubt primarily because of the result, but the Ryder Cup had been well received in the USA and there was a feeling on both sides that the format had a future. Philpot certainly remained enthusiastic, writing in *Golf Illustrated*: "If our young players profit by the experience, we can reasonably hope for a happier fate in the next match for the Ryder Cup."

He was soon to be proved right, and already a great sporting rivalry had begun.

DAY TWO

SATURDAY SINGLES

Bill Mehlhorn *beat* **Archie Compston** *by one hole*

Johnny Farrell *beat* **Aubrey Boomer,** *5 and 4*

Johnny Golden *beat* **Herbert Jolly,** *8 and 7*

Leo Diegel *beat* **Ted Ray,** *7 and 5*

Gene Sarazen *halved with* **Charles Whitcombe**

Walter Hagen *beat* **Arthur Havers,** *2 and 1*

Al Watrous *beat* **Fred Robson,** *3 and 2*

Joe Turnesa *lost to* **George Duncan** *by one hole*

Session Score: 6.5-1.5

Overall Score: USA 9.5, Great Britain 2.5

THE FIRST RYDER CUP TEAMS

USA

Walter Hagen (captain), 35: The swashbuckling figurehead of American golf professionals had already won two US Opens and two British Opens, and was destined to win in Britain, too (1928 and 1929).

Johnny Farrell, 26: Went on to win the US Open the following year.

Gene Sarazen, 25: Already a US Open champion, he went on to become a US golfing and Ryder Cup legend and is one of only five players to win a career Grand Slam of Majors.

Leo Diegel, 28: Went on to win the PGA Championship in 1928 and 1929.

Johnny Golden, 31: Not long a professional, he died aged just 39.

Joe Turnesa, 26: Only turned pro in 1925; five of his six brothers were also golfers.

Al Watrous, 26: Runner-up at the British Open in 1926. Remained club pro at Oakland Hills for 37 years.

Bill Mehlhorn, 28: Nicknamed "Wild Bill" for his love of wearing cowboy hats on course. He never won a Major but was runner-up at the PGA in 1926.

GREAT BRITAIN

Ted Ray (captain), 50: Won the US Open at the ripe old age of 43 (1920) and famously lost a play-off against winner Francis Ouimet and Harry Vardon at the same tournament in 1913 – a story Disney later turned into a movie called *The Greatest Game Ever Played* (2005).

George Duncan, 43: The Scottish golfer won the British Open in 1920 after one of the greatest comebacks in history, from 13 shots down to win.

Arthur Havers, 29: English golfer, who won the British Open in 1923.

Aubrey Boomer, 30: Brought up in Jersey, Boomer was to be runner-up to Bobby Jones in the British Open just months after the Ryder Cup. Won four French Opens during his career.

Fred Robson, 42: Never won a Major but finished in the top 10 of the British Open four times.

Archie Compston, 34: A renowned matchplay golfer, he famously went on to beat Walter Hagen in a challenge match in 1928.

Herbert Jolly, 42: Last-minute replacement for Abe Mitchell, he had been placed eighth at the British Open in 1923.

Charles Whitcombe, 33: The second of three famous golfing brothers, he went on to become a Ryder Cup captain.

George Gadd, 37: Malvern-born player, who won the British PGA Match Play Championship in 1922 (runner-up in 1924 and 1925).

OPPOSITE: *America's Leo Diegel in action on the 2nd tee against Ted Ray as the USA wins the Ryder Cup in Massachusetts.*

BELOW: *US captain Walter Hagen, surrounded by his victorious team-mates, picks up the Ryder Cup trophy after beating Great Britain.*

1929
Great Britain 7 USA 5

Moortown Golf Club, Leeds

April 26-27

THE COURSE

Moortown Golf Club
Location: Leeds,
West Yorkshire,
England
Par: 69
Yards: 6,980

A traditional club founded in 1909 and designed by Dr Alister MacKenzie with large, undulating seaside greens and numerous bunkers. To this day, the club's ladies' section plays annually for their own "Ryder Cup", also donated by Samuel Ryder.

There was no question that the Ryder Cup had caught the imagination of the British public. A huge crowd, which peaked at an unprecedented 15,000 on Saturday afternoon, turned up in 1929 to watch Great Britain win the trophy for the first time in front of founder Samuel Ryder at Moortown Golf Club in Leeds.

IT WAS SCOTLAND'S GEORGE DUNCAN who became the first British golfer to lift the now-famous golden trophy, and already it was clear the tournament was there to stay as the matches generated huge interest throughout the country.

The crowds that turned up to watch Duncan's side take on a US team captained by Walter Hagen were as great as they were unexpected, and those fans witnessed a thrilling match that saw Britain trail at the end of the first day but produce a hugely impressive performance on the Saturday to clinch overall victory by two points. There was a lot for golf's new fans to take in,

not least the arrival of a young 22-year-old Henry Cotton, who announced his arrival on the big stage by beating America's Al Watrous, 4 and 2 – and who would go on to win three British Open titles in an illustrious career.

The main problem facing both teams was the miserable, wintry weather. Cold, swirling winds and drizzling rain had affected practice sessions and although the wind abated as the teams approached the 1st tee, it was still unseasonably cold and not what the Americans were used to. Given those facts, Britain were disappointed with the first session, which saw the USA win the

LEFT: *The British Ryder Cup stars of 1929 line up for a team shot before the tournament in Leeds.*

OPPOSITE: *British captain George Duncan (left) and US captain Walter Hagen in action at Moortown.*

DAYS ONE AND TWO

CAPTAINS

Great Britain: George Duncan   **USA:** Walter Hagen

FRIDAY FOURSOMES

C. Whitcombe/Compston *halved with* **Farrell/Turnesa**

Boomer/Duncan *lost to* **Diegel/Espinosa,** *7 and 5*

Mitchell/Robson *beat* **Sarazen/Dudley,** *2 and 1*

E. Whitcombe/Cotton *lost to* **Golden/Hagen** *by two holes*

Session Score: 1.5-2.5

SATURDAY SINGLES

Charles Whitcombe *beat* **Johnny Farrell,** *8 and 6*

George Duncan *beat* **Walter Hagen,** *10 and 8*

Abe Mitchell *lost to* **Leo Diegel,** *8 and 6*

Archie Compston *beat* **Gene Sarazen,** *6 and 4*

Aubrey Boomer *beat* **Joe Turnesa,** *4 and 3*

Fred Robson *lost to* **Horton Smith,** *4 and 2*

Henry Cotton *beat* **Al Watrous,** *4 and 2*

Ernest Whitcombe *halved with* **Al Espinosa**

Session Score: 5.5-2.5

Overall Score: Great Britain 7, USA 5

Foursomes 2.5-1.5. The visitors opened with an encouraging half for Johnny Farrell and Joe Turnesa against Charles Whitcombe and Archie Compston, coming from one down at the last to avoid defeat. It proved a pivotal result as Leo Diegel and Al Espinosa waltzed to a 7 and 5 victory over Aubrey Boomer and Duncan, while Johnny Golden and Walter Hagen sealed victory over Ernest Whitcombe and Cotton.

With the match in the balance, US captain Walter Hagen's decision to give all his players at least one game during the weekend (which went on to become a tradition for the American side) perhaps ultimately cost him victory as British captain George Duncan proved more ruthless in leaving his weaker players out of the singles. The USA were further limited by a rule banning steel shafts (which had been in regular use in the States for some time but which were still frowned upon in England) meaning debutant Horton Smith, for instance, had to play with wooden-shafted clubs for the first time as he faced Fred Dobson in the singles. Mind you, it didn't seem to affect the up-and-coming star as he won, 4 and 2. It was a rare highlight for the Americans, who went down 5.5-2.5 to lose the cup they had won two years earlier, with Diegel their only other winner as he saw off Abe Mitchell, 8 and 6, in the third match off the tee.

The session, and indeed the match, hinged on a mammoth tussle between the two captains, which remains one of the greatest matches in Ryder Cup history. Legend has it that Duncan overheard his opposite number telling Gene Sarazen he would be guaranteed a point when he faced him in the singles and vowed to make his rival eat his words, eventually routing him 10 and 8 over 36 holes. This was a player rated the best (and certainly the most flamboyant) in the world and a man who just two weeks later went on to win The Open at Muirfield, so it was a hugely encouraging victory. Duncan accepted the trophy from Samuel Ryder himself after Compston cruised to victory over Sarazen, 6 and 4, and Cotton beat Watrous 4 and 2 to complete a memorable win for Great Britain. The Ryder Cup rivalry was now in full swing.

> **"***Well, boys, there's a point for our team right there.***"**

US captain Walter Hagen talks up his chances when facing British counterpart George Duncan

1931

USA 9
Great Britain 3

Scioto Country Club, Ohio

June 26-27

From a windswept and rainy Leeds, the Ryder Cup transferred to 100-degree sunshine in Ohio, 1931. The USA turned up the heat on their new rivals with a thoroughly ruthless and convincing six-point victory at the Scioto Country Club that left British captain Charles Whitcombe facing intense criticism.

OVER THE YEARS, controversy and media outrage has almost become a regular part of the Ryder Cup, adding to the drama and intensity of the tournament. For Britain, it began in 1931 with a strange decision over team selection.

The PGA decided to bring in a new rule insisting players selected for the Ryder Cup not only were born in Britain but also continued to live there – meaning those players who intended to stay in America after the matches in Columbus to play lucrative exhibition matches would have to return home with the team. It was a particularly tough call for Henry Cotton, who had a professional post in Belgium – especially when he was informed that if he accepted a 'free ride' to America, he would be required to share his exhibition match fees with the rest of the team. In a row that continued for months, Cotton even offered to pay his own fare to the States but was refused... and was subsequently de-selected from the team.

So, instead of playing in the Ryder Cup, Britain's best player organized an "unofficial" private tour of America with Percy Alliss and Aubrey Boomer. Even when an olive branch was offered, he refused to change his mind – leaving the British team seriously weakened and without three of its better players. It seemed an unnecessary row over a residency rule that was primarily aimed at ensuring the USA didn't pick British players based in the States for their Ryder Cup team and had never been designed to punish those players who were keen to play abroad. Samuel Ryder tried to clarify the situation by assuring the PGA that if they wanted to change the competition rules, it was possible.

Whatever the rights and wrongs of the situation it hardly did Britain any favours. Nor did the intense heat in Ohio, which topped 37.7°C (100°F), or a decision to overlook George Duncan, who had lifted the trophy in 1929, as captain in favour of Charles Whitcombe – who proved less than inspirational.

The US team, led once again by Walter Hagen and featuring a blend of youth and experience, were more than a match for their rivals. In-form players

> **"** *The Cup is the sole property of the PGA and they can alter the terms in any way they think fit at the time.* **"**
>
> *Founder Samuel Ryder clarifies the rules over team selection*

ABOVE: *The victorious US players in 1931 (from left): Burke, Sarazen, Wood, Hagen (with the trophy), Farrell, Shute, Espinosa, Diegel and Smith.*

OPPOSITE: *Great Britain's Duncan and Havers (both left) line up with the USA's Shute and Hagen at the Scioto Country Club.*

such as Craig Wood, Wiffy Cox, Denny Shute and Billy Burke (who had only earned selection a few weeks before the tournament began) were included.

Once the action started, it was clear the USA were heading for victory with Hagen avenging his huge singles defeat against opposing captain Duncan two years earlier in teaming up with Shute to defeat Duncan and Arthur Havers, 10 and 9. The USA won the Foursomes 3-1 before demolishing their rivals 6-2 in Saturday's singles matches, with some of the victories by huge margins. Burke demolished Archie Compston, 7 and 6, in the opening singles game, for instance. Gene Sarazen (who had already won 8 and 7 in the Foursomes a day earlier) added another point in beating Fred Robson, also by 7 and 6.

Once again failing to cope with the searing heat, Britain were able to muster just two victories – for Arthur Havers against Craig Wood once the trophy had already been lost and for William Davies, 4 and 3 against Johnny Farrell. In contrast the US team were majestic in victory, ending the matches 9-3 ahead to send their rivals home disconsolate. The Ryder Cup had now tasted victory, defeat, controversy and disappointment on both sides of the Atlantic and although on PGA insistence it would never again be played in the heat of an American summer, the matches were becoming ingrained in golfing folklore.

DAYS ONE AND TWO

CAPTAINS

USA: Walter Hagen   **Great Britain:** Charles Whitcombe

FRIDAY FOURSOMES

Sarazen/Farrell *beat* **Compston/Davies,** *8 and 7*

Hagen/Shute *beat* **Duncan/Havers,** *10 and 9*

Diegel/Espinosa *lost to* **Mitchell/Robson,** *3 and 1*

Burke/Cox *beat* **Easterbrook/E. Whitcombe,** *3 and 2*

Session Score: 3-1

SATURDAY SINGLES

Billy Burke *beat* **Archie Compston,** *7 and 6*

Gene Sarazen *beat* **Fred Robson,** *7 and 6*

Johnny Farrell *lost to* **William Davies,** *4 and 3*

Wiffy Cox *beat* **Abe Mitchell,** *3 and 1*

Walter Hagen *beat* **Charles Whitcombe,** *4 and 2*

Denny Shute *beat* **Bert Hodson,** *8 and 6*

Al Espinosa *beat* **Ernest Whitcombe,** *2 and 1*

Craig Wood *lost to* **Arthur Havers,** *4 and 3*

Session Score: 6-2

Overall Score: USA 9, Great Britain 3

Ryder Cup legends
Walter HAGEN

One of the greatest showmen golf has ever seen, Walter Hagen did as much as anyone to popularize the Ryder Cup in its early days, as both skilful player and enigmatic captain, but his influence on the game of golf goes far beyond that. In many ways, he was the world's first professional golfer and single-handedly propelled the sport into the modern era.

When Walter Hagen arrived at the British Open in 1920 there was still stuffiness about British golf, which viewed golf professionals with immense scepticism and even banned them from entering the clubhouse. But one story about the US legend sheds light on the true character of the man who transformed those opinions – and those ancient rules – during the course of his career. By then, Hagen was already making good money from playing exhibition golf back home and so rather than suffer the ignominy of being refused entry to the clubhouse at Deal, Kent, he hired himself a showy Daimler limousine, asked his chauffeur to park it on the drive of the club, where he used it as a changing room instead. One can only imagine the reaction he received from his British hosts but on his return two years later to win the British Open, he sparked an interest in US golf that would prove crucial to plans for a Britain v America challenge match.

Over the ensuing years Hagen became a true sporting legend. Known simply as "Sir Walter" or "The Haig", although exact figures are unavailable, it is quite possible he became golf's first millionaire such was his success on and off the course. He won 11 professional major championships, second only to Jack Nicklaus' total of 18, and between 1914 and 1929, won the PGA Championship five times, the British Open four times and twice-won the US Open. In the Ryder Cup, his record was won seven, lost one and halved one; he captained the USA in the first Ryder Cup in 1927, eventually playing in five contests, winning four. In fact, Hagen – one of the game's great scramblers – was instrumental in supporting the idea of a Britain v USA tournament from the start and it was his colourful personality and attitude to life that really caught the public's imagination.

Hagen made further strides in his stand against the establishment at the 1920 US Open in Toldo, Ohio, by encouraging players to donate a large grandfather clock to the host club in return for the professionals being allowed to use the clubhouse during the tournament; this showed he understood the need for diplomacy, too.

Born in Rochester, New York, on December 21, 1892, the son of a blacksmith, Walter Hagen hailed from a modest background and entered golf as a caddy, but always intended to live large. "I never wanted to be a millionaire," he famously said. "I just wanted to live like one." He looked like a millionaire on the golf course, too, sporting expensive tailored clothes in bright colours and plush fabrics, so perhaps it came as no surprise that his exhibition matches, which did so much to raise the profile of the game and the standing of golf professionals in the US, became hugely popular. Perhaps the only irony is that he also became so associated with the Ryder Cup – a tournament with no prize money, where players turned up for the glory of representing their country and the chance to hold the gold trophy aloft. Although one quote from the great man perhaps explains this decision for he said: "My game was my business and as a business, it demanded constant playing in the championship bracket for a current title was my selling commodity."

Hagen served as the first club professional at the now-legendary Oakland Hills Country Club, in Bloomfield Hills, Michigan from 1918 and also made money endorsing golf equipment and designing clubs for Wilson Sports, which bore his name (marketed either as "Walter Hagen" or "Haig Ultra"). But it would be unfair to remember him only as a player who made a big impact off the course. Despite his glitzy persona, he was focused and technical on the course, with such immense self-confidence that it seemed nothing could faze him. "I expect to make at least seven mistakes a round," he once declared. "Therefore, when I make a bad shot, it's just one of the seven."

In essence, Walter Hagen was an incredible player and an even more amazing character, whose celebrated philosophy was: "Don't hurry, don't worry – you're only here for a short visit, so be sure to smell the flowers along the way." The Ryder Cup, and professional golf, owes him a lot.

> **" All the professionals should say a silent thanks to Walter Hagen each time they stretch a cheque between their fingers. It was Walter who made professional golf what it is. "**
>
> *Gene Sarazen, Hagen's team-mate, pays tribute*

RYDER CUP RECORD

Ryder Cups: 1927 (winner, playing captain), 1929, 1931 (winner, playing captain), 1933, 1935 (winner, playing captain), 1937 (winner, non-playing captain)

Total wins: 4
Matches: 9 (won 7, halved 1, lost 1)
Total points: 7.5

1933

Great Britain 6.5
USA 5.5

Southport & Ainsdale Golf Club

June 26-27

THE COURSE

Southport & Ainsdale Golf Club
Location: Southport, Merseyside, England
Par: 72
Yards: 6,836

A true championship links course set among ranges of tall sandhills and smaller sand dunes, the club was founded in 1906. Its signature hole, the 16th, features a giant bunker nicknamed "Gumbley's" after a former member, who took 14 strokes to escape it and hole out.

The Ryder Cup's first-ever non-playing captain, John Henry Taylor, guided Great Britain to victory at Southport in 1933 as Syd Easterbrook converted a nerve-wracking putt in the very last match. In doing so, he secured a narrow win for the host nation. This meant that the number of wins for each side was tied at two trophies each after the opening four Ryder Cup tournaments.

BY 1933, THE FIERCE RIVALRY that is so familiar to modern Ryder Cup fans was already beginning to emerge and a remarkably close match at the Southport & Ainsdale Golf Club only served to intensify the increasing passion for the competition on both sides of the Atlantic Ocean.

The tension increased when Great Britain appointed traditionalist John Henry Taylor as captain - a man who had never found much in common with America's flamboyant and progressive leader Walter Hagen. It worsened again when Hagen only just missed hitting his rival with a practice swing on the 1st tee but once the golf began, it was incredibly tight.

Unlike their miserable performance of two years ago, and in windy conditions that felt more familiar at the coastal course, Great Britain looked intent on revenge. Even without Henry Cotton, still omitted because he was based abroad in Belgium, and even when the sun came out on the opening day, home advantage remained crucial.

Playing in front of 7,000 spectators, Great Britain led in three and were all square in the fourth after 18 holes of Foursomes with Percy Alliss and Charles Whitcombe going round in 72, and Abe Mitchell and Arthur Havers following suit. But an afternoon fight-back by America changed everything.

Hagen and Gene Sarazen started the ball rolling by coming back from one down with one to play to at least earn a half against Alliss and Whitcombe. They also edged victory in the final match as Ed Dudley and Billy Burke beat the two Alfs - Padgham and Perry - having been four-down at one stage. Those results sandwiched British victories for Mitchell and Havers; also William Davies and Syd Easterbrook, leaving the home side just one point ahead by the end of the first day.

The singles proved just as close, too, and it all came down to the final match with Easterbrook and Denny Shute all square on the final green and both facing long par putts to gain an advantage.

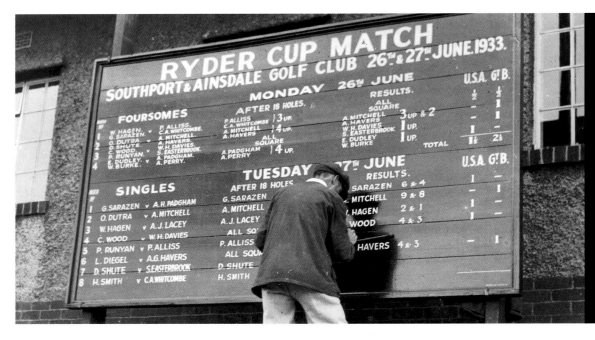

LEFT: *The Ryder Cup scoreboard is chalked up by an official at Southport in 1933, telling the story.*

OPPOSITE: *Crowds surround the green as Abe Mitchell tees off during the 1933 Ryder Cup.*

> **"***I am the proudest man in the British Commonwealth of people at this moment.***"**
>
> *British captain John Henry Taylor after regaining the Ryder Cup*

Indeed, the tension was palpable as Easterbrook left his effort close to the hole and Shute went four feet past before missing his second effort to hand Britain the trophy. Easterbrook had no problem finishing off the job and it proved a landmark in Ryder Cup history.

It's a mark of the competition's newfound status that the trophy was presented not by Samuel Ryder this time but by HRH The Prince of Wales in his capacity as president of the PGA, saying: "In giving this Cup, I am naturally impartial. But, of course, we over here are very pleased to have won." Players were also presented with medals before Taylor led a traditional "three cheers" salute to the weekend's special guest.

Despite the on-course rivalry, the speeches reflected the spirit of the matches as the Prince paid tribute to the US team, and Taylor in turn praised the Americans for their sporting attitude and the spectators for their good behaviour. US captain Hagen, too, congratulated Great Britain on their "excellent golf" and looked forward to winning the trophy back – a prediction that was soon to come true. But what he could not have predicted was that this was the last time Britain would win the trophy for 24 years, and also the last time that Samuel Ryder would attend – sadly, he died in 1936. But, judging by the events at the S&A, he had certainly left a remarkable legacy behind him.

DAYS ONE AND TWO

CAPTAINS

Great Britain: John Henry Taylor   **USA:** Walter Hagen

MONDAY FOURSOMES

Alliss/C. Whitcombe *halved with* **Sarazen/Hagen**

Mitchell/Havers *beat* **Dutra/Shute,** *3 and 2*

Davies/Easterbrook *beat* **Wood/Runyan** *by one hole*

Padgham/Perry *lost to* **Dudley/Burke** *by one hole*

Session Score: 2.5-1.5

TUESDAY SINGLES

Alf Padgham *lost to* **Gene Sarazen,** *6 and 4*

Abe Mitchell *beat* **Olin Dutra,** *9 and 8*

Arthur Lacey *lost to* **Walter Hagen,** *2 and 1*

William Davies *lost to* **Craig Wood,** *4 and 3*

Percy Alliss *beat* **Paul Runyan,** *2 and 1*

Arthur Havers *beat* **Leo Diegel,** *4 and 3*

Syd Easterbrook *beat* **Denny Shute** *by one hole*

Charles Whitcombe *lost to* **Horton Smith,** *2 and 1*

Session Score: 4-4

Overall Score: Great Britain 6.5, USA 5.5

1935

**USA 9
Great Britain 3**

Ridgewood Country Club, New Jersey

September 28-29

The legendary Walter Hagen led the USA to another impressive home victory in 1935 as he played in his last Ryder Cup. He combined effectively with Gene Sarazen to comprehensively end Great Britain's challenge. It was a match that saw all three Whitcombe brothers – Charles, Ernest and Reg – compete for the losing side at New Jersey's Ridgewood Country Club.

GREAT BRITAIN MAY HAVE ENJOYED their victory in front of royalty in 1933 but they soon found playing in America – where a larger ball was used – a completely different prospect. They were royally beaten by Hagen's team, with Paul Runyan and Horton Smith playing superbly to clinch a six-point victory for the second time in a row on US soil.

Hagen combined with his old rival Gene Sarazen (the two were never the greatest of friends but were able to put differences aside to compete effectively together) to beat Jack Busson and Alf Perry by a mammoth 7 and 6 in the opening day's Foursomes. However, the captain was honest enough about his own form, at the age of 42, to leave himself out of the singles, allowing others to finish off the job. Hagen went on to become non-playing captain in 1937, but this was his last on-course action in the Ryder Cup – the tournament he had helped to instigate. He bowed out with a record of seven victories, one half and one defeat, having lifted the trophy three times out of five. It's a record that makes him one of the competition's all-time greats.

Great Britain, still without Henry Cotton because of selection issues over players who were based abroad, went for family connections this time in a bid to stop the Americans. Captain Charles Whitcombe chose both his brothers, Ernest and Reg, for the team. But even family know-how – and drizzling rain to make the Brits feel at home – was not enough to prevent the USA from running away with victory.

Following the lead of their captain, Paul Runyan and Horton Smith added a Foursomes victory for the States, as did Henry Picard and Johnny Revolta. At the end of the opening day, the home team led 3-1, just as they had four years earlier. Charles and Ernest Whitcombe combined for Britain's only point – a one-up

> ## "The British team could not hole out in a hole the size of the Atlantic."

The London Mail explains Great Britain's defeat

OPPOSITE: *Britain's trio of Ryder Cup brothers (left to right), Reg, Ernest and Charles Whitcombe in New Jersey in 1935.*

RIGHT: *Sam Parks and Alf Perry (driving) in action at Ridgewood during the Ryder Cup singles matches.*

victory over Olin Dutra and Ky Laffoon. Afterwards, Charles sat out the singles and could only watch despairingly as his team were demolished 6-2 to relinquish the trophy that they had won so dramatically in Southport.

Percy Alliss was one of the few British success stories with a victory over Craig Wood. The Americans, cheered on by a crowd of up to 8,000 on the Sunday afternoon, were too good for their rivals, though. Windy conditions made matters more difficult, highlighted by the fact that Horton Smith was the only player to go under 70 as he carded 69 for his first 18 against Bill Cox – and even he had to settle for a half as the wind picked up later in the day, amazingly carding 83 for the second round. Sarazen was widely credited with the "Shot of the Day" as he played a miraculous shot from beneath overhanging branches, using only a restricted backswing to drop the ball inches from the hole on his way to a hard-fought victory over Busson. In all, America won five of the eight matches, with Runyan, Revolta, Dutra and Picard all adding to Sarazen's opening point, while Sam Parks added a half in a high-quality match against Alf Perry.

It was a hugely convincing victory in which the British players struggled to deal with patches of wet clover on the course, which often made ball striking more difficult. There were also signs of American superiority on the putting greens: there was no doubting the USA were worthy winners and it was a feeling they soon became highly accustomed to.

DAYS ONE AND TWO

CAPTAINS

USA: Walter Hagen   **Great Britain:** Charles Whitcombe

SATURDAY FOURSOMES

Sarazen/Hagen *beat* **Perry/Busson,** *7 and 6*

Picard/Revolta *beat* **Padgham/Alliss,** *6 and 5*

Runyan/Smith *beat* **Cox/Jarman,** *9 and 8*

Dutra/Laffoon *lost to* **C. Whitcombe/E. Whitcombe** *by one hole*

Session Score: 3-1

SUNDAY SINGLES

Gene Sarazen *beat* **Jack Busson,** *3 and 2*

Paul Runyan *beat* **Dick Burton,** *5 and 3*

Johnny Revolta *beat* **Reg Whitcombe,** *2 and 1*

Olin Dutra *beat* **Alf Padgham,** *4 and 2*

Craig Wood *lost to* **Percy Alliss** *by one hole*

Horton Smith *halved with* **Bill Cox**

Henry Picard *beat* **Ernest Whitcombe,** *3 and 2*

Sam Parks *halved with* **Alf Perry**

Session Score: 6-2

Overall Score: USA 9, Great Britain 3

Ryder Cup legends
Gene **SARAZEN**

The influence of Gene Sarazen, a true golfing hero, extends way beyond the Ryder Cup but during those transatlantic battles the man affectionately known as "The Squire" helped make the USA the world's dominant golfing power.

Born Eugenio Saraceni, Gene Sarazen formed part of a supremely talented US triumvirate with Bobby Jones and Walter Hagen, who tussled for titles throughout the 1920s and 30s – rivalries that extended the interest in the sport of golf across the globe. Sarazen, one of just five players to win all four Majors – the "Grand Slam" of golf – as an individual, was similarly imperious as part of the USA team competing in the Ryder Cup.

In his first two Ryder Cup appearances of 1927 and 1929, Sarazen picked up just half a point from the singles, but won four in a row, 1931–37. The most notable of his singles triumphs came at Southport & Ainsdale Golf Club. In the build-up to the tournament, the 1937 US side was described by *Golf Monthly* as "the greatest golfing force which has ever come to this country". But Britain had other ideas and were indeed level with their opponents, with only the final four singles matches left to play. In the first of these, Sarazen faced Percy Alliss and found himself three shots down just after lunch. The Squire fought back to draw level before a major stroke of luck on the 15th swung the match and the tournament in the USA's favour. Alliss could only watch in horror as Sarazen's shot bounced off an unwitting spectator and onto the green. His disappointment was compounded when his US opponent nonchalantly sunk the putt to edge himself ahead for the first time in the contest. Sarazen held on tight to claim a one-up victory, which put his team into a 5-4 lead – and on the way to an 8-4 triumph.

Sarazen's Ryder Cup legacy was also mirrored in his overall contribution to golf. Only two years before this memorable round at Southport, he hit the "shot heard round the world" (an albatross – double eagle inAmerica – on the 15th hole) to ultimately claim the 1935 Masters. He is also credited with the invention of the modern sand wedge (which he debuted in the 1932 British Open) and held a 75-year endorsement contract with Wilson, the longest in professional sport.

RYDER CUP RECORD

Ryder Cups: 1927 (winner), 1929, 1931 (winner), 1933, 1935 (winner), 1937 (winner)
Total wins: 4
Matches: 12 (won 7, halved 3, lost 2)
Total points: 8.5

Archie **COMPSTON**

Sacked for idleness at 16 by Kidderminster Golf Club, Archie Compston went on to become one of Britain's leading lights in the Ryder Cup's early years and even became a personal coach and close friend of Edward VIII.

Despite being described as a fiery, volatile character, Compston – a towering figure – was much loved by golf fans and became arguably the sport's first British celebrity but his association with the game started in somewhat inauspicious circumstances in the small town of Kidderminster in Worcestershire.

His obvious talent, both as a player and a coach, prompted the club committee to make the "lad-from-down-the-road in Wolverhampton" their first-ever pro in 1909. He was paid 18 shillings (about $4.50) a week for his role as "pro and groundsman", but was sacked for his lamentable attitude towards keeping the greens. It proved no more than a minor blip on his journey to the top of both the sport and England's social ladder as a result of his close association with Edward VIII, later the Duke of Windsor, who also played at Coombe Hill Golf Club. However, Compston's reputation was not built on social profile alone, with performances in his three campaigns in Great Britain's Ryder Cup team marking him out as one of the world's finest players, during which time he forged a particular rivalry with the US's Gene Sarazen.

In 1927's inaugural edition, Compston lost in the Foursomes and the singles as the USA triumphed at the Worcester Country Club in Massachusetts. It was not until two years later, in the heavy rain drenching the Moortown Golf Club in Yorkshire, that the two men's paths first crossed. Having halved his Foursome alongside Charlie Whitcombe on the first day, Compston scored his first and only point against Sarazen with a 6 and 4 victory in the singles. Two years later, in 1931, the American would have his revenge in the heat of Ohio, when he and Johnny Farrell thrashed Compston – alongside W.H. Davies – 8 and 7 in the Foursomes. American Billy Burke also beat the Englishman 7 and 6 in what proved to be his last Ryder Cup.

RIGHT: Britain's Archie Compston poses at Moortown, Leeds, during the final day's practice before heading to America for the 1927 Ryder Cup.

RYDER CUP RECORD

Ryder Cups: 1927, 1929 (winner), 1931
Total wins: 1
Matches: 6 (won 1, halved 1, lost 4)
Total points: 1.5

1937
Great Britain 4
USA 8

Southport & Ainsdale Golf Club

June 29-30

For the first time in Ryder Cup history, the host team suffered defeat as the legendary Walter Hagen, now a non-playing captain, took his US side to Southport. The Americans returned home with an emphatic 8-4 victory that, due to World War II, proved to be the last time the two teams would meet for another decade.

THE COURSE

Southport & Ainsdale Golf Club
Location: Southport, Merseyside, England
Par: 72
Yards: 6,836

Staging the Ryder Cup for the second time in a row, Great Britain hoped that the S&A would once more prove a lucky course for them. But despite terrible storms, the Americans, more accustomed to sunnier climes, still came out on top.

HAVING WON SUCH A MEMORABLE VICTORY at Southport in 1933, Great Britain must have gone into the matches four years later dreaming of a similar result. Having tied at 4-4, with only four games remaining on course, there seemed no reason at all why it could not be repeated. But what happened on the second afternoon will be forever remembered on both sides of the Atlantic, albeit for opposite reasons. The USA won all four of those matches through Gene Sarazen, Sam Snead, Ed Dudley and Henry Picard to turn a tight encounter into a hugely impressive victory that proved once and for all that the Americans were no longer golf's apprentices, they were rapidly becoming masters.

Even the return of British talisman Henry Cotton, overlooked for the previous three Ryder Cups because of a residency rule, was not enough to inspire the hosts although he certainly made an impact

by beating Tony Manero, 5 and 3. Quite clearly, Cotton was Britain's best golfer of the 1930s, having won The Open in 1934 – and he went on to win the trophy again, just weeks after the 1937 Ryder Cup was completed. But having accepted a role as a professional in Belgium, he was ruled ineligible for the Ryder Cup until he returned to Britain to take up a post at Ashridge Golf Club, near London.

Cotton formed part of a strong British side that included up-and-coming stars Dai Rees and Sam King and was captained by Charles Whitcombe. Having guided his team to defeats in America (1931 and 1935), Whitcombe was looking to make it third time lucky.

The Americans, featuring rookies Sam Snead (runner-up in that year's US Open), Byron Nelson and Ed Dudley, began well, despite stormy seaside conditions that made the opening day's play difficult for both teams. Cotton's disappointing and surprising defeat with Alf

ABOVE: *Crowds flock to watch Great Britain's Dai Rees putting on a wet 18th green at Southport during the 1937 Ryder Cup.*

DAYS ONE AND TWO

CAPTAINS

Great Britain: Charles Whitcombe   **USA:** Walter Hagen

TUESDAY FOURSOMES

Padgham/Cotton *lost to* **Dudley/Nelson**, *4 and 2*

Lacey/Cox *lost to* **Guldahl/Manero**, *2 and 1*

C. Whitcombe/Rees *halved with* **Sarazen/Shute**

Alliss/Burton *beat* **Picard/Revolta**, *2 and 1*

Session Score: 1.5-2.5

WEDNESDAY SINGLES

Alf Padgham *lost to* **Ralph Guldahl**, *8 and 7*

Sam King *halved with* **Denny Shute**

Dai Rees *beat* **Byron Nelson**, *3 and 1*

Henry Cotton *beat* **Tony Manero**, *5 and 3*

Percy Alliss *lost to* **Gene Sarazen** *by one hole*

Dick Burton *lost to* **Sam Snead**, *5 and 4*

Alf Perry *lost to* **Ed Dudley**, *2 and 1*

Arthur Lacey *lost to* **Henry Picard**, *2 and 1*

Session Score: 2.5-5.5

Overall Score: Great Britain 4, USA 8

ABOVE: *Captain Charles Whitcombe (left) welcomes Ryder Cup debutant Henry Cotton to the Great Britain team.*

Padgham against new boys Dudley and Nelson, going down 4 and 2, set the tone. The USA ended Day One leading 2.5-1.5.

But with the rain still pouring down on the second day, the British reached lunch in what seemed an encouraging position. Already Cotton had secured victory over Manero and Rees beat Nelson, 3 and 1. By mid-afternoon the scores were tied at 4-4, with everything to play for, but then the Americans simply stepped up a gear with Snead the hero (as he was so often to become in the future).

There was an element of fate about the result, too – especially when Sarazen's narrow victory over Percy Alliss was achieved thanks to a birdie at the 15th when his tee shot landed in the lap of a female spectator and bounced back onto the green as she stood up to shake it off! But in fairness, Sarazen had already worked hard to come back from three-down and there was no luck involved in Snead's convincing 5 and 4 victory over Dick Burton, Dudley's 2 and 1 triumph over Alf Perry, or Picard's 2 and 1 win against Arthur Lacey.

This match proved to be the final Ryder Cup before the intervention of the World War II, with the 1939 event (planned for Ponte Vedra Country Club, Florida) cancelled. But the Americans ended the first period in Ryder Cup history on a major high and they certainly enjoyed it.

With the British Open staged in Carnoustie that year, most of the US team were due to stay in England for two more weeks. Together, they headed for Scotland by bus – it must have been quite a journey.

> **❝We left no pub un-stoned on that ride.❞**

The US team celebrate their Ryder Cup win on their way to play in the British Open at Carnoustie

CHAPTER THREE

THE HOGAN ERA

The 1937 Ryder Cup proved to be the last before World War II made the postponement of the event inevitable. Play did not resume until 1947, when the Great Britain team discovered that the game had taken great steps forwards in the USA. And so started a period of American dominance, inspired by Ben Hogan, that would last another decade.

1947

USA 11
Great Britain 1

Portland Golf Club, Oregon

November 1-2

Eleven years after the death of founder Samuel Ryder, the competition needed a new benefactor to bring it back to life after the upheaval caused by World War II. It found one in the shape of American merchant Robert Hudson, who funded the 1947 Ryder Cup and watched proudly as the USA stormed to an overwhelming victory in his hometown of Portland, Oregon.

LIKE HIS GREAT PREDECESSOR, Hudson had come to golf late in life and loved the game as much for the atmosphere between the players as for the sport itself. He had a vision to take the Ryder Cup forward. Having made his money from food processing, he first sponsored the Portland Open and then the 1946 PGA Championship. On hearing that the Ryder Cup was struggling for finance, he agreed to fund the whole event provided it was staged in his hometown.

Under the agreement, Hudson not only paid for the British team to travel to America on the *Queen Mary*, he also laid on a glitzy pre-match banquet, offered the players gifts and joined them on the long train journey from New York to Oregon. A hospitable and flamboyant character, with contacts in high society (film star Dorothy Lamour was invited to join in the celebrations), Robert Hudson's contribution was crucial in keeping the Ryder Cup alive at a time when war and not sport had been the focus of everyone's lives.

The British team knew they faced a tough task. Most of the side had been serving in the Armed Forces during the war, while America continued to stage tournaments, with Byron Nelson –

excused from military service due to haemophilia – winning 31 times between 1945 and 1946. The visitors included just three players who had been involved in the last Ryder Cup of 1937 – Dai Rees, Sam King and Henry Cotton – and the team was selected by committee. The US chose a side based on tournament performances between 1946 and 1947, meaning playing-captain Ben Hogan could boast such star names as Nelson, Lloyd Mangrum, Jimmy Demaret, Herman Barron and Sam Snead.

Britain's task was made more difficult by the weather – heavy downpours soaked the Portland course to the point of waterlogging to leave the longer-hitting Americans as firm favourites. It was a tag that proved justified because Hogan's men ran away with victory and in a match restricted to just four Foursomes on Saturday and eight singles on the Sunday (played over 36 holes), the US won all but one of the ties. Only Sam King (who beat Herman Keiser, 4 and 3) contributed for the British.

The ability to stop a ball dead on the green using back-spin proved a crucial factor and Great Britain's captain Henry Cotton even went so far as to demand that all US golf clubs be checked for illegally deep grooves on the last day of practice. Nothing

LEFT: US captain Ben Hogan receives the Ryder Cup from sponsor Robert Hudson, watched by Ed Dudley (second left) and British captain Henry Cotton (right).

> **"***I do not think we can ever win a match in your country but all the same, golf is a wonderful game and we all love it.***"**
>
> *Henry Cotton, Captain of Great Britain, after the 11–1 defeat at Portland*

DAYS ONE AND TWO

CAPTAINS

USA: Ben Hogan   **Great Britain:** Henry Cotton

SATURDAY FOURSOMES

Oliver/Worsham *beat* **Cotton/Lees,** *10 and 9*

Snead/Mangrum *beat* **Daly/Ward,** *6 and 5*

Hogan/Demaret *beat* **Adams/Faulkner** *by two holes*

Nelson/Barron *beat* **Rees/King,** *2 and 1*

Session Score: 4-0

SUNDAY SINGLES

E.J. Harrison *beat* **Fred Daly,** *5 and 4*

Lew Worsham *beat* **Jimmy Adams,** *3 and 2*

Lloyd Mangrum *beat* **Max Faulkner,** *6 and 5*

Ed Oliver *beat* **Charlie Ward,** *4 and 3*

Byron Nelson *beat* **Arthur Lees,** *2 and 1*

Sam Snead *beat* **Henry Cotton,** *5 and 4*

Jimmy Demaret *beat* **Dai Rees,** *3 and 2*

Herman Keiser *lost to* **Sam King,** *4 and 3*

Session Score: 7-1

Overall Score: USA 11, Great Britain 1

ABOVE: *Fred Daly drives off the golf deck of the* Queen Mary *as the British team prepare to sail for America in 1947.*

was found amiss, however. The rout began with a humiliating 10 and 9 defeat for Cotton and Arthur Lees against Ed Oliver and Lew Worsham. From that point on, the Americans never looked back. Snead and Mangrum also won by a large margin, 6 and 5 against Charlie Ward and Fred Daly, and the US were 4-0 up by the end of play.

The singles were just as convincing. Cotton chose to stick with his experienced men despite being so badly beaten, 24 hours earlier. His decision proved to be a mistake as all bar King suffered defeat and not a single player made it to the last green. Young Sam Snead was particularly impressive for the US, beating the experienced Cotton, 5 and 4. But in truth there was a gaping chasm in class between the Americans and their opponents, which left the British side stunned by the margin of victory. It was a sign of things to come.

1949
Great Britain 5 USA 7

Ganton Golf Club, Scarborough

September 16-17

THE COURSE

Ganton Golf Club
Location: Scarborough, North Yorkshire, England
Par: 72
Yards: 6,935

Founded in 1891, the inland course (9 miles (14 km) from the sea) was designed by Tom Chisholm and Robert Bird, then modified by Ted Ray, James Braid and J.H. Taylor. Notorious for its 100 bunkers, it was once home to the great Harry Vardon.

Despite missing some of its top players, the USA posted a second consecutive win in Britain - although 12 years apart due to World War II - as they edged to a narrow victory in Yorkshire under the captaincy of Ben Hogan. However, the matches were dogged by controversy, both on and off the course.

HAVING WON SO HANDSOMELY in Portland, two years earlier, it was fair to say the Americans arrived in England as favourites to defend their trophy - but not everything was going their way. Ben Hogan was involved in a near-fatal car crash in February 1949 and although fit enough by the September to captain at Ganton, he was not able to play. He was joined on the sidelines by former star player Byron Nelson (now retired) and US Open winner Cary Middlecoff, who was not a PGA member and therefore ineligible for selection.

Despite his injuries, Hogan certainly caused a stir when he made an official complaint about the clubs that were being used by the British golfers, claiming that the grooves were too deep. He remembered only too well that Henry Cotton had issued the same complaint about US players in Portland, so perhaps it was a case of sweet revenge. In Oregon, the referee had dismissed Britain's complaint but at Ganton, Hogan was proved right. Therefore, the British team sought advice from Royal and Ancient Rules of Golf Committee member Bernard Darwin before calling in host professional Jock Ballantine to file away the prohibited grooves overnight.

Ill feeling between the teams was starting to build and not least because a row had already erupted over the news that the US side had brought 600 steaks with them from home out of fear that post-war meat rationing in Britain would limit their dining options. The meat had been paid for by benefactor Robert Hudson (the merchant who underwrote the 1949 Ryder Cup) and in what the visitors saw as a friendly gesture, they offered to share with their hosts. To the proud British, however, it was a suggestion that smacked of unwanted charity. Perhaps it was just a clash of cultures - to some traditional English golfers, the confident and fashionably dressed Americans appeared brash in times of austerity - but in the truth, the row over the illegally grooved golf clubs proved more damaging as the media debated who was to blame.

RIGHT: *US captain Ben Hogan, pictured ahead of the matches at Ganton Golf Club in 1949.*

DAYS ONE AND TWO

ABOVE: *US star Lloyd Mangrum on the way to victory, as his team clinch Ryder Cup victory.*

CAPTAINS

Great Britain: Charles Whitcombe   **USA:** Ben Hogan

FRIDAY FOURSOMES

Faulkner/Adams *beat* **Harrison/Palmer,** *2 and 1*

Daly/Bousfield *beat* **Hamilton/Alexander,** *4 and 2*

Ward/King *lost to* **Demaret/Heafner,** *4 and 3*

Burton/Lees *beat* **Snead/Mangrum** *by one hole*

Session Score: 3-1

SATURDAY SINGLES

Max Faulkner *lost to* **E.J. Harrison,** *8 and 7*

Jimmy Adams *beat* **Johnny Palmer,** *2 and 1*

Charlie Ward *lost to* **Sam Snead,** *6 and 5*

Dai Rees *beat* **Bob Hamilton,** *6 and 4*

Dick Burton *lost to* **Clayton Heafner,** *3 and 2*

Sam King *lost to* **Chick Harbert,** *4 and 3*

Arthur Lees *lost to* **Jimmy Demaret,** *7 and 6*

Fred Daly *lost to* **Lloyd Mangrum,** *4 and 3*

Session Score: 2-6

Overall Score: Great Britain 5, USA 7

None of this controversy affected the Great Britain team. With their newly filed clubs, they took a heartening 3-1 lead by the end of the opening day's Foursomes – and all this without talisman Cotton, who was so upset at being overlooked as captain that he refused to play under his replacement, Charles Whitcombe.

Playing in front of huge and excited crowds, Max Faulkner starred in the opening match, partnering Jimmy Adams to a 2 and 1 victory over E.J. Harrison and Johnny Palmer, and going round in just 69. It was a result that inspired Irishman Fred Daly and Ken Bousfield to play even better, winning 4 and 2 against Skip Alexander and Bob Hamilton. The Americans fought back with an important victory for Jimmy Demaret and Clayton Heafner, but Britain needed only three-and-a-half points in the Sunday's singles to win back the trophy. It proved an impossible task, however, as the US won the session 6-2, starting with a quite remarkable performance from Harrison, who played some outstanding golf to beat Faulkner – rated Britain's top player.

Heafner's birdie-strewn four-hole finish to defeat Richard Burton 3 and 2, followed by Demaret's 7 and 6 rout of Arthur Lees and then Lloyd Mangrum's victory over Daly clinched the Ryder Cup – even though Dai Rees' round of 65 as he beat Bob Hamilton was possibly the golfing highlight of the day. In the end, however, the Americans were just too strong. Maybe all those steaks had done the trick.

RYDER CUP RECORD

Ryder Cups: 1947 (winner, playing captain), 1949 (winner, non-playing captain), 1951 (winner), 1967 (winner, non-playing captain)

Total wins: 4
Matches: 3 (won 3, halved 0, lost 0)
Total points: 3

Ryder Cup legends
Ben HOGAN

Against a backdrop of childhood tragedy, World War II and a near-fatal car accident, the quiet Ben Hogan became one of history's most celebrated golfers, with a swing that is still hailed as perhaps the finest ever.

OPPOSITE: America's iconic golfer Ben Hogan receives the Ryder Cup trophy as winning team captain in 1949.

Ben Hogan was just 9 years old when his father - a blacksmith - committed suicide with a gunshot to the chest on Valentine's Day of 1922, plunging the family into turmoil. The young Ben and his siblings were forced to go out to work to ease the financial burden on his mother, Clara, and it was then that he discovered that he could make a handsome profit as a caddy at the nearby Glen Garden Country Club, Fort Worth, Texas - and so began his love affair with golf at the age of 11.

As a youngster, Hogan would often practise with his brother Royal and their friend, Byron Nelson - himself a future golfing star - but he was not averse to honing his skills alone, with an approach to training that frequently bordered on the obsessive. Indeed, this would become a trademark of his time, both as player and captain, and the fruit of his labours was the putative perfect swing. Life was not always easy for Hogan, who struggled financially as a young pro, because of a hook that undermined all his good work on the course, although he worked incredibly hard to correct the problem.

Like many, Hogan's job was put on hold when the USA entered World War II, where he fought between 1942 and 1945. Up until then, he had busied himself in racking up tour victories and it seemed to take him no time at all to get back into the swing of things when he returned from the conflict. That said, he was still without the holy grail of a Major title, winning a record 30 tournaments before finally landing a big one. Success came at the Portland Golf Club, where he lifted the 1946 PGA Championship and then the following year, Hogan began a Ryder Cup career that would span 20 years, both as player and captain. As the USA's leading moneymaker and arguably his country's finest player, Hogan was appointed playing captain and set the perfect example in turning around a four-shot deficit to take his Foursomes match two-up on the final green. He chose to drop himself for the singles but the decision mattered little, with America claiming a crushing 11-1 overall victory.

In his mid-thirties, Hogan's singles career went from strength to strength, winning the second and third Majors of his career at the PGA Championship and the US Open. But on the morning of February 2, 1949, Hogan and his beloved Valerie were driving just outside Texas when a Greyhound bus, attempting to overtake a truck, collided head-on with their car. Just before impact, the three-time Major-winning golfer dived across to shield his wife from the impact, saving her life as well as his own for the steering column punctured the seat where he had been sitting just a split-second beforehand.

As a result of the many injuries he sustained in the crash, doctors said he might never walk again, but Hogan proved them wrong. After 59 days in hospital, he returned home on April 1 and when the eighth Ryder Cup kicked off in September of that year, the man known as "The Hawk" was ready to captain his fellow countrymen in a non-playing role. This was the first Ryder Cup played on British soil (at Ganton Golf Club in Yorkshire) for 12 years and Hogan's crop contained just three players with previous experience of playing across the pond. Despite being on crutches and only able to reach the holes nearest to the clubhouse, the captain inspired his team to a 7-5 overall win.

His final outing as a Ryder Cup player came two years later at Pinehurst, North Carolina, under captain Sam Snead. Having won the Masters earlier in 1951, Hogan was the star of a USA team considered superior to their opponents in almost every way. And so it was on the course, with the USA romping to a 9.5- 2.5 victory with Hogan, alongside Jimmy Demaret, cruising to a 5 and 4 Foursomes win before beating Charlie Ward, 3 and 2, in the singles.

After a 16-year hiatus he made a return to the Ryder Cup in 1967 to captain the US team that he famously introduced as "the finest golfers in the world". In the event, his words could not have been any more accurate for his team, containing such stars as Arnold Palmer and Gene Littler, humiliated Europe with a record 23.5-8.5 victory. It was a fitting way for Ben Hogan to bow out.

> **"** *I hate a hook – it nauseates me, I could vomit when I see one. It's like a rattlesnake in your pocket.* **"**
>
> *Ben Hogan battles against the hook shot*

1951

USA 9.5
Great Britain 2.5

Pinehurst Resort, North Carolina

November 2-4

The USA made it five-in-a-row by yet again winning comfortably at Pinehurst in 1951. Led by inspirational player-captain Sam Snead and star performer Jimmy Demaret, it was a Ryder Cup that bizarrely included a rest day in between the Foursomes and Singles matches to allow both teams to attend a college football match.

ABOVE: *Ben Hogan of the USA and Dai Rees of Great Britain before the opening day's play of the 1951 Ryder Cup.*

OPPOSITE: *From left, Fred Daly, Sam Snead, Charles Ward and Lloyd Mangrum brave the weather with umbrellas and waterproofs in North Carolina.*

THINGS WERE CERTAINLY DIFFERENT in the early days of the Ryder Cup and the competition in 1951 would probably seem almost unrecognizable from the mass media, ultra-hyped event that grips the world every two years, these days. Although the matches were growing in popularity, the competition at Pinehurst was watched by around 6,000 supporters and reported on by a select group of just 30 golf writers. Astonishingly, the complex remained open to club golfers during the entire weekend with members and guests allowed to play on the resort's other courses while the Ryder Cup greats did battle.

As was the early tradition, there were only 12 matches to be played but strangest of all was a blank Saturday, built into the schedule to allow the players to attend a football game. At Chapel Hill, they witnessed a college match between North Carolina and Tennessee, in which Carolina were crushed 27-0. Britain's golfers ended up routed, too – swept aside by an American team that once again dominated the first-day Foursomes despite unseasonably cold weather that must have made the visitors feel at home. The day opened to heavy mist but their hosts never looked back, going on to claim a convincing 9.5-2.5 victory.

Sam Snead was the inspiration, partnering Lloyd Mangrum to a 5 and 4 victory over Jimmy Adams and John Panton on the Friday and beating new British Open champion Max Faulkner, 4 and 3, in the singles. Most of the American team, which included rookies Jack Burke Jnr. and Henry Ransom, contributed to a fine win against a Great Britain team now captained by Arthur Lacey. The last time that Great Britain had visited the USA (in 1947), they were so badly beaten that only one of the matches even reached the last green – this time was not much better, with only two matches going the distance.

Arthur Lees scored two of Britain's 2.5 points and perhaps the highlight for the visitors was his Foursomes match alongside Charlie Ward against Henry Ransom and Ed Oliver, which featured the British pair going round in 69 and producing a string of birdies in the final six holes of a 2 and 1 victory. But there were plenty more heroes on the opposite team, with America's Jimmy Demaret producing an excellent personal display to win twice and conclude his Ryder Cup career with a perfect record of played six, won six. Demaret produced the shot of the tournament, too – holing out for

DAYS ONE AND TWO

CAPTAINS

USA: Sam Snead   **Great Britain:** Arthur Lacey

FRIDAY FOURSOMES

Heafner/Burke beat **Faulkner/Rees**, 5 and 3

Oliver/Ransom lost to **Ward/Lees**, 2 and 1

Snead/Mangrum beat **Adams/Panton**, 5 and 4

Hogan/Demaret beat **Daly/Bousfield**, 5 and 4

Session Score: 3-1

SUNDAY SINGLES

Jack Burke beat **Jimmy Adams**, 4 and 2

Jimmy Demaret beat **Dai Rees** by two holes

Clayton Heafner halved with **Fred Daly**

Lloyd Mangrum beat **Harry Weetman**, 6 and 5

Ed Oliver lost to **Arthur Lees**, 2 and 1

Ben Hogan beat **Charlie Ward**, 3 and 2

Skip Alexander beat **John Panton**, 8 and 7

Sam Snead beat **Max Faulkner**, 4 and 3

Session Score: 6.5-1.5

Overall Score: USA 9.5, Great Britain 2.5

a birdie from a greenside bunker at the 17th despite his ball being buried deep into the sand. And it wasn't a one-off – the flamboyant American successfully got up-and-down from sand on 10 out of 11 occasions. No wonder he offered his sand wedge as a gift to rival Rees when the match was over.

Burke Jnr. and Ben Hogan (now back to playing after a full recovery from a car crash in 1949, and as ruthless and focused as ever, beating Charlie Ward 3 and 2) joined a select group of players with a 100 per cent record over the weekend.

Even the staunchest British supporter had to admit that it was a hugely convincing victory for the USA and a another very demoralizing defeat for the visitors. Already, people were beginning to question whether the Ryder Cup was losing its competitive edge.

1953

Great Britain 5.5
USA 6.5

Wentworth Golf Club, Surrey

October 2-3

THE COURSE

Wentworth Golf Club
Location: West Course,
Virginia Water,
Surrey, England
Par: 72
Yards: 7,308

*Designed by Harry Colt,
the legendary course now
home to the headquarters
of the PGA European Tour
was built in 1926. Today, it
is surrounded by the private
and exclusive Wentworth
Estate, where many golfers
have bought second homes.*

In 1953, the Ryder Cup returned to the course where it all began – a full 27 years after the unofficial challenge match between Great Britain and the USA created a brand new competition. It proved to be a battle worthy of the occasion as Great Britain pushed their rivals to the limit in a match won at the very last hole by Lloyd Mangrum's American side.

IF SAMUEL RYDER (1858-1936) was looking down on Wentworth almost two decades later, he would surely have been proud of what he witnessed as Great Britain and America produced a Ryder Cup to remember. Despite recent losses there was a feeling of optimism in Britain following the crowning of Queen Elizabeth II, while explorer Edmund Hillary had just conquered Everest – so why not the Ryder Cup next? Local enthusiasm was boosted by the news that America's Ben Hogan had insisted, despite winning all three Majors since recovering from a car crash, that he would play no more 36-hole matches and therefore was not available for selection.

US captain Lloyd Mangrum therefore had an inexperienced team at his disposal, with five newcomers: Dale Douglas, Ted Kroll, Fred Haas, Cary Middlecoff and Walter Burkemo. And for once, the British team – led by non-playing captain Henry Cotton – felt that they were an even match for their rivals, especially as rookies Peter Alliss, Eric Brown, Ireland's Harry Bradshaw and Bernard Hunt promised to be a talented group.

Cotton proved himself a thorough captain, organizing luxury accommodation and catering for his players. He also went to the extent of accompanying them on a team-bonding trip to London's West End, and emphasized the need for team spirit. On the opening day, however, he placed huge pressure on Alliss – at this stage the youngest player ever to appear in the Ryder Cup – by asking him to open the Foursomes alongside Weetman against Douglas and Oliver. It was a tall order but the two new boys played well and led by one hole at lunch, eventually going down 2 and 1.

> **"** *My mind was full of nothing but feet. Rows and rows of feet... the shoes of the people perched on the front seat of the grandstand.* **"**
>
> *Peter Alliss describes the surreal pressure on the last green*

ABOVE: *Dave Douglas of the USA takes a drive at the 1953 Ryder Cup at Wentworth.*

LEFT: *Harry Weetman of Great Britain plays from the rough at the 3rd hole on the way to his one hole defeat of Sam Snead.*

DAYS ONE AND TWO

CAPTAINS

Great Britain: Henry Cotton   **USA:** Lloyd Mangrum

FRIDAY FOURSOMES

Weetman/Alliss *lost to* **Douglas/Oliver**, *2 and 1*

Brown/Panton *lost to* **Mangrum/Snead**, *8 and 7*

Adams/Hunt *lost to* **Kroll/Burke**, *7 and 5*

Daly/Bradshaw *beat* **Burkemo/Middlecoff** *by one hole*

Session Score: 1-3

SATURDAY SINGLES

Dai Rees *lost to* **Jack Burke**, *2 and 1*

Fred Daly *beat* **Ted Kroll**, *9 and 7*

Eric Brown *beat* **Lloyd Mangrum** *by two holes*

Harry Weetman *beat* **Sam Snead** *by one hole*

Max Faulkner *lost to* **Cary Middlecoff**, *3 and 1*

Peter Alliss *lost to* **Jim Turnesa** *by one hole*

Bernard Hunt *halved with* **Dave Douglas**

Harry Bradshaw *beat* **Fred Haas**, *3 and 2*

Session Score: 4.5-3.5

Overall Score: Great Britain 5.5, USA 6.5

The match was affected by an unusual decision from adjudicator Admiral Sir Charles Forbes when, at the third hole of the afternoon, the Americans' ball nestled at the base of a tree. But Forbes ruled it was sitting in a rabbit scrape and therefore awarded a free drop – a decision that was hotly contested by the British team. It was a big decision, too, because it helped the USA to a 3-1 first-day lead, with Lloyd Mangrum and Sam Snead soon afterwards demolishing Eric Brown and John Panton, 8 and 7. Fred Daly and Harry Bradshaw – the first Ryder Cup partnership to be taken from both Northern and Southern Ireland – did provide a welcome victory for the hosts against Walter Burkemo and Cary Middlecoff, however.

The singles matches, however, were to prove much, much closer, with the Americans gaining a nail-biting victory as darkness closed in on the 18th green. It was Bernard Hunt who missed the putt that handed the USA victory as he halved against Dave Douglas, with nerves jangling on both sides. But young Alliss also missed vital shots at the same hole when he took a double-bogey six to go from all square to one-down against Jim Turnesa right at the death. For the British, who fought tooth and nail, it was hard to take – especially when Weetman produced one of the Ryder Cup's greatest fight-backs, coming from four-down with five to play to beat Snead at the last.

When Bradshaw triumphed over Fred Haas, the home team suddenly realized they could win. Maybe that pressure was too much for Alliss as he made such a hash of the 18th, meaning a tie was the best that Britain could hope for. A huge crowd gathered around the 18th as Hunt over-shot the green with his approach shot in the final match and then, agonizingly, took three putts – when even two would have won the match – to give the USA a half and overall victory in one of the most pressurized and exciting Ryder Cups of all time.

Spectators gather in front of the main Wentworth scoreboard as the results for the final day of the 1953 Ryder Cup are mounted.

1955
Thunderbird CC, California

USA 8
Great Britain 4

November 5-6

In 1955, American domination of the Ryder Cup continued in California as captain Chick Harbert guided his side to an 8-4 victory. This meant the trophy had now resided in the USA for an astonishing 21 years, but at least Great Britain put up a fight in probably their best performance so far on American soil.

THE COURSE

Thunderbird Country Club
Location: Palm Springs, California, USA
Par: 72
Yards: 6,512

Designed by John Dawson and Larry Hughes and opened in 1952, this desert course features stunning views of the surrounding mountains. A favourite with celebrities, Lucille Ball once lived in a house facing the 18th fairway and Bing Crosby was club champion in 1958.

IT IS A SIGN OF JUST HOW STRONG America were in the 1950s that gaining four points, even in defeat, was seen as something of a triumph by the British, who were led by captain Dai Rees and picked up four victories in the USA for the first time. Contrast that to their last two visits to the States, where they collected a total of just three points!

Great Britain were determined to at least be competitive and had decided to select seven players for their team based on points awarded for performances in five key tournaments. The other three were selected by committee and this time there was no place for Peter Alliss or Bernard Hunt, the two men who had crumbled under pressure at Wentworth two years earlier, or for

> *"We've learned a lot, although we have lost, and we are going back to practise in the streets and on the beaches."*
>
> Lord Brabazon, president of the British PGA, makes his post-match speech

LEFT: *Harry Weetman is filmed by his wife as the British team practise before sailing to America for the 1955 Ryder Cup.*

ABOVE: *US captain Chick Harbert holds the Ryder Cup with pride, watched on by sponsor Robert Hudson and Great Britain's Dai Rees (right).*

DAYS ONE AND TWO

CAPTAINS

USA: Chick Harbert   **Great Britain:** Dai Rees

SATURDAY FOURSOMES

Harper/Barber *lost to* **Fallon/Jacobs** *by one hole*

Ford/Kroll *beat* **Brown/Scott,** *5 and 4*

Burke/Bolt *beat* **Lees/Weetman** *by one hole*

Snead/Middlecoff *beat* **Bradshaw/Rees,** *3 and 2*

Session Score: 3-1

SUNDAY SINGLES

Tommy Bolt *beat* **Christy O'Connor,** *4 and 2*

Chick Harbert *beat* **Syd Scott,** *3 and 2*

Cary Middlecoff *lost to* **John Jacobs** *by one hole*

Sam Snead *beat* **Dai Rees,** *3 and 1*

Marty Furgol *lost to* **Arthur Lees,** *3 and 2*

Jerry Barber *lost to* **Eric Brown,** *3 and 2*

Jack Burke *beat* **Harry Bradshaw,** *3 and 2*

Doug Ford *beat* **Harry Weetman,** *3 and 2*

Session Score: 5-3

Overall Score: USA 8, Great Britain 4

48-year-old Henry Cotton, now considered too old. Instead four new players – John Jacobs, Syd Scott, Christy O'Connor Snr. and Johnny Fallon – joined the ranks.

Having dominated the tournament for so long, the Americans were also keen to make changes: not to their team, but to the format itself. Sam Snead suggested Fourballs should replace the more traditional Foursomes, for instance. However, the proposal received short shrift from the British PGA. That year's American team was not considered one of its strongest. Even taking into consideration rookies Jerry Barber, Marty Furgol, Doug Ford, Chandler Harper and Tommy Bolt, the average age was 37 and without the likes of Ben Hogan and Byron Nelson, it lacked star quality. The impressive Thunderbird Country Club had enough glamour to make up for that, however. In the celebrity heartland of Palm Springs, it had a touch of Hollywood glitz about it. A fleet of electric buggies followed players around the course, which was surrounded by homes owned by film stars and celebrities. Water hazards featured around the greens, narrow fairways and punishing areas of rough. It was very different to what the British team were used to back home.

Maybe they took time to grow accustomed to their new surroundings because the USA raced into a 3-1 lead on the opening day despite an exciting and hard-fought victory for Britain's Fallon and Jacobs in the first Foursomes match against Harper and

Barber. The match was a real battle all the way, with some stunning displays of short-game genius from Barber, who time and again was able to chip in from off the green. But in the end the British held firm for a narrow one-up victory. Their team-mates could not follow suit, however, because America's Doug Ford and Ted Kroll, Jack Burke Jnr. and Tommy Bolt, and Sam Snead and Cary Middlecoff all won their matches to take a healthy lead into the singles.

Perhaps the turning point was a combative display from Tommy "Lightning" Bolt, whose gritty play helped his team come from behind to snatch victory against Harry Weetman and Arthur Lees. And the same player kicked off the singles by beating O'Connor, 4 and 2. It took a spirited fight-back from Great Britain to make their hosts sweat in front of a large and increasingly vocal crowd. Jacobs began with an important victory against Middlecoff, thanks to birdies at the 12th and 13th before Lees added a 3 and 2 win against Furgol, and Eric Brown beat Jerry Barber. But the Americans were too strong to throw it all away and their attitude was typified by Sam Snead, who when faced with what seemed an impossible shot up against a palm tree at the 7th against Dai Rees still managed to produce a miraculous recovery shot to make an eagle and take the hole. By the time Burke beat Bradshaw and Ford beat Weetman, overall victory was already assured and the status quo was safe – but there were at least signs that Britain could fight back.

1957

Great Britain 7.5
USA 4.5

Lindrick Golf Club, Rotherham

October 4-5

THE COURSE

Lindrick Golf Club
Location: Rotherham, South Yorkshire, England
Par: 71
Yards: 6,541

The South Yorkshire course, founded in 1891, was a controversial choice because many critics in Britain feared it would suit the USA more than their own team. But they were proved wrong as Great Britain produced a rare and memorable Ryder Cup win.

Roared on by a vociferous crowd that upset American sensibilities, Great Britain produced possibly their greatest singles session ever in the Ryder Cup of 1957. Led by playing captain Dai Rees, they won six of the eight matches to lift the trophy for the first time in 24 years.

THE PERFORMANCE AT LINDRICK GOLF CLUB will always be remembered by the British as one of their finest, even against some of the incredible displays in the modern era; Rees' team came from 3-1 down to win 7.5-4.5 on an incredible Saturday that saw the US side routed. All this on a course selected after Sir Stuart Goodwin, a Yorkshire businessman, had donated £10,000 ($28,000 at mid-1950s exchange rates) to help finance the British team on condition the competition was staged at his local club. But it proved no barrier to a British victory for with a strong team (selected based on performances in professional stroke-play tournaments), captain Rees was able to call on players of the quality of Max Faulkner, Ken Bousfield, Christy O'Connor Snr., Harry Weetman and Eric Brown.

The American team, led by Jack Burke Jnr., perhaps lacked star names after Sam Snead and Ben Hogan both opted against taking part, while Cary Middlecoff and Julius Boros were ignored after controversially choosing to play in a lucrative exhibition match instead of the USPGA Championship. Even so, after seven victories in a row they were strong favourites.

Things started badly for Britain when Peter Alliss and Bernard Hunt – recalled despite their infamous collapses, four years earlier – went down to Doug Ford and Dow Finsterwald, 2 and 1, in the opening match. There were further defeats for Faulkner and Weetman (against Ted Kroll and Burke) and for O'Connor and Brown (a crushing 7 and 5 reverse against Dick Mayer and Tommy Bolt). The one ray of hope as the USA went 3-1 up was a battling performance from Rees, who, partnered by Bousfield, came from two-down to beat Art Wall and Fred Hawkins; but when a row over selection broke out on the Friday night, the outlook appeared bleak.

Following a team meeting, Rees had left Faulkner and Weetman out of his singles line-up after both men apparently volunteered

> ❝ *The worst I have ever seen in my life.* ❞

America's Tommy Bolt describes the crowd at Lindrick after they cheered his missed putts

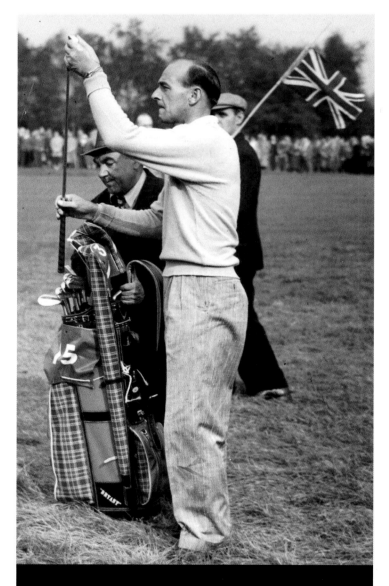

ABOVE: *Britain's Eric Brown chooses a club during his singles match against Tommy Bolt.*

LEFT: *Great Britain's jubilant captain Dai Rees is surrounded by happy team-mates after winning the trophy.*

DAYS ONE AND TWO

CAPTAINS

Great Britain: Dai Rees   **USA:** Jack Burke Jnr.

FRIDAY FOURSOMES

Alliss/Hunt *lost to* **Ford/Finsterwald,** *2 and 1*

Bousfield/Rees *beat* **Wall/Hawkins,** *3 and 2*

Faulkner/Weetman *lost to* **Kroll/Burke,** *4 and 3*

O'Connor/Brown *lost to* **Mayer/Bolt,** *7 and 5*

Session Score: 1-3

SATURDAY SINGLES

Eric Brown *beat* **Tommy Bolt,** *4 and 3*

Peter Mills *beat* **Jack Burke,** *5 and 3*

Peter Alliss *lost to* **Fred Hawkins,** *2 and 1*

Ken Bousfield *beat* **Lionel Hebert,** *4 and 3*

Dai Rees *beat* **Ed Furgol,** *7 and 6*

Bernard Hunt *beat* **Doug Ford,** *6 and 4*

Christy O'Connor *beat* **Dow Finsterwald,** *7 and 6*

Harry Bradshaw *halved with* **Dick Mayer**

Session Score: 6.5-1.5

Overall Score: Great Britain 7.5, USA 4.5

to drop out. Later, he was stunned when a furious Weetman told journalists he would never play under his captaincy again. The two men had been long-time friends and the controversy was lapped up by the English media, with Weetman later being called to a disciplinary hearing by the PGA and subsequently banned from playing for a year. Without him, however, Britain produced their best-ever singles display to justify Rees' decision. They began with an early win for Brown in an ill-humoured match against the volatile, but talented Bolt. Roared on by an increasingly raucous home crowd, Brown won 4 and 3 with Bolt clearly rattled by the way the home supporters cheered missed putts. He even broke a golf club shaft over his knee in frustration.

That particular tie set the tone but perhaps the biggest shock came as rookie Peter Mills beat US captain Burke, 5 and 3, to level the scores at 3-3, with Bousfield, Hunt and O'Connor all leading as he did so. Fred Hawkins showed great resolve to beat Alliss and stem the tide but that result proved to be the US's last win of the day as Great Britain roared to victory. O'Connor crushed Finsterwald 7 and 6 in another ill-humoured match that saw both men refuse to shake hands, while Rees continued his own excellent Ryder Cup in beating Ed Furgol by the same margin.

Bernard Hunt scored a morale-boosting victory over Ford to make up for his disappointment of four years earlier and with the score now 6-4, Britain needed only a half from either Bousfield – who appeared to be on a slide after losing three holes in a row, having once been seven-up against Lionel Hebert – or Harry Bradshaw against Dick Mayer. But after Faulkner and Rees raced across the course to let Bousfield know the importance of his result, he regained his nerve to seal a victory that meant the Ryder Cup was, at last, returning to Britain. It had been a long, long wait.

Ryder Cup legends
Sam **SNEAD** and Lloyd **MANGRUM**

Sam Snead and Lloyd Mangrum were quite the double act. "Slammin'" Sammy was renowned for his ferocity, while "Icicle" Lloyd's natty attire, distinctive moustache and never-say-die attitude endeared him to the golfing fraternity. And both were Ryder Cup heroes – Snead made eight American sides and captained his team on three occasions, while Mangrum played four times and captained the USA once.

In 1949, Snead and Mangrum took on the dangerous pairing of Dick Burton and Arthur Lees for Great Britain at the Ganton Golf Club in Scarborough. They were part of the US team who once again took home the trophy despite the absence of Ben Hogan, who acted as non-playing captain after having suffered injuries in a car crash. Snead's drive and authority was clear for all to see and it was no surprise when he captained the US side two years later at the Pinehurst Resort in North Carolina. Under his stewardship, the team romped to victory 9.5-2.5, with Snead and Mangrum winning their Foursomes battle with ease before going on to win in the singles, too. Snead downed Max Faulkner in the singles, 4 and 3, while Mangrum saw off the challenge of Harry Weetman to keep the USA on course for a crushing win.

If Snead oversaw a thumping victory for the USA in 1951, the going proved much tougher when Mangrum played captain in 1953 and paired with his friend again at Wentworth. The USA triumphed, but such was the tension – they won 6.5-5.5 – that the Americans didn't gain victory until the final singles match when Bernard Hunt missed a putt to halve with Dave Douglas. Mangrum

was an honorary captain in 1955 when Snead once again stole the show. Combining with the imperious Tommy Bolt, Jack Burke Jr. and Doug Ford, they had two victories apiece to account for all of the American points, while Mangrum watched on with pride.

Sam Snead's devoted approach to golf was the reason he captained the US Ryder Cup side three times (in 1951, 1959 and 1969). Snead's legacy is the incredible magnitude of his victories – as his 82 tour wins testify – and his swing is constantly recalled with a mixture of awe and envy.

Mangrum won enough tournaments to be ranked among the legends of the game but these successes seem trivial when compared to what he achieved off the course. Mangrum also fought in World War II, where he won four Battle Stars and two Purple Hearts for his service. Sam Snead's contribution should not be overlooked either, for he also served in the US military during World War II.

Lloyd Mangrum died of a heart attack, aged 59, in 1973 – his twelfth attack in total. He just didn't do anything in moderation. And like his friend, the only thing that could stop Sam Snead in his tracks was Father Time. Indeed, he played golf at an elite level longer than any other player, winning the most PGA Tour events (82). That kept his trademark straw hat, which was always perched serenely on top of his head, in the public eye for a long time.

RYDER CUP RECORD

Sam SNEAD
Ryder Cups: 1937 (winner), 1947 (winner), 1949 (winner), 1951 (winner, playing captain), 1953 (winner), 1955 (winner), 1959 (winner, playing captain), 1969 (winner, non-playing captain)
Total wins: 8
Matches: 13 (won 10, halved 1, lost 2)
Total points: 10.5

Lloyd MANGRUM
Ryder Cups: 1947 (winner), 1949 (winner), 1951 (winner), 1953 (winner, playing captain)
Total wins: 4
Matches: 8 (won 6, halved 0, lost 2)
Total points: 6

AS A PAIR:
Matches: 4 (won 3, halved 0, lost 1)
Total points: 3

> **"***I'll never, never captain an American team again because of the 9,000 deaths I suffered in the last hour.***"**
>
> *Lloyd Mangrum's nerves in 1953*

BELOW: *Lloyd Mangrum (left) and Sam Snead pictured during a practice round ahead of the 1949 Ryder Cup.*

1959

USA 8.5
Great Britain 3.5

Eldorado Golf Club, California

November 6-7

Buoyed by their morale-boosting victory at Lindrick, just when Great Britain believed they were now on a par with their American rivals, they were in for a shock. Sam Snead's US side romped to a victory that included six out of eight points in the singles, putting the British right back to square one at Indian Wells.

HAVING WAITED SO LONG TO WIN BACK the famous golden trophy - 24 years, to be precise - Great Britain took just 24 months to hand it back as they continued a miserable run of performances on American soil to lose convincingly at the Eldorado Golf Club. But in many ways the 13th Ryder Cup matches were overshadowed by a harrowing journey for the British team, which began with a choppy crossing on the *Queen Elizabeth* that left many of the players sick. Then, even more horrifically, the plane taking them from Los Angeles to Palm Springs plunged 1.2km (4,000ft) in severe turbulence before the pilot was finally able to regain control and return to base.

Such a nerve-wracking experience - the plane had run into the tail end of a hurricane that had already devastated parts of Mexico - would be bad enough at any time but coming just a year after English soccer club Manchester United were involved in a fatal airplane crash in Munich, which killed 23 people, it was particularly difficult. Many of the players were clearly shaken. Rather than catch a connecting flight, the team travelled by bus for the final leg, but were never able to find top form against a ruthless American side led by Sam Snead and inspired by Dow Finsterwald, PGA Champion Bob Rosburg and Mike Souchak, who each won two points.

OPPOSITE: *US player Rob Rosburg collected two points in his only Ryder Cup appearance.*

LEFT: *Sam Snead, US captain, shows team-mates a list of the pairings for the opening day's matches.*

DAYS ONE AND TWO

CAPTAINS

USA: Sam Snead **Great Britain:** Dai Rees

FRIDAY FOURSOMES

Rosburg/Souchak *beat* **Hunt/Brown,** *5 and 4*

Boros/Finsterwald *beat* **Rees/Bousfield** *by two holes*

Wall/Ford *lost to* **O'Connor/Alliss,** *3 and 2*

Snead/Middlecoff *halved with* **Weetman/Thomas**

Session Score: 2.5-1.5

SATURDAY SINGLES

Doug Ford *halved with* **Norman Drew**

Mike Souchak *beat* **Ken Bousfield,** *3 and 2*

Bob Rosburg *beat* **Harry Weetman,** *6 and 5*

Sam Snead *beat* **Dave Thomas,** *6 and 5*

Art Wall *beat* **Christy O'Connor,** *7 and 6*

Dow Finsterwald *beat* **Dai Rees** *by one hole*

Jay Hebert *halved with* **Peter Alliss**

Cary Middlecoff *lost to* **Eric Brown,** *4 and 3*

Session Score: 6-2

Overall Score: USA 8.5, Great Britain 3.5

> **"** *I didn't play safe, I never do – it's not my game. I just didn't hit the right shot.* **"**

Great Britain's Harry Weetman on the stroke that cost his side dearly

The American team, completely revamped from 1957, took a 2.5-1.5 lead in the opening day's Foursomes, with Christy O'Connor Snr. and Peter Alliss Britain's only winners against Art Wall and Doug Ford, 3 and 2. Rosburg and Souchak were comfortable victors for the USA as they overcame Bernard Hunt and Eric Brown, 5 and 4; Julius Boros and Dow Finsterwald saw off Dai Rees and Ken Bousfield by two holes. Perhaps the key moment, however, came in the last match of the day when the Americans were handed a half they hardly expected as Snead and Cary Middlecoff arrived at the 18th already one-down against Harry Weetman and Dave Thomas.

Things looked bad for the USA when Snead's approach shot found water with little hope of making better than a five. Strangely, Weetman – instead of laying up safely and taking a steady route to victory – went for glory with a five-iron and saw his shot also land in the lake. He was made to pay as Snead holed a 10-foot putt to win the hole with a bogey, putting his side 3-1 ahead. It was a psychologically vital point, too: although the

British were still within touching distance, they went into the final day knowing it could have been closer. They soon found the Americans, with memories of a singles drubbing at Lindrick still fresh in their minds, were in the mood for revenge.

Five of the matches ended in US victories and two were halved, leaving Eric Brown as Great Britain's only winner when he beat Middlecoff, 4 and 3. By that time the trophy was long gone. Finsterwald held out to beat Rees at the last despite seeing his opponent come back from six holes down, while Rosburg, Souchak, Snead and Wall contributed victories to regain the trophy for the US. In some ways, this was a landmark Ryder Cup – the last time ever that matches were played over 36 holes. But in many others it was a routine victory, and one the American home crowd had now become accustomed to witnessing.

1961

Great Britain 9.5
USA 14.5

Royal Lytham & St Annes Golf Club

October 13-14

THE COURSE

Royal Lytham & St Annes Golf Club
Location: Lytham St Annes, Lancashire, England
Par: 70
Yards: 7,118

Royal Lytham & St Annes was the first Open Championship course to play host to the Ryder Cup, bringing prestige to the event with its new-look format.

In an historic Ryder Cup, the previous format was changed into two sets of 18-hole Foursomes and singles matches, doubling the number of points available from 12 to 24. It made no difference to the overall result, however, as Jerry Barber's US side produced yet another focused and assured performance to defend their trophy at Royal Lytham & St Annes, winning by five points.

THE NEW-LOOK RYDER CUP - proposed by Lord Brabazon - saw the scrapping of 36-hole matches to streamline the tournament, making it more marketable. It featured two sets of Foursomes on the opening day and eight singles matches on the second. In fact, if the Americans had their way, it would also have been extended to a third day, with two sessions of Fourballs added to the mix, but this proposal was vetoed by the British, at least for now.

The matches were to be staged at Royal Lytham & St Annes and attracted renewed interest from golf fans curious as to which side would benefit most from the changes. With more points up for grabs, perhaps America's greater strength in depth would count, or would the shorter games give British golfers a chance?

The home team were boosted by the news that their rivals had surprisingly - and controversially - omitted Sam Snead (one of their most famous and successful players) after he played in an unauthorized Pro-Am tournament in a breach of USPGA rules. In fact, Snead was fined and banned from tournament golf for six months, a harsh punishment that was later reduced to 45 days. Meanwhile, his place in the US Ryder Cup team went to Doug Ford. A furious Snead was reported as saying, "This is the worst slap in the face I have ever had!" A fine Ryder Cup playing career came abruptly to an end when his appeal was scheduled for after the 1961 tournament and so the man who had played in seven Ryder Cups and won 10.5 points missed out.

ABOVE: *Great Britain's captain Dai Rees in putting action in front of packed crowds at Royal Lytham & St Annes.*

Even without the talismanic Sam Snead, however, the Americans proved too strong for Great Britain, with impressive debutant Arnold Palmer and big-hitting Mike Souchak contributing three-and-a-half points each as the visitors eased to victory. As usual, the USA took an early lead, romping to 6-2 after the opening day's Foursomes, but there was at least an early boost for Britain in the opening match as Peter Alliss and Christy O'Connor beat Doug Ford and Gene Littler, 4 and 3.

But the home collapse was alarming for captain Dai Rees, who was in charge of the British team for the fourth Ryder Cup in a row, as they lost the next three matches. Strangely, the Welshman sent out exactly the same pairings in the afternoon (including himself) – and saw his team go down 3-1 again. Rees did contribute Britain's only point, partnering Ken Bousfield to victory against Mike Souchak and Bill Collins. Having spent so much time on course, however, he was in no position to monitor the form of his players as the singles draw was made. Consequently, the USA dominated the morning singles, too, with Ford, Souchak, Billy Casper and Dow Finsterwald extending the lead to six points before Souchak and Palmer wrapped up victory in the afternoon. There was a sting in the tale as the British side won four afternoon matches to narrow the scores, but all the same this was a convincing win and a sign of what was to come.

ABOVE: *US captain Jerry Barber is held aloft as he celebrates victory at the end of the 1961 Ryder Cup.*

DAYS ONE AND TWO

CAPTAINS

Great Britain: Dai Rees   **USA:** Jerry Barber

FRIDAY MORNING FOURSOMES
O'Connor/Alliss *beat* **Ford/Littler**, *4 and 3*
Panton/Hunt *lost to* **Wall/Hebert**, *4 and 3*
Rees/Bousfield *lost to* **Casper/Palmer**, *2 and 1*
Haliburton/Coles *lost to* **Collins/Souchak** *by one hole*
Session Score: 1-3

SATURDAY MORNING SINGLES
Harry Weetman *lost to* **Doug Ford** *by one hole*
Ralph Moffitt *lost to* **Mike Souchak**, *5 and 4*
Peter Alliss *halved with* **Arnold Palmer**
Ken Bousfield *lost to* **Billy Casper**, *5 and 3*
Dai Rees *beat* **Jay Hebert**, *2 and 1*
Neil Coles *halved with* **Gene Littler**
Bernard Hunt *beat* **Jerry Barber**, *5 and 4*
Christy O'Connor *lost to* **Dow Finsterwald**, *2 and 1*
Session Score: 3-5

FRIDAY AFTERNOON FOURSOMES
O'Connor/Alliss *lost to* **Wall/Hebert** *by one hole*
Panton/Hunt *lost to* **Casper/Palmer**, *5 and 4*
Rees/Bousfield *beat* **Collins/Souchak**, *2 and 1*
Haliburton/Coles *lost to* **Barber/Finsterwald** *by one hole*
Session Score: 1-3

SATURDAY AFTERNOON SINGLES
Harry Weetman *lost to* **Art Wall** *by one hole*
Peter Alliss *beat* **Bill Collins**, *3 and 2*
Bernard Hunt *lost to* **Mike Souchak**, *2 and 1*
Tom Haliburton *lost to* **Arnold Palmer**, *2 and 1*
Dai Rees *beat* **Doug Ford**, *4 and 3*
Ken Bousfield *beat* **Jerry Barber** *by one hole*
Neil Coles *beat* **Dow Finsterwald** *by one hole*
Christy O'Connor *halved with* **Gene Littler**
Session Score: 4.5-3.5
Overall Score: Great Britain 9.5, USA 14.5

Billy Capser of the USA studies a putt during the Friday afternoon Fourballs, which he and Gay Brewer lost 3 and 2 to Great Britain's Tony Jacklin and Peter Oosterhuis, in the 1973 Ryder Cup at Muirfield.

CHAPTER FOUR
THE USA RETAINS CONTROL

As the Ryder Cup moved into the 1960s and 1970s, American dominance showed no sign of diminishing. Even the inclusion of Irish players in the British team couldn't close the huge gap that had opened up. Eventually, questions were raised about the competition's future.

1963

USA 23
Great Britain 9

Atlanta Athletic Club, Georgia

October 11-13

Although drastic changes had been made to make the Ryder Cup more competitive, more alterations came in 1963 when two sets of Fourballs were introduced. However, nothing could stop the USA – led by inspired player-captain Arnold Palmer – from storming to what remains the second-biggest victory in Ryder Cup history, as they demolished their bewildered opponents in Atlanta.

IF EVER THERE WAS ANY DOUBT about the chasm in class between the US and British teams in the 1960s, this was certainly confirmed by a Ryder Cup that was to prove historically important for so many reasons in 1963. For a start it saw the introduction of Fourballs to attract greater television interest in the US, where Foursomes – played mostly in Scotland – were a largely unknown format and had long been regarded with some scepticism by the US PGA. Repeated requests to replace them were previously ignored by the British, who feared doing so would make their team even less competitive and so a compromise was reached as the matches were extended to two series of

DAYS ONE AND TWO

CAPTAINS

USA: Arnold Palmer   **Great Britain:** John Fallon

FRIDAY MORNING FOURSOMES
Palmer/Pott *lost to* **Huggett/Will**, *3 and 2*
Casper/Ragan *beat* **Alliss/O'Connor** *by one hole*
Boros/Lema *halved with* **Coles/Hunt**
Littler/Finsterwald *halved with* **Thomas/Weetman**
Session Score: 2-2

FRIDAY AFTERNOON FOURSOMES
Maxwell/Goalby *beat* **Thomas/Weetman**, *4 and 3*
Palmer/Casper *beat* **Huggett/Will**, *5 and 4*
Littler/Finsterwald *lost to* **Coles/B. Hunt**, *2 and 1*
Boros/Lema *beat* **Haliburton/G. Hunt** *by one hole*
Session Score: 3-1

SATURDAY MORNING FOURBALLS
Palmer/Finsterwald *beat* **Huggett/Thomas**, *5 and 4*
Littler/Boros *halved with* **Alliss/B. Hunt**
Casper/Maxwell *beat* **Weetman/Will**, *3 and 2*
Goalby/Ragan *beat* **Coles/O'Connor** *by one hole*
Session Score: 3.5-0.5

SATURDAY AFTERNOON FOURBALLS
Palmer/Finsterwald *beat* **Coles/O'Connor**, *3 and 2*
Lema/Pott *beat* **Alliss/B. Hunt** *by one hole*
Casper/Maxwell *beat* **Haliburton/G. Hunt**, *2 and 1*
Goalby/Ragan *halved with* **Huggett/Thomas**
Session Score: 3.5-0.5

DAY THREE

SUNDAY MORNING SINGLES

Tony Lema *beat* **Geoff Hunt**, *5 and 3*
Johnny Pott *lost to* **Brian Huggett**, *3 and 1*
Arnold Palmer *lost to* **Peter Alliss** *by one hole*
Billy Casper *halved with* **Neil Coles**
Bob Goalby *beat* **Dave Thomas**, *3 and 2*
Gene Littler *beat* **Christy O'Connor** *by one hole*
Julius Boros *lost to* **Harry Weetman** *by one hole*
Dow Finsterwald *lost to* **Bernard Hunt** *by two holes*
Session Score: 3.5-4.5

SUNDAY AFTERNOON SINGLES

Arnold Palmer *beat* **George Will**, *3 and 2*
Dave Ragan *beat* **Neil Coles**, *2 and 1*
Tony Lema *halved with* **Peter Alliss**
Gene Littler *beat* **Tom Haliburton**, *6 and 4*
Julius Boros *beat* **Harry Weetman**, *2 and 1*
Billy Maxwell *beat* **Christy O'Connor**, *2 and 1*
Dow Finsterwald *beat* **Dave Thomas**, *4 and 3*
Bob Goalby *beat* **Bernard Hunt**, *2 and 1*
Session Score: 7.5-0.5
Overall Score: USA 23, Great Britain 9

OPPOSITE: *The US Ryder Cup team of 1963 pose for the cameras complete with their golf bags ahead of the matches in Georgia.*

ABOVE: *Arnold Palmer throws down his putter in frustration during his Day One Foursomes match. He and partner Johnny Pott lost to Great Britain's Brian Huggett and George Will.*

Fourballs, two series of Foursomes and a series of singles. It meant there were now 32 points at stake instead of 24 and the Ryder Cup, for the first time, would be played over three days rather than two.

This particular Ryder Cup also proved to be the last time a playing captain took charge of either team. The British had already dispensed with that tradition, choosing John Fallon as a non-playing captain in Atlanta, but the legendary Arnold Palmer (who had already won the Masters three times, the US Open once and the British Open twice) gave it one last go. He won four points, including a singles victory over George Will, as he guided his team to victory.

Great Britain at least made a decent start, squaring the opening session of Foursomes 2-2, with a surprise win for Will and Brian Huggett against Palmer and Johnny Pott. The Americans won the afternoon session 3-1 (Fallon having surprisingly and controversially broken up his successful partnerships from the morning), before the home team completely dominated the Fourballs, winning seven out of eight points available to lead 12-4 at the end of the second day.

The Ryder Cup was all but over for the British side but the USA were ruthless in keeping their foot on the accelerator and thundered to a 14-point victory, winning 10 of the singles matches, including seven out of eight in the final session. For Great Britain, the only highlights were a memorable win for Peter Alliss against Palmer and a sweet triumph for Harry Weetman against US Open champion Julius Boros, but the gap between the two sides was cavernous. Palmer had introduced his men by saying: "This team would beat the rest of the world combined." And he wasn't overstating his case.

1965

Great Britain 12.5
USA 19.5

Royal Birkdale, Southport

October 7-9

THE COURSE

Royal Birkdale Golf Club
Location: Southport, Merseyside, England
Par: 72
Yards: 6,817

A sprawling course built in a valley between large dunes, Royal Birkdale was chosen because it provided natural vantage points to watch the action. It was designed by three generations of the Hawthorn family of golf architects, guided by legendary British golfer J.H. Taylor.

The Ryder Cup entered the modern era of commercialism at Royal Birkdale in 1965 when a sponsorship deal saw a large tented village spring up on course and increased numbers of spectators arrived to cheer on the teams. Although Great Britain would this time put up more of a fight, nothing could change the fact that the USA, who dominated the singles matches, were just too good for their opponents.

IN SOME WAYS, the 1965 Ryder Cup was the one that got away for the British side, who put up a real fight on the opening two days and went into the Saturday singles only two points behind. But by the time the match was over there were the usual inquests into why American golfers seemed so much more adept at finishing off games.

The matches were given extra profile after Royal Birkdale member and PGA vice-president Brian Park made a donation of £11,000 ($31,000 at mid-1960s exchange rates) towards the building of an on-course hospitality pavilion and vast tented village. Park had travelled to America to see how tournaments were hosted and his vision was to completely modernize golf in Britain. Indeed, his efforts astonished local fans who had never seen anything like it. Luncheon areas, marquees, colourful flower borders, an information tent, a 160-page commemorative programme, a Post Office, an

observation tower for press photographers and a trade exhibition all added to the Ryder Cup experience and became a blueprint for future tournaments.

Britain's team, captained by Harry Weetman, had four newcomers: Lionel Platts, Peter Butler, Jimmy Martin and Jimmy Hitchcock. All were in high spirits after their amateur counterparts had drawn 11-11 with the Americans in the Walker Cup in Baltimore. In contrast, the US side had problems. Johnny Pott ruptured a muscle in his lower back during practice, meaning he would miss the tournament, and Ken Venturi, the 1964 US Open champion, had only just had surgery for circulatory problems in his hands.

> ❝*It's no domestic tabby of a course, but a full-grown tiger.*❞
>
> *Golf Digest gives its verdict on the course*

DAY ONE

CAPTAINS
Great Britain: Harry Weetman   **USA:** Byron Nelson

THURSDAY MORNING FOURSOMES

Platts/Butler *lost to* **Boros /Lema** *by one hole*
Thomas/Will *beat* **Palmer/Marr,** *6 and 5*
B. Hunt/Coles *lost to* **Casper/Littler,** *2 and 1*
Alliss/O'Connor *beat* **Venturi/January,** *5 and 4*
Session Score: 2-2

THURSDAY AFTERNOON FOURSOMES

Thomas/Will *lost to* **Palmer/Marr,** *6 and 5*
Alliss/O'Connor *beat* **Casper/Littler,** *2 and 1*
Martin/Hitchcock *lost to* **Boros/Lema,** *5 and 4*
B. Hunt/Coles *beat* **Venturi/January,** *3 and 2*
Session Score: 2-2

LEFT: *US captain Byron Nelson (left) meets British Prime Minister Harold Wilson at Royal Birkdale.*

DAYS TWO AND THREE

FRIDAY MORNING FOURBALLS

Thomas/Will *lost to* **January/Jacobs** *by one hole*

Platts/Butler *halved with* **Casper/Littler**

Alliss/O'Connor *lost to* **Palmer/Marr,** *6 and 4*

Hunt/Coles *beat* **Boros/Lema** *by one hole*

Session Score: 1.5-2.5

SATURDAY MORNING SINGLES

Jimmy Hitchcock *lost to* **Arnold Palmer,** *3 and 2*

Lionel Platts *lost to* **Julius Boros,** *4 and 2*

Peter Butler *lost to* **Tony Lema** *by one hole*

Neil Coles *lost to* **Dave Marr** *by two holes*

Bernard Hunt *beat* **Gene Littler** *by two holes*

Dave Thomas *lost to* **Tommy Jacobs,** *2 and 1*

Peter Alliss *beat* **Billy Casper** *by one hole*

George Will *halved with* **Don January**

Session Score: 2.5-5.5

FRIDAY AFTERNOON FOURBALLS

Alliss/O'Connor *beat* **Palmer/Marr** *by two holes*

Thomas/Will *lost to* **January/Jacobs** *by one hole*

Platts/Butler *halved with* **Casper/Littler**

Hunt/Coles *lost to* **Venturi/Lema** *by one hole*

Session Score: 1.5-2.5

SATURDAY AFTERNOON SINGLES

Christy O'Connor *lost to* **Tony Lema,** *6 and 4*

Jimmy Hitchcock *lost to* **Julius Boros,** *2 and 1*

Peter Butler *lost to* **Arnold Palmer** *by two holes*

Peter Alliss *beat* **Ken Venturi,** *3 and 1*

Neil Coles *beat* **Billy Casper,** *3 and 2*

George Will *lost to* **Gene Littler,** *2 and 1*

Bernard Hunt *lost to* **Dave Marr** *by one hole*

Lionel Platts *beat* **Tommy Jacobs** *by one hole*

Session Score: 3-5

Overall Score: Great Britain 12.5, USA 19.5

So, the opportunity was there for an upset, especially when the early sessions went well for the hosts.

The opening day Foursomes were shared, finishing 2-2 in both sessions. Highlights included a 6 and 5 victory for Britain's Dave Thomas and George Will over Dave Marr and Arnold Palmer, and a 5 and 4 win for Peter Alliss and Christy O'Connor Snr. against Venturi/January in the morning. However, Tony Lema – who was to win five points out of six – holed a tough putt on the final green to beat Platts and Butler to keep the holders in contention.

In the afternoon, it was Arnold Palmer who was the hero, however. He spent his lunch break on the practice ground after losing in the morning and played some astonishing golf on his return – going six-under-par as he again partnered Marr to victory against Will and Thomas. The second-day Fourballs matches were equally close and although the USA ended with a 5-3 lead, seven of the eight matches went to the 18th green. Perhaps the crucial results came when Thomas/Will threw away a four-hole lead against Don January and Tommy Jacobs to lose by one hole – before Lionel Platts and Peter Butler went from four-up with four to play to earn just a half against Billy Casper and Gene Littler. Even an afternoon victory for Alliss and O'Connor over Palmer/Marr couldn't quite make up for it and the USA duly cemented victory with an excellent display in the singles.

Britain would have won the Ryder Cup comfortably, had all the matches been played over nine holes, but when the pressure was on, their rivals held their nerve. The US team mastered local conditions far better than the British and skipper Byron Nelson saw victory all but assured as his first four players came back with a point each.

Ryder Cup legends
Arnold **PALMER** and Gardner **DICKINSON**

US tennis star Peter Fleming once stated the best doubles partnership in the world was "John McEnroe and anybody" – generously self-deprecating from a man who partnered his fellow American to numerous major tennis titles. Golf's closest equivalent to McEnroe might be Arnold Palmer, but it was really only with the relatively unheralded Gardner Dickinson that "The King" was truly invincible.

Gardner Dickinson and Arnold Palmer are America's most successful Ryder Cup partnership. They played together five times, won five times and were on the winning team by comfortable margins when competing as members of the 1967 and 1971 US sides. Palmer is possibly America's greatest-ever Ryder Cup player in terms of games played and points won. Dickinson had a 9-1 overall record in Ryder Cup play – the best winning percentage for anyone participating in at least seven matches in the biennial team event.

US captain Ben Hogan paired the rookie Dickinson with the near million-dollar prizewinner Palmer for the 1967 Ryder Cup. His faith, however, was returned as Dickinson and "The

RIGHT: *Arnold Palmer (right) helps team-mate Gardner Dickinson line up a putt at the Ryder Cup in St. Louis in 1971.*

King returned with their country's first point of the competition in beating Peter Alliss and Christy O'Connor Snr., 2 and 1. Indeed, it was the start of a beautiful relationship. Afterwards, they went out in the afternoon and thrashed Malcolm Gregson and Hugh Boyle, 5 and 4. The following morning, Hogan rested Palmer, but Dickinson maintained his winning debut by pairing Doug Sanders to a 3 and 2 win over Brian Huggett and George Will. The same pair beat Alliss/Gregson in the afternoon. The results must surely have helped to inspire Palmer and Dickinson to win both their singles matches against prize scalp Tony Jacklin on the final day. Palmer even found time to beat Brian Huggett, too, at a time when two rounds of eight separate singles matches were played on the same day.

> ❝*I loved the Ryder Cup because it simply wasn't about playing for money — it was about playing for something far grander and more personal.*❞
>
> *Arnold Palmer*

The unbeaten – and unbeatable – duo contributed more than any other US players in leading their country to a 23.5-8.5 win – the biggest win in the history of the competition. Two years later, the Ryder Cup was in danger of losing its allure, such was the one-sided nature of the event, and so it was possibly fortunate the two countries played out a draw at Royal Birkdale, albeit without Dickinson in the US side. He played his way back into 1971 side for the September meet at Old Warson Country Club, St. Louis, Missouri and captain Jay Herbert was sensible enough to reunite him with Palmer in the opening morning's Fourballs games. The pair continued to maintain their unbeaten streak with a two-up win over Peter Townsend and rookie Peter Oosterhuis. They went on to beat the same pair by the same score in the afternoon Foursomes.

The following morning featured America's most dynamic-ever duo in a controversial 5 and 4 win over Oosterhuis and Bernard Gallacher. Palmer tried to calm the argument after Gallacher's young caddie asked him what club he used for a stunning tee-shot and the referee subsequently awarded the USA the hole for the youngster's infringement. The rest is history and it proved to be Dickinson and Palmer's fifth – and final – match together. Palmer, who successfully partnered Dow Finsterwald in earlier Ryder Cups, was later paired with fellow legend and World No. 1 Jack Nicklaus, although he never achieved the same success or synergy as he had with Dickinson. He did, however, end up with a Ryder Cup record of 22 matches won against eight losses, with two ties and a total of 23 points. It was a mark that would stand from 1973 until Nick Faldo won two more points at Valderrama in 1997.

RYDER CUP RECORD

Arnold PALMER
Ryder Cups: 1961, 1963 (winner, playing captain), 1965, 1967 (winner), 1971 (winner), 1973 (winner), 1975 (winner, non-playing captain)
Total wins: 5
Matches: 32 (won 22, halved 2, lost 8)
Total points: 23

Gardner DICKINSON
Ryder Cups: 1967 (winner), 1971 (winner)
Total wins: 2
Matches: 10 (won 9, halved 0, lost 1)
Total points: 9

AS A PAIR:
Matches: 5 (won 5, halved 0, lost 0)
Total points: 5

1967

Champions Golf Club, Texas

October 20-22

THE COURSE

Cypress Creek Course, Champions Golf Club
Location: Houston, Texas, USA
Par: 71
Yards: 7,200

Designed by Ralph Plummer and opened in 1959, this golf club features more than 70,000 trees and is noted for its wide fairways and enormous greens.

US captain Ben Hogan introduced his players as the finest golfers in the world and they more than lived up to that tag in 1967. Indeed, with a breath-taking performance, they inflicted what remains the heaviest defeat ever suffered by a British or European Ryder Cup team.

THE USA'S 15-POINT VICTORY at the Champions Golf Club in Houston was all the more remarkable because it was achieved without their best player, Jack Nicklaus, who despite having won seven Major championships had yet to complete his five-year period as a PGA member and was therefore ineligible for selection. But Gardner Dickinson and Arnold Palmer neatly stepped into his shoes as both went unbeaten in five matches to steer the US team to a memorable victory.

Captain Hogan set the tone for a dominant performance at a team dinner on the eve of the tournament. Having listened patiently to a long introduction from British captain Dai Rees, outlining the achievements of his players one by one, he calmly rose to introduce his squad in just a single sentence. And as he sat down to raucous applause, the demolition of Great Britain began.

Rees had been a controversial choice as a former captain – indeed, the hot-headed Harry Weetman refused to play under him. By contrast, Hogan was an impressive leader, single-handedly choosing his team (not by committee, unlike the British), insisting on long practice hours and introducing a 10.30 p.m. curfew for the players. Even world superstar Palmer was put firmly in his place when he questioned an order to practise with the smaller British-sized ball, only to be told: "Who said you are playing?"

Of course Palmer did play, but every player in the US side got the message from their captain. With rookies Gardner Dickinson,

ABOVE: *Tony Jacklin of Great Britain chips out of a bunker on the second hole in Houston during the 1967 Ryder Cup.*

DAY ONE

CAPTAINS

USA: Ben Hogan   **Great Britain:** Dai Rees

FRIDAY MORNING FOURSOMES

Casper/Boros *halved with* **Huggett/Will**
Palmer/Dickinson *beat* **Alliss/O'Connor**, *2 and 1*
Sanders/Brewer *lost to* **Jacklin/Thomas**, *4 and 3*
Nichols/Pott *beat* **Hunt/Coles**, *6 and 5*
Session Score: 2.5-1.5

FRIDAY AFTERNOON FOURSOMES

Casper/Boros *beat* **Huggett/Will** *by one hole*
Dickinson/Palmer *beat* **Gregson/Boyle**, *5 and 4*
Littler/Geiberger *lost to* **Jacklin/Thomas**, *3 and 2*
Nichols/Pott *beat* **Alliss/O'Connor**, *2 and 1*
Session Score: 3-1

Bobby Nichols, Al Geiberger, Doug Sanders and Gay Brewer joining established stars such as Palmer and Billy Casper, the American team boasted a formidable line-up. Although Britain introduced a young Tony Jacklin, fresh from scoring the first televised hole-in-one at the Dunlop Masters weeks earlier, they were soon to be outplayed.

Huggett/Will did give the visitors an early half against Casper/Boros, while Jacklin/Thomas sealed a 4 and 3 victory over Sanders/Brewer. Any joy was short-lived, however, for the Americans won the afternoon Foursomes 3-1 before taking seven out of eight Fourballs matches on the Saturday to set up a 13-3 lead. By the end of the final day, the USA – with Dickinson, Palmer and Geiberger all winning twice in the singles – had added another 10.5 points to their total to complete a record-breaking victory. For Great Britain, it was an all-time low.

With the exception of Palmer's 5 and 3 demolition of Huggett, most of the matches had been close. All the same, the result had never been in doubt and the scoreline told a sorry story for

Great Britain (and maybe for the competition itself). It had been a ruthless, top-quality performance from the victors, but could the Ryder Cup carry on like this?

DAYS TWO AND THREE

SATURDAY MORNING FOURBALLS
Casper/Brewer *beat* **Alliss/O'Connor,** *3 and 2*
Nichols/Pott *beat* **Hunt/Coles** *by one hole*
Littler/Geiberger *beat* **Jacklin/Thomas** *by one hole*
Dickinson/Sanders *beat* **Huggett/Will,** *3 and 2*
Session Score: 4-0

SATURDAY AFTERNOON FOURBALLS
Casper/Brewer *beat* **Hunt/Coles,** *5 and 3*
Dickinson/Sanders *beat* **Alliss/Gregson,** *3 and 2*
Palmer/Boros *beat* **Will/Boyle** *by one hole*
Littler/Geiberger *halved with* **Jacklin/Thomas**
Session Score: 3.5-0.5

SUNDAY MORNING SINGLES
Gay Brewer *beat* **Hugh Boyle,** *4 and 3*
Billy Casper *beat* **Peter Alliss,** *2 and 1*
Arnold Palmer *beat* **Tony Jacklin,** *3 and 2*
Julius Boros *lost to* **Brian Huggett** *by one hole*
Doug Sanders *lost to* **Neil Coles,** *2 and 1*
Al Geiberger *beat* **Malcolm Gregson,** *4 and 2*
Gene Littler *halved with* **Dave Thomas**
Bobby Nichols *halved with* **Bernard Hunt**
Session Score: 5-3

SUNDAY AFTERNOON SINGLES
Arnold Palmer *beat* **Brian Huggett,** *5 and 3*
Gay Brewer *lost to* **Peter Alliss,** *2 and 1*
Gardner Dickinson *beat* **Tony Jacklin,** *3 and 2*
Bobby Nichols *beat* **Christy O'Connor,** *3 and 2*
Johnny Pott *beat* **George Will,** *3 and 1*
Al Geiberger *beat* **Malcolm Gregson,** *2 and 1*
Julius Boros *halved with* **Bernard Hunt**
Doug Sanders *lost to* **Neil Coles,** *2 and 1*
Session Score: 5.5-2.5
Overall Score: USA 23.5, Great Britain 8.5

ABOVE: *Dense fog at the Champions Course didn't prevent Arnold Palmer getting in some practice ahead of the Sunday games.*

“ *Ladies and gentlemen, the United States Ryder Cup team – the finest golfers in the world!* ”

Ben Hogan introduces his star-studded team

1969

Great Britain 16 USA 16

Royal Birkdale, Southport

September 18-20

THE COURSE

Royal Birkdale Golf Club
Location: Southport,
Merseyside, England
Par: 72
Yards: 6,817

Staging its second Ryder Cup, the Royal Birkdale strengthened its reputation as one of the most atmospheric places to watch golf as it is built among sand dunes with the wind blowing in off the Irish Sea. And it certainly hosted an incredible tournament.

The Ryder Cup went from its most one-sided contest in 1967 to the closest-ever in 1969. Indeed, it will be forever remembered for the moment Jack Nicklaus, in one of the greatest examples of sportsmanship in history, conceded a missable putt to Britain's Tony Jacklin at the very last hole to leave the matches tied.

"THE CONCESSION", AS IT HAS BECOME KNOWN, holds a special place in Ryder Cup history. It was the moment when the spirit of golf and of Sam Ryder himself combined to create something truly unique - even if US captain Sam Snead, a competitive and feisty character, was said to be furious. Nicklaus, who knew a tie would guarantee the trophy was retained, had too much respect for his opponent to ask him to putt from two feet.

This gesture led to a life-long friendship between the two legends, who went on to design the Concession Golf Club in Florida together.

Even without that iconic moment this Ryder Cup was a classic, with 17 of the 32 matches going to the 18th. And not all of it was played in a friendly spirit. British captain Eric Brown set the tone by telling his players not to help search for American balls if they ended in the rough. American Ken Still also courted controversy in failing to own up when hit by the ball and then instigating an ugly argument during Saturday's Fourballs when his playing partner David Hill putted out of turn.

Even so, the action was fascinating as Britain, spurred on by young guns Peter Townsend - aged 22 - and Bernard Gallacher - at 20 years old, the youngest golfer ever to play in the Ryder Cup - took a 3.5-0.5 lead on the first morning. Nicklaus was surprisingly benched for that session, which proved a mistake.

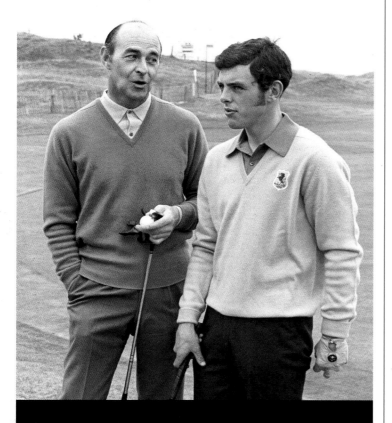

ABOVE: *British captain Eric Brown (left) has a quiet word with the youngest player in his team, 20-year-old Bernard Gallacher.*

DAY ONE

CAPTAINS
Great Britain: Eric Brown   **USA:** Sam Snead

THURSDAY MORNING FOURSOMES
Coles/Huggett beat **Barber/Floyd**, *3 and 2*
Gallacher/Bembridge beat **Trevino/Still**, *2 and 1*
Jacklin/Townsend beat **Hill/Aaron**, *3 and 1*
O'Connor/Alliss halved with **Casper/Beard**
Session Score: 3.5-0.5

THURSDAY AFTERNOON FOURSOMES
Coles/Huggett lost to **Hill/Aaron** by one hole
Gallacher/Bembridge lost to **Trevino/Littler** by one hole
Jacklin/Townsend beat **Casper/Beard** by one hole
Butler/Hunt lost to **Nicklaus/Sikes** by one hole
Session Score: 1-3

DAYS TWO AND THREE

FRIDAY MORNING FOURBALLS

O'Connor/Townsend *beat* **Hill/Douglass** *by one hole*

Huggett/Caygill *halved with* **Floyd/Barber**

Barnes/Alliss *lost to* **Trevino/Littler** *by one hole*

Jacklin/Coles *beat* **Nicklaus/Sikes** *by one hole*

Session Score: 2.5-1.5

SATURDAY MORNING SINGLES

Peter Alliss *lost to* **Lee Trevino,** *2 and 1*

Peter Townsend *lost to* **Dave Hill,** *5 and 4*

Neil Coles *beat* **Tommy Aaron** *by one hole*

Brian Barnes *lost to* **Billy Casper** *by one hole*

Christy O'Connor *beat* **Frank Beard,** *5 and 4*

Maurice Bembridge *beat* **Ken Still** *by one hole*

Peter Butler *beat* **Ray Floyd** *by one hole*

Tony Jacklin *beat* **Jack Nicklaus,** *4 and 3*

Session Score: 5-3

FRIDAY AFTERNOON FOURBALLS

Butler/Townsend *lost to* **Casper/Beard** *by two holes*

Huggett/Gallacher *lost to* **Hill/Still,** *2 and 1*

Bembridge/B. Hunt *halved with* **Aaron/Floyd**

Jacklin/Coles *halved with* **Trevino/Barber**

Session Score: 1-3

SATURDAY AFTERNOON SINGLES

Brian Barnes *lost to* **Dave Hill,** *4 and 2*

Bernard Gallacher *beat* **Lee Trevino,** *4 and 2*

Maurice Bembridge *lost to* **Miller Barber,** *7 and 6*

Peter Butler *beat* **Dale Douglass,** *3 and 2*

Neil Coles *lost to* **Dan Sikes,** *4 and 3*

Christy O'Connor *lost to* **Gene Littler,** *2 and 1*

Brian Huggett *halved with* **Billy Casper**

Tony Jacklin *halved with* **Jack Nicklaus**

Session Score: 3-5

Overall Score: Great Britain 16, USA 16

Having chosen Ray Floyd and Miller Barber to lead off against Neil Coles and Brian Huggett, Snead saw his pairing lose 3 and 2. The USA fought back, however, winning the second session 3-1. Nicklaus was finally called into action and reached the final day tied at 8-8. Even when Great Britain won five of the eight morning singles matches, the USA recovered again. By the time Huggett and Casper halved their match, it was all square with only Nicklaus and Jacklin to finish.

Nicklaus famously asked his rival, who had just eagled the 17th to draw level, how he felt as they walked the final fairway. "Bloody awful!" Jacklin replied. But both men got to the green in two, and with 10,000 fans and both teams crowding there to watch the match-decider, made history as Nicklaus' eagle putt slipped past the hole and Jacklin's missed by two foot. With nerves of steel, Nicklaus then sent his final shot into the back of the cup to secure a tie and the trophy itself. No one expected what happened next for he picked up Jacklin's marker and shook hands on an honourable draw. It was a sporting gesture that will never be forgotten.

> **❝***I don't think you would have missed that Tony, but I didn't want to give you the chance!***❞**
>
> *Jack Nicklaus' famous concession*

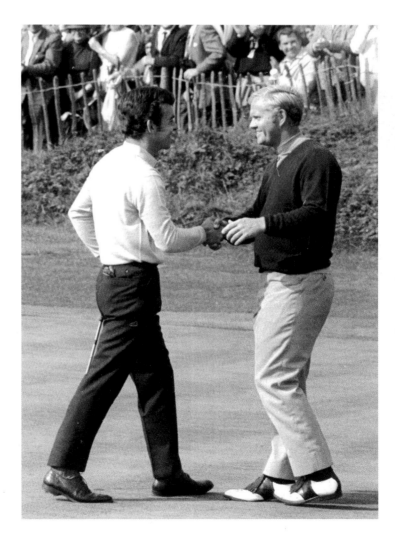

RIGHT: *Jack Nicklaus (right) and Tony Jacklin shake hands after the famous concession that left their match and the scores tied.*

Great Britain's Tony Jacklin (right) gives the USA's Jack Nicklaus a lift after beating him 4 and 3 in their singles match in 1969. The pair played again in the afternoon in a match that was famously halved.

1971

USA 18.5
Great Britain 13.5

Old Warson CC, Missouri

September 16-18

After all the high drama of "The Concession" in 1969, it was business as usual two years later. Inspired by Lee Trevino, the USA completed a straightforward victory in St. Louis. But the British team could at least hold their heads high after a competitive performance that maintained the interest of the American public and with it, that of the television networks.

THE COURSE

Old Warson Country Club
Location: St. Louis, Missouri, USA
Par: 71
Yards: 6,718

Designed by Robert Trent Jones Snr, the par-four 14th from an elevated tee requires a 200-yard shot across a lake to a narrow landing area. Naturally, it is one of the great holes on any golf course in the world.

THE EXCITEMENT OF ROYAL BIRKDALE was still in the air in 1971 and, with Tony Jacklin having won the US Open in 1970, American broadcasters televised the Ryder Cup for the first time. The tournament will be remembered for the bizarre weather conditions. Starting with a 37.7°C (100°F) heat wave during practice sessions, it continued with a deluge of rain, which resulted in the opening ceremony being cancelled.

Great Britain captain Eric Brown had called up rookies Harry Bannerman, John Garner and Peter Oosterhuis, and got off to a glorious start with Neil Coles and Christy O'Connor Snr. producing a shock 2 and 1 victory over Billy Casper and Miller Barber. There was even better to come when Tony Jacklin and Brian Huggett beat Nicklaus/Stockton, 3 and 2 (a match in which the Americans failed to register a single birdie) before Maurice Bembridge and Peter Butler put their side 3-1 up with victory over Charles Coody and Frank Beard.

ABOVE: *British captain Eric Brown poses for the cameras ahead of the 1971 Ryder Cup in Missouri.*

DAY ONE

CAPTAINS
Great Britain: Eric Brown   **USA:** Jay Hebert

THURSDAY MORNING FOURSOMES
Casper/Barber *lost to* **Coles/O'Connor,** *2 and 1*
Palmer/Dickinson *beat* **Townsend/Oosterhuis** *by one hole*
Nicklaus/Stockton *lost to* **Huggett/Jacklin,** *3 and 2*
Coody/Beard *lost to* **Bembridge/Butler** *by one hole*
Session Score: 1-3

THURSDAY AFTERNOON FOURSOMES
Casper/Barber *lost to* **Bannerman/Gallacher,** *2 and 1*
Palmer/Dickinson *beat* **Townsend/Oosterhuis** *by one hole*
Trevino/Rudolph *halved with* **Huggett/Jacklin**
Nicklaus/Snead *beat* **Bembridge/Butler,** *5 and 3*
Session Score: 2.5-1.5

The Americans were stunned. Captain Jay Hebert had included rookies Coody, Dave Stockton, Mason Rudolph and J.C. Snead (nephew of the legendary Sam Snead) but could still call on the world's top four golfers in Jack Nicklaus, Lee Trevino, Billy Casper and Arnold Palmer – even if Trevino was still recovering from an appendix operation and Casper was nursing a broken toe. In the end, quality counted. The British had one last hurrah when Harry Bannerman and Bernard Gallacher opened the afternoon Foursomes by beating Casper/Barber, 2 and 1. The momentum shifted, however, when the USA won the session 2.5-1.5 to leave their rivals just a single point ahead.

As so often in the past, the Fourballs proved to be America's trump card, winning Friday's morning session 4-0 and the afternoon session 2.5-1.5 to lead by 10-6. There was controversy, too, when Gallacher's caddie – impressed by a shot from Palmer – asked him what club he had used on the par-three 7th – an infringement of Rule 9a, the giving of advice. After much discussion, the match referee awarded the hole to the Americans despite Palmer's attempts at diplomacy.

With British confidence drained, the singles proved a formality. Trevino crushed Brian Huggett, 7 and 6 (his fourth point of the week), before Snead's one-hole win against Jacklin retained the trophy. Though Britain managed to end on a high with wins for Barnes, Gallacher, Oosterhuis and Bannerman, the coveted trophy was long gone and at 18.5-13.5, the Americans underlined their superiority.

ABOVE: *Great Britain's Tony Jacklin plays out of a bunker on a practice day prior to the 1971 tournament at the Old Warson Country Club.*

DAYS TWO AND THREE

FRIDAY MORNING FOURBALLS
Trevino/Rudolph *beat* **O'Connor/Barnes,** *2 and 1*
Beard/Snead *beat* **Coles/Garner,** *2 and 1*
Palmer/Dickinson *beat* **Oosterhuis/Gallacher,** *5 and 4*
Nicklaus/Littler *beat* **Townsend/Bannerman,** *2 and 1*
Session Score: 4-0

SATURDAY MORNING SINGLES
Lee Trevino *beat* **Tony Jacklin** *by one hole*
Dave Stockton *halved with* **Bernard Gallacher**
Mason Rudolph *lost to* **Brian Barnes** *by one hole*
Gene Littler *lost to* **Peter Oosterhuis,** *4 and 3*
Jack Nicklaus *beat* **Peter Townsend,** *3 and 2*
Gardner Dickinson *beat* **Christy O'Connor,** *5 and 4*
Arnold Palmer *halved with* **Harry Bannerman**
Frank Beard *halved with* **Neil Coles**
Session Score: 4.5-3.5

FRIDAY AFTERNOON FOURBALLS
Trevino/Casper *lost to* **Gallacher/Oosterhuis** *by one hole*
Littler/Snead *beat* **Jacklin/Huggett,** *2 and 1*
Palmer/Nicklaus *beat* **Townsend/Bannerman** *by one hole*
Coody/Beard *halved with* **Coles/O'Connor**
Session Score: 2.5-1.5

SATURDAY AFTERNOON SINGLES
Lee Trevino *beat* **Brian Huggett,** *7 and 6*
J.C. Snead *beat* **Tony Jacklin** *by one hole*
Miller Barber *lost to* **Brian Barnes,** *2 and 1*
Dave Stockton *beat* **Peter Townsend** *by one hole*
Charles Coody *lost to* **Bernard Gallacher,** *2 and 1*
Jack Nicklaus *beat* **Neil Coles,** *5 and 3*
Arnold Palmer *lost to* **Peter Oosterhuis,** *3 and 2*
Gardner Dickinson *lost to* **Harry Bannerman,** *2 and 1*
Session Score: 4-4
Overall Score: USA 18.5, Great Britain 13.5

1973
GB & Ireland 13
USA 19

Muirfield, East Lothian

September 20-22

Finally, in 1973, the Ryder Cup went "home" to the birthplace of golf – Scotland. It was also the first time the hosts competed officially as Great Britain & Ireland, even though Irish players had been eligible to play for many years. The result was a familiar one, however, as a strong US side won by six points to retain the trophy.

THE AMERICAN TEAM AT MUIRFIELD, captained by Jack Burke Jnr., was regarded as the strongest ever to cross the Atlantic for the Ryder Cup. It included such superstars as Jack Nicklaus, Billy Casper, Lee Trevino and the new British Open champion, Tom Weiskopf. Between them, they boasted 28 Majors (compared to Tony Jacklin's two for Britain), and the US team was heavily backed to defend the trophy. In fact, the media was so convinced of an American victory that it was debating the one-sided nature of the Ryder Cup even before the matches got underway.

A few changes had been made to the format, including mixing up Foursomes and Fourballs on the opening two days and altering the name of the British team to Great Britain & Ireland. It was little more than a gesture because Irish players had been selected since 1953 and Northern Irish players since 1947, though it was nevertheless an important landmark.

The British team, which included rookies Eddie Polland, Clive Clark and Tommy Horton, made an encouraging start under new captain Bernard Hunt. Indeed, the good news started at the very first hole, where Trevino and Casper three-putted to go one down against Bernard Gallacher and Brian Barnes, who eventually sealed a narrow victory. Christy O'Connor and Neil Coles then produced an encouraging 3 and 2 victory over Weiskopf and J.C. Snead before a

DAY ONE

CAPTAINS

GB & Ireland: Bernard Hunt   **USA:** Jack Burke Jnr.

THURSDAY MORNING FOURSOMES

Barnes/Gallacher *beat* **Trevino/Casper** *by one hole*
O'Connor/Coles *beat* **Weiskopf/Snead,** *3 and 2*
Jacklin/Oosterhuis *halved with* **Rodríguez/Graham**
Bembridge/Polland *lost to* **Nicklaus/Palmer,** *6 and 5*
Session Score: 2.5-1.5

THURSDAY AFTERNOON FOURBALLS

Barnes/Gallacher *beat* **Aaron/Brewer,** *5 and 4*
Bembridge/Huggett *beat* **Palmer/Nicklaus,** *3 and 1*
Jacklin/Oosterhuis *beat* **Weiskopf/Casper,** *3 and 1*
O'Connor/Coles *lost to* **Trevino/Blancas,** *2 and 1*
Session Score: 3-1

DAYS TWO AND THREE

FRIDAY MORNING FOURSOMES

Barnes/Butler *lost to* **Nicklaus/Weiskopf** *by one hole*

Oosterhuis/Jacklin *beat* **Palmer/Hill** *by two holes*

Bembridge/Huggett *beat* **Rodríguez/Graham**, *5 and 4*

Coles/O'Connor *lost to* **Trevino/Casper**, *2 and 1*

Session Score: 2-2

SATURDAY MORNING SINGLES

Brian Barnes *lost to* **Billy Casper**, *2 and 1*

Bernard Gallacher *lost to* **Tom Weiskopf**, *3 and 1*

Peter Butler *lost to* **Homero Blancas**, *5 and 4*

Tony Jacklin *beat* **Tommy Aaron**, *3 and 1*

Neil Coles *halved with* **Gay Brewer**

Christy O'Connor *lost to* **J.C. Snead** *by one hole*

Maurice Bembridge *halved with* **Jack Nicklaus**

Peter Oosterhuis *halved with* **Lee Trevino**

Session Score: 2.5-5.5

FRIDAY AFTERNOON FOURBALLS

Barnes/Butler *lost to* **Snead/Palmer** *by two holes*

Jacklin/Oosterhuis *lost to* **Brewer/Casper**, *3 and 2*

Clark/Polland *lost to* **Nicklaus/Weiskopf**, *3 and 2*

Bembridge/Huggett *halved with* **Trevino/Blancas**

Session Score: 0.5-3.5

SATURDAY AFTERNOON SINGLES

Brian Huggett *beat* **Homero Blancas**, *4 and 2*

Brian Barnes *lost to* **J.C. Snead**, *3 and 1*

Bernard Gallacher *lost to* **Gay Brewer**, *6 and 5*

Tony Jacklin *lost to* **Billy Casper**, *2 and 1*

Neil Coles *lost to* **Lee Trevino**, *6 and 5*

Christy O'Connor *halved with* **Tom Weiskopf**

Maurice Bembridge *lost to* **Jack Nicklaus** *by two holes*

Peter Oosterhuis *beat* **Arnold Palmer**, *4 and 2*

Session Score: 2.5-5.5

Overall Score: Great Britain 13, USA 19

crushing win for the powerful pairing of Nicklaus/Palmer (6 and 5 against Polland and Maurice Bembridge) restored American pride.

The Great Britain & Ireland team ended the day three points ahead, including another win for Barnes/Gallacher in the afternoon Fourballs, but disaster struck when Gallacher contracted food poisoning overnight. He was replaced at short notice by Peter Butler who, playing alongside Barnes the next day, was to make an instant impact. Butler made Ryder Cup history when he became the first player ever to score a hole-in-one in the competition. He aced the par-three 16th in a Friday Foursomes match against Nicklaus and Weiskopf. However, defeat at the last against Nicklaus/Weiskopf

was to set the tone for an American revival, as the second day ended with the scores tied at 8-8.

The opening two singles matches proved crucial to the final result, with Casper easing past a tired-looking Barnes and Gallacher (back from illness but still looking pale) before succumbing to a 3 and 1 defeat against Weiskopf. So, by the time Homero Blancas crushed Butler, 5 and 4, the writing was on the wall. America won the session 5.5-2.5 before taking the afternoon singles by exactly the same margin, thanks to a crucial run of victories for Snead, Gay Brewer, Casper and Trevino. The Ryder Cup might have come home but the trophy would not linger there.

OPPOSITE: *Peter Butler of Great Britain celebrates his momentous hole-in-one – the first in Ryder Cup history.*

RIGHT: *US team captain Jack Burke Jnr. holds the Ryder Cup, flanked by his victorious players at Muirfield.*

Ryder Cup legends
Peter **ALLISS** and Christy **O'CONNOR**

After switching his putter for a microphone in the early 1960s, Englishman Peter Alliss soon established himself as the voice of golf. Meanwhile, Christy O'Connor Snr. (affectionately known as "Himself") is one of Ireland's favourite sons and counts among his country's finest sportsmen. But it was as a Ryder Cup pairing that both men truly excelled as the tournament's second most successful team.

The incomparable Spanish partnership of Severiano Ballesteros and José María Olazábal will probably never be challenged as the greatest-ever in the Ryder Cup but more recent successes have featured Nick Faldo and Ian Woosnam, as well as Darren Clarke and Lee Westwood. Before them, however, came the genial double act of Peter Alliss and Christy O'Connor. They played together 12 times, winning five and halving one match. In comparison, the best-ever US team of Arnold Palmer and Gardner Dickinson won only five points. Between 1953 and 1969, Alliss played in a total of eight Ryder Cups while O'Connor appeared in 10 consecutive competitions from 1955-73 – a record that would be surpassed only by Nick Faldo in 1997.

RYDER CUP RECORD

Peter ALLISS
Ryder Cups: 1953, 1957 (winner), 1959, 1961, 1963, 1965, 1967, 1969 (tied but USA retain trophy)
Total wins: 1
Matches: 30 (won 10, halved 5, lost 15)
Total points: 12.5

Christy O'CONNOR Snr.
Ryder Cups: 1955, 1957 (winner), 1959, 1961, 1963, 1965, 1967, 1969 (tied but USA retain trophy), 1971, 1973
Total wins: 1
Matches: 36 (won 11, halved 4, lost 21)
Total points: 13

AS A PAIR:
Matches: 12 (won 5, halved 1, lost 6)
Total points: 5.5

ABOVE: *Christy O'Connor drives the 10th watched by partner Peter Alliss (left) at the 1965 Ryder Cup matches at Royal Birkdale.*

Although not paired, both players were on the same team in 1957 and O'Connor, in particular, played a key part in helping to secure the Cup at Lindrick Golf Club in Yorkshire. With an impressive second-day comeback, the British team won the event for the first time since 1933 when O'Connor thrashed Dow Finsterwald, 7 and 6. Two years later, the British failed to retain the trophy when attending the Eldorado Country Club in Indian Wells, California, but the significance of their one Foursome victory should not be underestimated for it came from the new team of Christy O'Connor and Peter Alliss, who beat Art Wall and Doug Ford, 3 and 2. America retained the title in 1961, although O'Connor and Alliss were again winners together. For the promising Great Britain side, the one-sided US victory of 1963 was one to forget, however.

Fourballs were introduced in 1965 and it was in that year, at Royal Lytham & St Annes, Lancashire, when Alliss and O'Connor combined to win three matches out of four and lose just one. At a time when the American golfers were so dominant, this was an outstanding feat - one that would not be achieved again for more than 20 years.

For Alliss and O'Connor, life (and golf) was fairly simple for both were naturals who took to the game from an early age and played with seemingly effortless ease. Former US captain and Ryder Cup player Lee Trevino said of O'Connor: "Christy flows through the ball like fine wine." Despite winning over 20 professional tournaments and finishing in the top five of the British Open five times, Peter Alliss still places the event above all others, admitting that his greatest (and worst) moments came in the Ryder Cup. As he explained: "Worst was in the 1953 Ryder Cup, the 18th at Wentworth, when I took four to get down. Best was in the final hole of the 1965 Ryder Cup. It was Alliss and O'Connor against Palmer and Marr - I hit a four-wood to within 10 feet." His father, Percy, also played for Great Britain and the two men are one of only two father-and-son duos to compete in the Ryder Cup (Antonio and Ignacio Garrido of Spain being the other).

Christy O'Connor was one of Europe's most respected Ryder Cup players (although against such tough opposition, he holds the record for most matches lost at 21). It was in his final appearance at the Ryder Cup of 1973 at Muirfield in Scotland that he excelled. On the morning of the final day, O'Connor lost to J.C. Snead by one hole and reportedly asked to sit out the afternoon singles but captain Bernard Hunt wanted him to play against Tom Weiskopf, winner of The Open Championship and six other tournaments that year. O'Connor, approaching his 49th birthday, held the strongest US player to a tie, earning half a point for his team in the process with a spectacular half on the final hole. Peter Alliss has said of his former partner, "'Himself' was a genius - a legend of Irish golf, and golf in general."

At the age of 38, Alliss retired from full-time tour golf and swiftly moved on to the commentary duties, for which he is possibly more widely known than his on-course talents. However, his Ryder Cup record, especially in partnership with Christy O'Connor, will never be forgotten.

"It would be very easy to drool with sentimentality over the Ryder Cup but at the end of the day, it is simply two teams trying to knock seven bells out of each other in the nicest possible way."

Peter Alliss on the Ryder Cup

1975

USA 21
GB & Ireland 11

Laurel Valley Golf Club, Pennsylvania

September 19-21

THE COURSE

Laurel Valley Golf Club
Location: Ligonier,
                   Pennsylvania, USA
Par: 71
Yards: 7,154

The course was originally designed by Dick Wilson, though reshaped by Paul Erath in 1965. Arnold Palmer, who captained the USA to victory in 1975, went on to redesign it once more in the late 1980s. The signature hole is the par-four 10th.

Arnold Palmer's imperious US team strolled to yet another convincing victory in 1975, which led to further questions on the competitiveness of the matches and what could be done to make them closer in future. At least Great Britain & Ireland could cling to an historic singles victory for Brian Barnes against the great Jack Nicklaus.

IN FACT, ENGLISHMAN BARNES beat the "Golden Bear" twice in Sunday's singles sessions, results which many golf historians regard as the biggest individual upsets in the competition's history. But sadly for Great Britain & Ireland it was a rare and isolated highlight in yet another convincing American victory.

To make things tougher for British captain Bernard Hunt, his team included six Ryder Cup rookies in Eamonn Darcy, Norman Wood, Tommy Horton, John O'Leary, Guy Hunt and Christy O'Connor Jnr. (nephew of his namesake). By contrast, the Americans included no fewer than seven US Open champions, including Hale Irwin, Gene Littler, Johnny Miller and Lou Graham – not to mention the big four of Nicklaus, Billy Casper, Ray Floyd and Lee Trevino. Indeed, it was an awesome collection of golfers.

The weather set the tone for Britain's challenge, which was washed away just as quickly as a heavy downpour flooded the

ABOVE: *Palmer watches his US team on the third day of practice.*

DAYS ONE AND TWO

CAPTAINS

USA: Arnold Palmer   **GB & Ireland:** Bernard Hunt

FRIDAY MORNING FOURSOMES

Nicklaus/Weiskopf *beat* **Barnes/Gallacher**, *5 and 4*
Littler/Irwin *beat* **Wood/Bembridge**, *4 and 3*
Geiberger/Miller *beat* **Jacklin/Oosterhuis**, *3 and 1*
Trevino/Snead *beat* **Horton/O'Leary**, *2 and 1*
Session Score: 4-0

FRIDAY AFTERNOON FOURBALLS

Casper/Floyd *lost to* **Oosterhuis/Jacklin**, *2 and 1*
Weiskopf/Graham *beat* **Darcy/O'Connor**, *3 and 2*
Nicklaus/Murphy *halved with* **Barnes/Gallacher**
Trevino/Irwin *beat* **Horton/O'Leary**, *2 and 1*
Session Score: 2.5-1.5

SATURDAY MORNING FOURBALLS

Casper/Miller *halved with* **Oosterhuis/Jacklin**
Nicklaus/Snead *beat* **Horton/Wood**, *4 and 2*
Littler/Graham *beat* **Barnes/Gallacher**, *5 and 3*
Geiberger/Floyd *halved with* **Darcy/G. Hunt**
Session Score: 3-1

SATURDAY AFTERNOON FOURSOMES

Trevino/Murphy *lost to* **Jacklin/Barnes**, *3 and 2*
Weiskopf/Miller *beat* **O'Connor/O'Leary**, *5 and 3*
Irwin/Casper *beat* **Oosterhuis/Bembridge**, *3 and 2*
Geiberger/Graham *beat* **Darcy/G. Hunt**, *3 and 2*
Session Score: 3-1

DAY THREE

SUNDAY MORNING SINGLES

Bob Murphy *beat* **Tony Jacklin,** *2 and 1*
Johnny Miller *lost to* **Peter Oosterhuis** *by two holes*
Lee Trevino *halved with* **Bernard Gallacher**
Hale Irwin *halved with* **Tommy Horton**
Gene Littler *beat* **Brian Huggett,** *4 and 2*
Billy Casper *beat* **Eamonn Darcy,** *3 and 2*
Tom Weiskopf *beat* **Guy Hunt,** *5 and 3*
Jack Nicklaus *lost to* **Brian Barnes,** *4 and 2*

Session Score: 5-3

SUNDAY AFTERNOON SINGLES

Ray Floyd *beat* **Tony Jacklin** *by one hole*
J.C. Snead *lost to* **Peter Oosterhuis,** *3 and 2*
Al Geiberger *halved with* **Bernard Gallacher**
Lou Graham *lost to* **Tommy Horton,** *2 and 1*
Hale Irwin *beat* **John O'Leary,** *2 and 1*
Bob Murphy *beat* **Maurice Bembridge,** *2 and 1*
Lee Trevino *lost to* **Norman Wood,** *2 and 1*
Jack Nicklaus *lost to* **Brian Barnes,** *2 and 1*

Session Score: 3.5-4.5
Overall Score: USA 21, Great Britain 11

ABOVE: *Britain's Brian Barnes, pipe in mouth, blasts his way out of a bunker as he beats the legendary Jack Nicklaus.*

Laurel Valley course, making practice almost impossible. A miserable opening session for the visitors ended with America cruising to victory in all four of the morning Foursomes matches – a whitewash instigated by Nicklaus and Tom Weiskopf's 5 and 4 demolition of Brian Barnes and Bernard Gallacher. And by the end of the day, the USA led 6.5-1.5, with Great Britain's only victory coming when Tony Jacklin and Peter Oosterhuis beat Billy Casper and Ray Floyd in the opening match of the afternoon Fourballs.

The Americans then won both Saturday's sessions 3-1 to take their lead to 12.5-3.5, with the singles still to come. Even their weakest pairing, Lou Graham and Gene Littler (only just back from surgery for cancer), contributed a win against Bernard Gallacher and Brian Barnes to leave the visitors demoralised. On the Sunday, the USA added another 8.5 points but there was a brief moment of joy for Britain, thanks to Barnes' display. He beat reigning Masters champion Nicklaus, 4 and 2, in the morning session. Then, when Nicklaus pleaded with his captain to be paired against the same player in the afternoon to gain revenge, the Englishman repeated the act: winning 2 and 1, despite Nicklaus starting his round with consecutive birdies. In the end, though, that result was merely a quirky postscript and not enough to save Great Britain & Ireland from defeat as Tom Weiskopf and Bob Murphy both won twice for the States as the match closed at 21-11. Debate over the relevance of the Ryder Cup was about to intensify.

> **❝** *You've beaten me once, but there ain't no way you're going to beat me again!* **❞**

Jack Nicklaus comes out fighting against Brian Barnes

Ryder Cup legends
Billy CASPER

Billy Casper is probably the most underrated golfer in the history of the game. Though he did not win as many Majors as Tiger Woods, Jack Nicklaus, Arnold Palmer or Gary Player, he beats them in almost every other statistical analysis and is unequivocally America's greatest-ever Ryder Cup performer.

Casper, who also captained the US team in 1979, played in eight consecutive winning sides from 1961-75. He competed in 37 matches, winning 20 and gaining seven halves for a record 23.5 points. Since he never featured on a losing Ryder Cup team as player or captain, it is perhaps only because of his desire to keep a relatively low profile compared to his 1960s rivals that he is not such a household name as his peers.

Quite possibly, it was Casper's unusual childhood in New Mexico and San Diego that persuaded him to become such a family man when he later had the chance. Born during the Depression to teenage parents who soon separated, he was largely raised by close relatives, although his father did start a sporting legend when he stuck a golf club in his hand, aged four. Golf would prove to be his escape from childhood troubles, not that he ever seemed disturbed on, or off, a golf course. He also found salvation in his childhood sweetheart, Shirley, who he married over 60 years ago before going on to have 11 children, six of them adopted. Add 34 grandchildren and 11 great-grandchildren to the equation and it is easier to understand why he claims he was always happiest at home as opposed to chasing media and commercial opportunities.

Few golfers were calmer under pressure than Casper, the unchallenged king of the putter. His two US Open and one Masters' triumphs were impressive but kept him in the Majors shadow of the "Big Three": Nicklaus, Palmer and Player. That said, between 1964 and 1970, Casper won 27 tournaments on the PGA Tour – two more than Nicklaus and six more than Palmer and Player combined. It is particularly revealing to hear what some of his fellow golfing greats say of him, although this testament to his putting, from Chi Chi Rodríguez, is perhaps the best: "Casper was the greatest putter I ever saw. When golf balls used to leave the factory, they prayed they would get to be putted by Billy!"

In all, Casper, who was sometimes known as "Buffalo Bill" for his love of buffalo meat, won 51 times in his career. Only Sam Snead, Jack Nicklaus, Tiger Woods, Ben Hogan, Arnold Palmer and Byron Nelson won more PGA Tour titles. And one of his three Majors goes down in history as being among the greatest feats in modern golf and came against the legendary Palmer, his first Ryder Cup playing partner. It was at the 1966 US Open when Casper trailed Palmer by seven shots with nine holes to play. His nerve and putting enabled him to draw level and force an 18-hole play-off, which he won relatively comfortably.

Casper's final PGA Tour win came in 1975, and he went on to win eight more times on the Senior Tour. His post-playing career has included designing many golf courses through his company,

Billy Casper Golf. He was the second player to reach $1 million in career tour earnings (Arnold Palmer being the first), attaining that mark on January 11, 1970, with his win at the Los Angeles Open. But his Ryder Cup debut came back in 1961, when he teamed up with Arnold Palmer to defeat Dai Rees and Ken Bousfield, 2 and 1. It was the start of a beautiful friendship between Casper and the tournament for he went on to win three of America's points in their 14.5-9.5 victory at Lytham St Annes.

Casper was also responsible for four-and-a-half points as America retained the trophy, two years later in Atlanta. He suffered his first Ryder Cup defeat in his second Foursomes match of the 1965 event at Royal Birkdale when British stalwarts Peter Alliss and Christy O'Connor Snr. were the victors over Casper partnered by Gene Littler. In 1967, he responded at the Champions Golf Club in Houston in going undefeated with four-and-a-half points in the thumping 23.5 to 8.5 victory. Casper also notched up three points in the infamous drawn Ryder Cup of 1969, fading only in 1971 when he failed to score. Further good scoring in 1973 and 1975 proved his star was far from burnt out, though.

He proved equally adept at captaining the 1979 side when the USA faced a European team for the very first time and saw them off by a 17-11 scoreline. Billy Casper's Ryder Cup legacy was certainly now assured, if not already.

> *" Casper was always there. He was a great player and a really great player under pressure."*
>
> *US player and captain Jack Nicklaus*

RYDER CUP RECORD

Ryder Cups: 1961, 1963, 1965, 1967, 1969, 1971, 1973, 1975,
1979 (non-playing captain). All won except
1969 (tied but USA retained trophy)
Wins: 8 (plus 1 tie to retain the trophy, 1969)
Matches: 37 (won 20, halved 7, lost 10)
Points: 23.5

1977

GB & Ireland 7.5
USA 12.5

Royal Lytham & St Annes Golf Club

September 15-17

THE COURSE

Royal Lytham & St Annes Golf Club
Location: Lytham St Annes, Lancashire, England
Par: 70
Yards: 7,118

A true links course founded in 1886, the club was first used for the Ryder Cup in 1961. Featuring 203 bunkers, the course has hosted the British Open.

In 1977, the USA completed its 20th Ryder Cup victory at a canter at Royal Lytham & St Annes and it proved to be their last against the Great Britain & Ireland team. The result was a landmark moment in Ryder Cup history as it sparked a series of vociferous calls for players from continental Europe to be allowed to join the competition in the future.

IN ONE LAST DESPERATE BID to make the matches closer (and no doubt in an attempt to see off suggestions from America that players from the "rest of the world" be invited to join the British team), some major changes were made to the format as Dow Finsterwald's US side arrived in Lancashire ready to defend the trophy once again.

At the request of the British PGA, the number of matches was drastically reduced, with only five Foursomes and five Fourballs to be played over the opening two days, followed by just one session of 10 singles, with 20 points on offer in all. But if the tinkering was designed to give Great Britain & Ireland a chance of victory, it failed to reap dividends for the home side, captained this time by Brian Huggett, were once again truly beaten.

The American team started quickly, winning the Foursomes by two points and stretching their lead to five in the Fourballs. Even an improved display by their opponents in the singles, tying the session 5-5, was nowhere near enough to turn it around. However, the performances of a young Nick Faldo, who at the age of 20 won three points, at least gave a hint of a brighter future. Not bad for a player who just days earlier had been diagnosed with glandular fever.

In fact, Faldo went on to play in 11 Ryder Cups, winning a record 25 points. He made his debut on the same day that American great Tom Watson also took his Ryder Cup bow. Both lined up in the opening day of Foursomes, with Faldo partnering the more experienced Peter Oosterhuis to a 2 and 1 victory over Ray Floyd

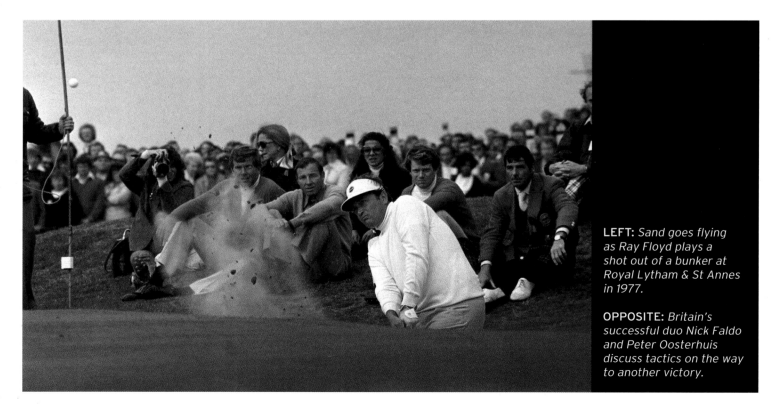

LEFT: *Sand goes flying as Ray Floyd plays a shot out of a bunker at Royal Lytham & St Annes in 1977.*

OPPOSITE: *Britain's successful duo Nick Faldo and Peter Oosterhuis discuss tactics on the way to another victory.*

and Lou Graham before Watson joined Jack Nicklaus to whip Tommy Horton and Mark James, 5 and 4. For both sides, a new era had begun. It couldn't come quick enough for Britain, though, as they went into the singles already five points behind and with little hope of winning the trophy. To add to their problems, Huggett had controversially dropped Tony Jacklin from his line-up and further upset the Englishman by openly criticizing him for failing to support his team-mates on course until the afternoon. Reports suggest the two men fell out badly over those comments and refused to speak to each other for many months.

Back on the course, victories for Graham, Lanny Wadkins, Dave Hill, Hubert Green and Ray Floyd completed victory for the US, with Peter Dawson, Brian Barnes, Faldo and Oosterhuis adding a touch of respectability to the scoreline for the hosts. And, just like two years earlier in Pennsylvania, there was a sweetener for Britain as the great Nicklaus was beaten, this time by a young Bernard Gallacher by one hole. The win was all the more remarkable because Gallacher was playing with a hastily purchased new putter after his own was stolen – such are the stories that make the Ryder Cup so special. But after another one-sided match, it was obvious to everyone on both sides of the Atlantic that major changes were needed to keep the format alive in the long term.

DAYS ONE TO THREE

CAPTAINS

GB & Ireland: Brian Huggett   **USA:** Dow Finsterwald

THURSDAY'S FOURSOMES

Gallacher/Barnes *lost to* **Wadkins/Irwin,** *3 and 1*

Coles/Dawson *lost to* **Stockton/McGee** *by one hole*

Faldo/Oosterhuis *beat* **Floyd/Graham,** *2 and 1*

Darcy/Jacklin *halved with* **Sneed/January**

Horton/James *lost to* **Nicklaus/Watson,** *5 and 4*

Session Score: 1.5-3.5

FRIDAY'S FOURBALLS

Barnes/Horton *lost to* **Watson/Green,** *5 and 4*

Coles/Dawson *lost to* **Sneed/Wadkins,** *5 and 3*

Faldo/Oosterhuis *beat* **Nicklaus/Floyd,** *3 and 1*

Jacklin/Darcy *lost to* **Hill/Stockton,** *5 and 3*

James/Brown *lost to* **Irwin/Graham** *by one hole*

Session Score: 1-4

SATURDAY'S SINGLES

Howard Clark *lost to* **Lanny Wadkins,** *4 and 3*

Neil Coles *lost to* **Lou Graham,** *5 and 3*

Peter Dawson *beat* **Don January,** *5 and 4*

Brian Barnes *beat* **Hale Irwin** *by one hole*

Tommy Horton *lost to* **Dave Hill,** *5 and 4*

Bernard Gallacher *beat* **Jack Nicklaus** *by one hole*

Eamonn Darcy *lost to* **Hubert Green** *by one hole*

Mark James *lost to* **Ray Floyd,** *2 and 1*

Nick Faldo *beat* **Tom Watson** *by one hole*

Peter Oosterhuis *beat* **Jerry McGee** *by two holes*

Session Score: 5-5

Overall Score: Great Britain 7.5, USA 12.5

> *"In America, the Ryder Cup now rates somewhere between Tennessee Frog Jumping and the Alabama Melon-Pip Spitting Championship."*
>
> *English writer Peter Dobereiner on the uncompetitive Ryder Cup*

Bernhard Langer celebrates as a putt from off the green finds the hole on the Saturday of the 1985 Ryder Cup at The Belfry. The German played five matches and picked up three points in Europe's 16.5-11.5 victory over the USA.

CHAPTER FIVE
ENTER THE EUROPEANS

With the USA dominant and matches often one-sided something had to be done to save the Ryder Cup. The answer came in 1979 as players from continental Europe were invited to join the Great Britain & Ireland team. It was a decision that eventually transformed the Ryder Cup into the spectacle it is today.

1979

USA 17
Europe 11

The Greenbrier, West Virginia

September 14-16

THE COURSE

The Greenbrier Course
Location: White Sulphur Springs, West Virginia, USA
Par: 72
Yards: 6,675

Set in 6,500 acres of rolling woodland, The Greenbrier was constructed in 1924 by Seth Raynor. In 1977, it was redesigned by Jack Nicklaus and was possibly the most luxurious resort to hold a Ryder Cup. In all, 26 US presidents stayed there.

By 1979, with the US team dominant and interest in an increasingly one-sided competition beginning to wane in America, the Ryder Cup had reached a crossroads. Something had to be done to save it. The solution, unveiled in West Virginia, came in the shape of a new-look Great Britain and Europe team that included star of the future, Severiano "Seve" Ballesteros.

AFTER 18 DEFEATS in the previous 22 Ryder Cups, it was clear that the British PGA needed to do something to make the event more competitive, or face the uncomfortable prospect that the tournament had no long-term future. In truth, discussions had been going on for the best part of a decade but maybe it was a statement from the great Jack Nicklaus that finally forced the issue. Having helped his team to yet another big away-win at Lytham St Annes, Nicklaus observed: "The Americans are quite happy to treat this match as a goodwill gesture, a get-together, a bit of fun, but here in Britain it's treated differently. The people here seem to want a serious knock-'em-down match. If that's

what's wanted, there has to be a stronger opposition."

He followed up these comments by writing to Lord Derby, President of the British PGA, and within a year two members of the British Ryder Cup committee – Brian Huggett and Peter Butler – were heading to Augusta National Golf Club in Georgia, USA to gain approval for plans to include Europeans in the side. Other options had been considered – a Commonwealth team, for instance, or even a "rest of the world" side, as suggested by Nicklaus – but both ideas involved matches in far-flung places such as South Africa or Australia. And with so many golfers to select from, how many British players would make the team?

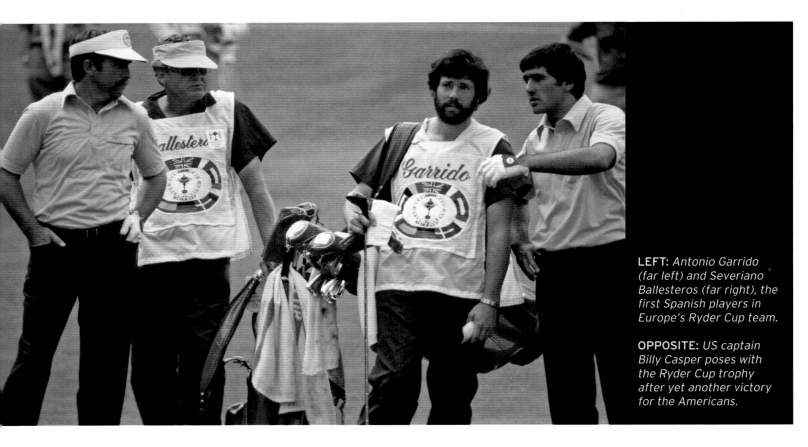

LEFT: *Antonio Garrido (far left) and Severiano Ballesteros (far right), the first Spanish players in Europe's Ryder Cup team.*

OPPOSITE: *US captain Billy Casper poses with the Ryder Cup trophy after yet another victory for the Americans.*

DAY ONE

CAPTAINS

USA: Billy Casper   **Europe:** John Jacobs

FRIDAY MORNING FOURBALLS

Wadkins/Nelson *beat* **Garrido/Ballesteros,** *2 and 1*

Trevino/Zoeller *beat* **Brown/James,** *3 and 2*

Bean/Elder *beat* **Oosterhuis/Faldo,** *2 and 1*

Irwin/Mahaffey *lost to* **Gallacher/Barnes,** *2 and 1*

Session Score: 3-1

FRIDAY AFTERNOON FOURSOMES

Irwin/Kite *beat* **Brown/Smyth,** *7 and 6*

Zoeller/Green *lost to* **Ballesteros/Garrido,** *3 and 2*

Trevino/Morgan *halved with* **Lyle/Jacklin**

Wadkins/Nelson *beat* **Gallacher/Barnes,** *4 and 3*

Session Score: 2.5-1.5

Overall Score: USA 5.5, Europe 2.5

> **"***Brown played like he didn't care.***"**

Hale Irwin expresses his surprise at the behaviour of Ken Brown

With the European Tour growing in stature and players such as a young Seve Ballesteros catching the eye, a European team was seen as a more attractive option, despite plenty of opposition from traditionalists on both sides of the Atlantic. Even the legendary Arnold Palmer objected, saying: "There are occasions even in professional sport when who wins by how much isn't everything." In the end, he was in the minority, though.

So, when the next Ryder Cup matches took place at The Greenbrier in West Virginia, the USA were up against new-look opposition that, for the first time, included two players from continental Europe: Spaniards Severiano Ballesteros and Antonio Garrido. Not that it made much difference to the result. With the format changed once again to include two sets of Foursomes and Fourballs followed by 12 singles matches, European captain John Jacobs had a brief boost when, after a rain-delayed start, he sent his Spaniards out together in the very first match and they duly won the opening two holes against Lanny Wadkins and Larry Nelson. Eventually they lost 2 and 1 in what proved to be yet another walkover for the Americans, led by captain Billy Casper.

There was, at least, an encouraging win for Brian Barnes and

Bernard Gallacher against Hale Irwin and John Mahaffey, but the USA were 3-1 up after the opening session. Europe were further embarrassed by the behaviour of two of their younger players, Ken Brown and Mark James, who, having turned up at the airport in casual clothes instead of team attire, then missed a team meeting to go shopping. Some critics demanded that the pair should be dropped after further disrespectful and disinterested antics during the opening ceremony, but instead they were sent out second in the morning and lost convincingly to Lee Trevino and "Fuzzy" Zoeller, with their body language once again criticized. In fact, Brown's petulant behaviour in an afternoon Foursomes match with Des Smyth (a new pairing because Mark James was suffering from a muscle injury) against Irwin and Tom Kite was so bad that the Europeans issued an apology after their team had lost, 7 and 6.

The European pair's behaviour dominated coverage in Britain, meaning a first-ever win for Ballesteros and Garrido over Zoeller and Hubert Green was overshadowed as the Americans went 5.5-2.5 ahead at the end of the first day of the first Ryder Cup to feature Europe instead of Great Britain.

PLAYER OF THE MATCH

Larry Nelson, who finished second to Tom Watson on the money list in 1979, was the USA's man of the weekend as he won a perfect five points from five matches in his very first Ryder Cup. He also secured four points in 1981 and went on to complete his Ryder Cup career with a record of nine victories, three defeats and one halved match – one of the ten best records of any American player in the history of the tournament.

> **"***The overall score wasn't that close, but many matches went down to the wire.***"**
>
> *US captain Billy Casper on the new-look Ryder Cup*

For the nervous organizers who were looking for signs that making changes to the Ryder Cup would eventually lead to it becoming more competitive, there was least some hope on the Saturday at Greenbrier. With a much-improved performance, Europe won the morning Foursomes session 3-1 to put themselves back in contention. Convincing wins for Tony Jacklin and Sandy Lyle (5 and 4 against Lee Elder and John Mahaffey) and for Nick Faldo and Peter Oosterhuis against Andy Bean and Tom Kite (this time by 6 and 5) gave the Europeans a morale-boosting start to the day. When Fuzzy Zoeller and Mark Hayes were beaten by Gallacher/Barnes 2 and 1, it seemed a clean sweep was on the cards – had Wadkins and the impressive Nelson not seen off Ballesteros and Garrido, 3 and 2.

The Americans continued their recovery in the afternoon as Wadkins and Nelson demolished Ballesteros and Garrido, 5 and 4,

to make it a difficult first Ryder Cup for the Spaniards. Irwin and Kite then teamed up to beat Jacklin/Lyle at the last but the session finished all square as Europe's most consistent performers – Faldo and Gallacher – fought back. Faldo again partnered Oosterhuis to a one-hole victory over Elder/Hayes, while Gallacher/Barnes made it three wins out of four as they beat Trevino/Zoeller.

With the US team only one point ahead going into the final day, there was still a chance that Europe could spring a surprise victory, but that hope was quickly demolished by a powerful display by the home side during Sunday's singles matches. Even without their leading money earner, Tom Watson – who had quit the team on the eve of the tournament as he rushed to attend the birth of his daughter – and despite fielding seven rookies, the USA were still, by some way, the better side.

Gallacher, with a 3 and 2 victory over Wadkins, gave Europe a good start, but the Americans hit back through the ever-consistent Larry Nelson (with his fifth win in three days), Kite, Hayes, Bean and Mahaffey all posting solid victories. Once the stoic Faldo had responded with a point for Europe, further victories for Irwin, Green and Trevino wrapped up the now-customary US victory parade. Only a late win for Brown against Zoeller gave Europe anything to smile about (although given his behaviour over the previous two days, there was an element of irony there). Clearly, there was a long way to go before the Ryder Cup matches would be as close as everyone dreamt of.

There had also been a gesture of sportsmanship from Europe captain Jacobs on the final day, which unlike previous years featured all 12 players in singles action. Both teams were asked to place the name of a player in a brown envelope in case an opponent was ill or injured, to even out the numbers. But Casper had clearly misunderstood the process and placed the name of his best player – Lee Trevino – in the envelope in error. James, to his credit, recognized it was a simple mistake and allowed his opposite number to rest Gil Morgan instead. The Ryder Cup was still not yet fully competitive, but it had certainly retained its spirit.

DAYS TWO AND THREE

SATURDAY MORNING FOURSOMES

Elder/Mahaffey lost to **Jacklin/Lyle**, 5 and 4

Bean/Kite lost to **Faldo/Oosterhuis**, 6 and 5

Zoeller/Hayes lost to **Gallacher/Barnes**, 2 and 1

Wadkins/Nelson beat **Ballesteros/Garrido**, 3 and 2

Session Score: 1-3

SATURDAY AFTERNOON FOURBALLS

Wadkins/Nelson beat **Ballesteros/Garrido**, 5 and 4

Irwin/Kite beat **Jacklin/Lyle** by one hole

Trevino/Zoeller lost to **Gallacher/Barnes**, 3 and 2

Elder/Hayes lost to **Faldo/Oosterhuis** by one hole

Session Score: 2-2

SUNDAY SINGLES

Lanny Wadkins lost to **Bernard Gallacher**, 3 and 2

Larry Nelson beat **Seve Ballesteros**, 3 and 2

Tom Kite beat **Tony Jacklin** by one hole

Mark Hayes beat **Antonio Garrido** by one hole

Andy Bean beat **Michael King**, 4 and 3

John Mahaffey beat **Brian Barnes** by one hole

Lee Elder lost to **Nick Faldo**, 3 and 2

Hale Irwin beat **Des Smyth**, 5 and 3

Hubert Green beat **Peter Oosterhuis** by two holes

Fuzzy Zoeller lost to **Ken Brown** by one hole

Lee Trevino beat **Sandy Lyle**, 2 and 1

Gil Morgan halved with **Mark James**

(Mark James injured, match not played)

Session Score: 8.5-3.5

Overall Score: USA 17, Europe 11

OPPOSITE: *Europe's controversial pair Ken Brown (far right) and Mark James (in red) shake after defeat to Fuzzy Zoeller (far left) and Lee Trevino.*

BELOW: *A young Sandy Lyle hits another sweet shot for Europe but he couldn't help his team to victory.*

1981

Europe 9.5
USA 18.5

Walton Heath Golf Club, Surrey

September 18-20

Just when the arrival of the Europeans provided hope of a more competitive tournament, the USA sent possibly its strongest-ever side to Walton Heath and demolished their opponents by a record margin. The result underlined their superiority and left the hosts regretting a row with Seve Ballesteros, which prevented the great Spaniard from taking part.

TO SAY THAT 1981 was a setback for the new-look Team Europe is an understatement. The Americans were so strong and so superior that John Jacobs' side were completely torn apart by a ruthless display of team golf in a performance that must surely rank as one of the finest in Ryder Cup history.

In truth, nothing went right for the home side during the build-up to the event, let alone on the golf course. For a start it was due to be staged at The Belfry - the new West Midlands headquarters of the Professional Golfers Association - but the course was neither ready nor suitable and so the Ryder Cup was switched at the last minute to Walton Heath, Surrey. Then there were huge issues over selection. The biggest of these involved Seve Ballesteros, who was now playing his golf on the American tour

but looked unlikely to qualify through the team by earnings alone and would need to be a captain's pick. Despite a shaky start to his Ryder Cup career two years earlier, the Spaniard would certainly have been a good addition to the team considering he had completed a dramatic Open victory at Royal Lytham in 1979 and clinched his first US Open a year later. His style of play - full of clever recovery shots, dramatic escapes from impossible positions and glorious touch-shots - made him popular, both in Europe and America. But there was a problem: a political one.

Seve had become embroiled in a huge row over appearance money: as a player on the US tour he had been demanding fees to play in events in Europe (as other American players did) which went against the principles of many of those running golf

LEFT: *Jack Nicklaus and Tom Watson take refuge under the umbrellas during a rainy opening day in Surrey.*

OPPOSITE: *Dave Marr and his victorious US team get their hands on the trophy after a convincing win at Walton Heath.*

in Britain and Europe. Even when captain Jacobs asked him to compete in two pre-Ryder Cup events in Europe as a gesture of goodwill, Ballesteros refused.

When the European team was announced, there was no Seve Ballesteros. And, just as surprisingly, Tony Jacklin had been left out in favour of Mark James, a player so heavily criticized for his behaviour two years earlier at The Greenbrier. And this despite Jacklin's incredible record of only eight defeats in 35 Ryder Cup matches. In contrast, the US team – hailed the best to come to England – could not have been stronger, with 36 major championships between them. It included golfing superstars such as Jack Nicklaus, Tom Watson, Ray Floyd, Lee Trevino, Hale Irwin, Ben Crenshaw and Tom Kite.

The difference in class soon showed, although not immediately. Astonishingly, given the way the match was to end, Europe finished the opening day with a one-point lead. Trevino and Larry Nelson started well enough for the US, beating debutants Bernhard Langer and Manuel Piñero by one hole, but the morning Foursomes ended 2-2. Sandy Lyle and Mark James beat Bill Rogers and Bruce Lietzke, while Bernard Gallacher and Des Smyth overcame Hale Irwin and Ray Floyd. The match of the day was a battle between Faldo and Oosterhuis against the "dream team" of Watson/Nicklaus, which proved hugely competitive. Nicklaus had already lost out to the same pairing four years earlier (when partnered by Floyd) and clearly sought revenge as the Americans came from two-down after four to win 4 and 3 with a flurry of birdies.

Surprisingly, Faldo and Oosterhuis were then "rested" for the afternoon session, which saw Europe – against all expectations – take the lead, as they were replaced by the untried pairing of Irishman Des Smyth and Spaniard José María Cañizares. It proved to be a wise decision as the Europeans won 6 and 5 before Sandy Lyle and Mark James beat Crenshaw and Jerry Pate, 3 and 2. Sam Torrance and Howard Clark halved with Kite and Johnny Miller. America's only victory came from the ever-reliable Irwin/Floyd. Suddenly, the Europeans were going into the second day 4.5-3.5 ahead.

DAY ONE

CAPTAINS

Europe: John Jacobs   **USA:** Dave Marr

FRIDAY MORNING FOURSOMES

Langer/Piñero *lost to* **Trevino/Nelson** *by one hole*

Lyle/James *beat* **Rogers/Lietzke**, *2 and 1*

Gallacher/Smyth *beat* **Irwin/Floyd**, *3 and 2*

Oosterhuis/Faldo *lost to* **Watson/Nicklaus**, *4 and 3*

Session Score: 2-2

FRIDAY AFTERNOON FOURBALLS

Torrance/Clark *halved with* **Kite/Miller**

Lyle/James *beat* **Crenshaw/Pate**, *3 and 2*

Smyth/Cañizares *beat* **Rogers/Lietzke**, *6 and 4*

Gallacher/Darcy *lost to* **Irwin/Floyd**, *2 and 1*

Session Score: 2.5-1.5

Overall Score: Europe 4.5, USA 3.5

"We've got a submarine on hand in case."

US captain Dave Marr on his escape plans if his team lost

DAYS TWO AND THREE

SATURDAY MORNING FOURBALLS

Faldo/Torrance *lost to* **Trevino/Pate,** *7 and 5*

Lyle/James *lost to* **Nelson/Kite** *by one hole*

Langer/Piñero *beat* **Floyd/Irwin,** *2 and 1*

Cañizares/Smyth *lost to* **Nicklaus/Watson,** *3 and 2*

Session Score: 1-3

SATURDAY AFTERNOON FOURSOMES

Oosterhuis/Torrance *lost to* **Trevino/Pate,** *2 and 1*

Langer/Piñero *lost to* **Nicklaus/Watson,** *3 and 2*

Lyle/James *lost to* **Rogers/Floyd,** *3 and 2*

Smyth/Gallacher *lost to* **Kite/Nelson,** *3 and 2*

Session Score: 0-4

SUNDAY SINGLES

Sam Torrance *lost to* **Lee Trevino,** *5 and 3*

Sandy Lyle *lost to* **Tom Kite,** *3 and 2*

Bernard Gallacher *halved with* **Bill Rogers**

Mark James *lost to* **Larry Nelson** *by two holes*

Des Smyth *lost to* **Ben Crenshaw,** *6 and 4*

Bernhard Langer *halved with* **Bruce Lietzke**

Manuel Piñero *beat* **Jerry Pate,** *4 and 2*

José María Cañizares *lost to* **Hale Irwin** *by one hole*

Nick Faldo *beat* **Johnny Miller,** *2 and 1*

Howard Clark *beat* **Tom Watson,** *4 and 3*

Peter Oosterhuis *lost to* **Ray Floyd** *by one hole*

Eamonn Darcy *lost to* **Jack Nicklaus,** *5 and 3*

Session Score: 4-8

Overall Score: Europe 9.5, USA 18.5

ABOVE: *Tom Kite of the USA rips through the ball on his way to a 3 and 2 victory over Sandy Lyle.*

RIGHT: *Lee Trevino strikes a pose as he tees off at Walton Heath as America storm to another impressive victory.*

Whether their opening-day performance was down to over-confidence or lack of concentration, the USA soon proved it would not be reflective of the match as a whole.

On the Saturday, they quickly took a stranglehold on the game, winning seven of the eight matches to produce one of the most convincing day's play ever seen by the Ryder Cup. Only Langer and Piñero managed a victory for the Europeans, beating Floyd and Irwin, 2 and 1, in the morning Fourballs. But the USA won the morning session 3-1, starting with a remarkable demolition of Faldo and new boy Torrance by Trevino and Pate, who won 7 and 5, and then whitewashed the afternoon Foursomes, 4-0. Meanwhile, the incomparable pairing of Watson and Nicklaus proved imperious, adding two more victories (3 and 2 against Smyth and Cañizares in the Fourballs, 3 and 2 against Langer and Piñero in the

Foursomes). Just as two years earlier when he won four points, Nelson also made an impact as he won twice alongside Kite to leave Europe shell-shocked and depressed by the time the singles arrived on Sunday.

With the USA already 10.5-5.5 up, it seemed the match was all but over when Trevino beat Torrance, 5 and 3, in the opening game of the last day to seize four points for himself over the weekend and a six-point lead for his team. Now Europe really knew their number was up. A procession of US victories soon followed, with Kite beating Lyle, Nelson overcoming James, Crenshaw whipping Smyth, 6 and 4, and Irwin edging past Cañizares at the last. And Nelson's victory – by two holes – set a new Ryder Cup record: the first player to win his first nine matches in the Ryder Cup.

Europe's highlights came as Langer earned a half with Lietzke, while Faldo added to his growing reputation by beating Miller, before Piñero (who made an impressive debut) beat Pate. And once the Americans had sealed victory, there was even a surprise win Clark against Watson. But it was never going to be enough against opponents of such class, who also seemed more confident than their rivals on the putting greens.

If Europe were looking for consolation it came in the quality of the golf on show and certainly, Jacobs refused to believe his team were as far behind their rivals as many critics suggested. US counterpart Dave Marr even suggested Europe's big mistake had been to injure American pride by going ahead on the first day. Whatever the truth, Europe knew they had been second whereas the Americans knew for certain they were still No. 1.

In England a debate raged over whether the addition of Ballesteros and Jacklin might have made a difference – both having been omitted from the team – and while critics were split on the answer to that question, they were certain the duo must be welcomed back by 1983. Thankfully, they were – Jacklin as captain and Seve as talisman – and over the ensuing years, that particular pair helped to completely transform the Ryder Cup into the tight and competitive battle it is today. After the record-winning margin of 1981, however, no one could have predicted this. As Nicklaus and Watson held the trophy aloft on September 20, there was really no one to touch them.

> **"** *None of them was intimidated, but they were not all able to produce their best.* **"**
>
> *European captain John Jacobs explains his team's defeat*

MATCH OF THE DAY

The match between Tom Kite and Sandy Lyle was one of true quality and although the records show Kite won comfortably, 3 and 2, he was made to produce his best golf to do so. Incredibly, Lyle was six-under-par for the round and carded eight birdies, but Kite went 10-under to take the match at the 16th with a round of 63.

Ryder Cup legends
Nick **FALDO** and Peter **OOSTERHUIS**

Nick Faldo is Mr Ryder Cup – most appearances, matches played, individual points, victories and fewest matches lost, there is barely a record he doesn't hold. Yet Ryder Cup folklore belongs both to Faldo and players such as Peter Oosterhuis, who competed in five successive European defeats, as they helped raise the competition to the exalted status it now holds.

When Scottish player Sam Torrance struck the winning putt in the 1985 Ryder Cup at The Belfry, it was not only a victory for the brilliant golfers present of the European side, but also a glorious triumph for all those who had battled so manfully towards inevitable defeat in the previous 28 years that the trophy had remained under US control. Few players embody the two sides to that particular coin better than Nick Faldo and Peter Oosterhuis.

For all of Faldo's triumphs, the man who put Welwyn Garden City on the map is well aware that he owes a debt of gratitude to characters such as "man mountain" Oosterhuis. The 6ft 5in Englishman played in every Ryder Cup from 1971-81 – and lost them all. Despite this, his personal record was 14 victories, 11 defeats and three halves. A man able to scramble a par from almost any position (and perhaps a European warning of what was to come when Seve Ballesteros arrived on the scene), Oosterhuis transformed from middling pro to a competitive lion when on Ryder Cup duty. His singles victims included the likes of Arnold Palmer, Johnny Miller and Gene Littler, but perhaps Oosterhuis' most famous match was against Lee Trevino in 1973. The night before they faced each other at Muirfield, East Lothian, Trevino told team-mates: "If I don't beat Oosterhuis, I'll kiss every ass in this room!" Needless to say, when he returned to the dressing room after halving the match, every one of them was there to greet him – with buttocks bared.

Yet perhaps Oosterhuis' greatest legacy was in teaching Faldo what the Ryder Cup really means, and quite why it gets under your skin and into the soul. Certainly, few would have blamed Faldo had he decided to pull out of the 1977 tournament for he was after all suffering with glandular fever. He himself was having none of it, however. It was his debut in the competition and he subsequently resolved to battle through – and did so in some style. Ultimately, this was a disappointing tournament for Great Britain and Ireland as they lost 12.5 to 7.5, but Faldo and Oosterhuis could come away with their heads up high as they won every match in which they competed. Raymond Floyd and Lou Graham were defeated in the Foursomes, Floyd and Jack Nicklaus in the Fourballs, then finally, Faldo and Oosterhuis claimed pyrrhic victories in the singles over Tom Watson and Jerry McGee respectively. It was an astonishing performance by the two men and it came as little surprise when they were paired together again in 1979. They had more of a mixed time in West Virginia, however, losing their Fourballs clash before claiming a stunning victory over Tom Kite and Andy Bean, 6 and 5.

> *"Years from now I want people to be able to say, 'I saw Faldo play.'"*

Nick Faldo's determination shines through

Unfortunately, Peter Oosterhuis' last appearance in the competition (1981) ultimately proved one to forget: he and Faldo were broken up as a partnership after losing 4 and 3 to Nicklaus and Watson before both lost while partnering Sam Torrance. Yet Faldo carried on the mantle of being the man that Europe rallied behind, the talismanic star who could take the fight to the Americans, as proven by his five Major titles between 1987 and 1992. And after being part of the team that made history in twice retaining the trophy Torrance sealed in 1985, Faldo's finest moment was still to come.

America had regained control of the Ryder Cup, winning in both 1991 and 1993, and went into the singles of 1995 ahead by two points. As the day went on, it became clear that victory hinged on Faldo beating Curtis Strange, yet on the 16th, he was one hole down and in the trees, while Strange was in the middle of the fairway. But the Faldo hit his approach to four feet and saved par. His opponent fell to pieces, and Faldo made another save for par at the last to seal a stunning victory. He became a figurehead for Europe, and his tally of points and appearances are unlikely to be matched. Not even defeat as captain in 2008 can change that.

RYDER CUP RECORD

Nick FALDO
Ryder Cups: 1977, 1979, 1981, 1983, 1985 (winner), 1987 (winner), 1989 (tied but Europe retains trophy), 1991, 1993, 1995 (winner), 1997 (winner), 2008 (non-playing captain)
Total wins: 4 (plus 1 tie to retain the trophy, 1989)
Matches: 46 (won 23, halved 4, lost 19)
Total points: 25

Peter OOSTERHUIS
Ryder Cups: 1971, 1973, 1975, 1977, 1979, 1981
Total wins: 0
Matches: 28 (won 14, halved 3, lost 11)
Points: 15.5

AS A PAIR:
Matches: 6 (won 4, halved 0, lost 2)
Total points: 4

ABOVE: *Ryder Cup all-time great Nick Faldo (right) with team-mate Peter Oosterhuis (left) at Royal Lytham & St Annes in 1997. Jack Nicklaus is centre.*

1983

USA 14.5
Europe 13.5

PGA National Golf Club, Florida

October 14-16

THE COURSE

The Champion Course
Location: PGA National Golf Club, Palm Beach Gardens, Florida, USA
Par: 72
Yards: 7,048

Created by Tom and George Fazio, the course was redesigned in 1990 by Jack Nicklaus, the man who led the USA to victory there. The original course featured a 578-yard final hole with cross-bunkers that played a huge part in the Ryder Cup.

America's dream team was finally made to put up a fight in 1983. With Tony Jacklin brought in as captain and Seve Ballesteros welcomed back, Europe produced a gallant attempt to win back the Ryder Cup as they went into the final day level at 8-8 in Florida - only to lose by a single point in the end. The genius of Lanny Wadkins helped captain Jack Nicklaus oversee his side's seventh victory in a row.

WITH THE US TEAM STRONGER than ever and having gone so many years without a trophy, the Europeans - whose side was this time selected based on the Order of Merit plus three captain's picks - knew that the 1983 Ryder Cup was a crucial one. It was time to show the golfing world that European Tour players could match their rivals across the Atlantic in the US. That aim was certainly achieved in Florida, and although the target of ending Europe's Ryder Cup drought would have to wait a while, no one - on either side of the Atlantic - was left in any doubt that future tournaments would be closely fought occasions. In fact, Europe were level with their rivals all the way through to the tenth singles match on the Sunday, and it took something special from Lanny Wadkins, who produced a classic wedge shot under pressure at the death, and a missed putt from Bernard Gallacher to deny them something more than just honour in defeat.

The USA went into the matches as strong favourites, not surprising considering their record of having won 20, lost three and tied one in recent Ryder Cup history; also taking into account that talismanic Nicklaus was their captain. No US captain had ever lost on home soil since the competition began in 1927, as Nicklaus bluntly reminded his players following a somewhat nervy start. However, Tony Jacklin was determined to lead an improved European side and insisted on a string of changes, from the players travelling on Concorde (accompanied by their loved ones) to smart new suits, a "team room" at the hotel to encourage team spirit and caddies paid for by the European Tour. But perhaps his biggest coup was in persuading Seve Ballesteros to reconsider his Ryder Cup future and join the team.

The USA also had new blood on board, including Curtis Strange and Calvin Peete (only the second black American to play in the

RIGHT: *The US team line up for the 1983 Ryder Cup complete with garish suits at the opening ceremony.*

DAY ONE

CAPTAINS

USA: Jack Nicklaus   **Europe:** Tony Jacklin

FRIDAY MORNING FOURSOMES

Watson/Crenshaw *beat* **Gallacher/Lyle**, *5 and 4*

Wadkins/Stadler *lost to* **Faldo/Langer**, *4 and 2*

Floyd/Gilder *lost to* **Cañizares/Torrance**, *4 and 2*

Kite/Peete *beat* **Ballesteros/Way**, *2 and 1*

Session Score: 2-2

FRIDAY AFTERNOON FOURBALLS

Morgan/Zoeller *lost to* **Waites/Brown**, *2 and 1*

Watson/Haas *beat* **Faldo/Langer**, *2 and 1*

Floyd/Strange *lost to* **Ballesteros/Way** *by one hole*

Crenshaw/Peete *halved with* **Torrance/Woosnam**

Session Score: 1.5-2.5

Overall Score: USA 3.5, Europe 4.5

ABOVE: *Europe's Seve Ballesteros gives youngster Paul Way a hand during a day of mixed fortunes.*

Ryder Cup after Lee Elder), but with Nicklaus, Lee Trevino and Johnny Miller no longer playing perhaps they were not as strong as two years previously. Nicklaus, as non-playing captain, had thought seriously about his tactics and realizing how important team spirit would be in this particular Ryder Cup, had opted to base many of his pairings on friendships rather than rankings. Indeed, his first line-up of Tom Watson and Ben Crenshaw got the side off to the best possible start by beating Gallacher and Sandy Lyle, 5 and 4.

Played in searing temperatures that regularly topped 32°C (90°F), it quickly became clear that this would be no walkover, though. Faldo/Langer beat Wadkins and Craig Stadler, 4 and 2, to level things up and the morning session ended 2-2, with Sam Torrance and José María Cañizares providing a shock victory over Ray Floyd and Bob Gilder before Peete/Kite calmed some of the hype surrounding Ballesteros in winning 2 and 1 against the Spaniard and the young Englishman, Paul Way.

Despite this setback, Jacklin proved his talent at man-management over lunch, coaxing Ballesteros back into action after reports that the Spaniard was unhappy at having been paired with Way rather than his compatriot Cañizares. As captain, Jacklin needed Seve to guide his younger team-mate (Way was just 20 years old at the time) through the afternoon session and the Spaniard did exactly that as they beat Floyd and Strange at the last.

Europe ended the day with a one-point lead as Brian Waites and Ken Brown also won (2 and 1 against Gil Morgan and Fuzzy Zoeller), while Torrance and Ian Woosnam held Crenshaw/Peete to a half. The big winners for the USA were Watson and Jay Haas, who won 2 and 1 against possibly Europe's top pairing of Faldo/Langer. Even so, Nicklaus knew he had a fight on his hands.

“I will not be the first captain to blow this thing. Now you guys, show me some brass!”

US captain Jack Nicklaus rallies his team

If the opening day had been close, it was no different on the Saturday because the USA came back to level at 8-8 by the end of the day. Probably for the first time since 1969, the result remained inconclusive going into the final session.

The morning Fourballs were won 2.5-1.5 by Nicklaus' men, with Craig Stadler showing the kind of determination and never-say-die spirit his captain had called for. He and Wadkins were three-down at one stage against Waites/Brown but came back to win at the last, thanks to a wonderful chip-in by Stadler at the 18th. Watson/Gilder also won against Torrance/Woosnam. But it wasn't only the Americans showing their mettle: Ballesteros produced two stunning woods to reach the par-five 18th in two against Morgan and Haas, knowing he needed to win the hole to earn a half. Playing alongside Way, the Spaniard was inspired as he chipped and putted to clinch a birdie and save his team from defeat. The pair won again in the afternoon, this time beating Watson/Gilder as another tight session was drawn 2-2. Sunday arrived with the teams all square and the Europeans dreaming of their first victory since 1957.

Jacklin opted to lead with his big guns up front in the singles, while Nicklaus placed his most experienced players further down the list to plug any holes in an emergency. Maybe the American made the right move because the match proved very close indeed. Early on, Ballesteros was on fire against Zoeller in the opening match, birdying four holes in a row to be three-up after 11 – only for the American to reply with four in a row and reach the 18th narrowly ahead. But Seve produced a quite remarkable shot from the bunker to set up a birdie and an all-important half at the death.

The rest of the singles then unfolded with the lead constantly changing hands. Faldo beat Haas, 2 and 1; Crenshaw replied by beating Lyle, 3 and 1. Then Langer beat Morgan to re-take the lead; Gilder responded by finishing off Gordon J. Brand before Peete sealed a one-up thriller against Waites. Finally, the USA led, but when Way beat fellow rookie Curtis Strange the seesaw was swinging again – and so it continued until the score reached 12.5-all and Nicklaus, buzzing around the course in his buggy, one ear glued to a walkie-talkie, started to fret.

In fact, when Torrance hit a stunning pitch at the 18th to halve his match with Kite, Europe appeared to be heading for a tie at the very least – unless Lanny Wadkins, who was one down against

SHOT OF THE DAY

Severiano Ballesteros' incredible bunker shot at the 18th against Fuzzy Zoeller is often listed as one of the best in Ryder Cup history. In fact, Bernhard Langer describes it as "the greatest shot I ever experienced". Seve, one down and fighting for a half, chose to take a three-wood from the sand – in a deep-linked bunker – and sent the ball 240 yards to the edge of the green.

LEFT: *Tom Watson takes aim at Palm Beach as the USA hold their nerve against an improving Europe.*

ABOVE: *Calvin Peete (partly hidden) congratulates his US team-mate Lanny Wadkins after a dramatic half against Spain's José María Cañizares.*

José María Cañizares, could produce something special. And that he did.

The American players and partners raced to the 18th fairway to watch as Wadkins left himself an 80-yard wedge to a pin guarded by a large bunker. He not only nailed the shot but almost holed it as Nicklaus rushed over and kissed the divot his player had left behind. Even then there was almost late drama as Watson allowed a two-hole lead to slip against Gallacher. Had the Scotsman not double-bogeyed the 17th, it could have been even closer. But the real moment when America's victory was sealed came with that incredible shot from Wadkins, who described it as "the most important of my life". It was a shot that kept Europe at bay for another two years – but at least they were getting closer.

> **❝***It's the first tournament I've ever been to when I wasn't playing and couldn't do anything about what was happening. This was the damnedest thing I was ever involved in!* **❞**
>
> *US captain Jack Nicklaus*

DAYS TWO AND THREE

SATURDAY MORNING FOURBALLS

Wadkins/Stadler *beat* **Waites/Brown** *by one hole*

Crenshaw/Peete *lost to* **Faldo/Langer**, *4 and 2*

Morgan/Haas *halved with* **Ballesteros/Way**

Watson/Gilder *beat* **Torrance/Woosnam**, *5 and 4*

Session Score: 2.5-1.5

SATURDAY AFTERNOON FOURSOMES

Kite/Floyd *lost to* **Faldo/Langer**, *3 and 2*

Morgan/Wadkins *beat* **Torrance/Cañizares**, *7 and 5*

Watson/Gilder *lost to* **Ballesteros/Way**, *2 and 1*

Haas/Strange *beat* **Waites/Brown**, *3 and 2*

Session Score: 2-2

SUNDAY SINGLES

Fuzzy Zoeller *halved with* **Severiano Ballesteros**

Jay Haas *lost to* **Nick Faldo**, *2 and 1*

Gil Morgan *lost to* **Bernhard Langer** *by two holes*

Bob Gilder *beat* **Gordon J. Brand** *by two holes*

Ben Crenshaw *beat* **Sandy Lyle**, *3 and 1*

Calvin Peete *beat* **Brian Waites** *by one hole*

Curtis Strange *lost to* **Paul Way**, *2 and 1*

Tom Kite *halved with* **Sam Torrance**

Craig Stadler *beat* **Ian Woosnam**, *3 and 2*

Lanny Wadkins *halved with* **José María Cañizares**

Ray Floyd *lost to* **Ken Brown**, *4 and 3*

Tom Watson *beat* **Bernard Gallacher**, *2 and 1*

Session Score: 6.5-5.5

Overall Score: USA 14.5, Europe 13.5

Severiano Ballesteros of Europe plays a shot out of a bunker during his 1983 Ryder Cup singles match against Fuzzy Zoeller at the PGA National course in Palm Beach Gardens, Florida.

1985
Europe 16.5
USA 11.5

The Belfry, Sutton Coldfield

September 13-15

For Europe, 28 years of waiting and the accompanying frustration finally ended when Sam Torrance sank a putt on the 18th at The Belfry in 1985 and raised his arms aloft in celebration. For the first time since 1957, the Ryder Cup was no longer in the hands of the US team and a new era in the history of golf's greatest team competition had just begun. The architect of Europe's win, Tony Jacklin, became a hero.

IN 1985, GOLF FANS IN ENGLAND and all over Europe sensed a change in the tide as their team prepared for the 26th Ryder Cup matches with a growing sense of optimism and excitement. Having come so close two years earlier at Palm Beach Gardens in Florida, European belief had been strengthened by Bernhard Langer's victory at the Masters in Augusta and Sandy Lyle's triumph at the British Open. Could this be the year when everything changed?

Record crowds of more than 25,000 flocked to The Belfry each day to cheer on their heroes, creating an atmosphere rarely experienced in the Ryder Cup before. It came as quite a shock to some of the American players, more accustomed to sedate British crowds who understood the etiquette of the game, when missed shots were cheered by the galleries and the volume grew louder, the nearer Europe came to victory. Suddenly, less than a decade after many critics suggested the event was too one-sided to survive for much longer, it was now so passionate and so competitive that a completely new generation of fans were giving it an edge hitherto unimagined.

Opinions were mixed on whether this new phenomenon was a good thing, with some players, including American Peter Jacobsen, complained it was off-putting and disappointing. US captain Lee Trevino was made of sterner stuff, however, and accused his own team members of being "cry babies". Whatever the behaviour of the crowd, the USA knew they had under-achieved at The Belfry because the side they sent to England was still a strong one, if perhaps lacking a real star name. It was missing talisman Tom Watson, who had narrowly failed to qualify, but captained by the experienced Trevino. US Open champion Andy North, PGA winner Hubert Green and new boys Mark O'Meara, Peter Jacobsen and Hal Sutton now added to the mix.

Once again captained by Tony Jacklin after his impressive leadership of two years earlier, the home side was largely similar

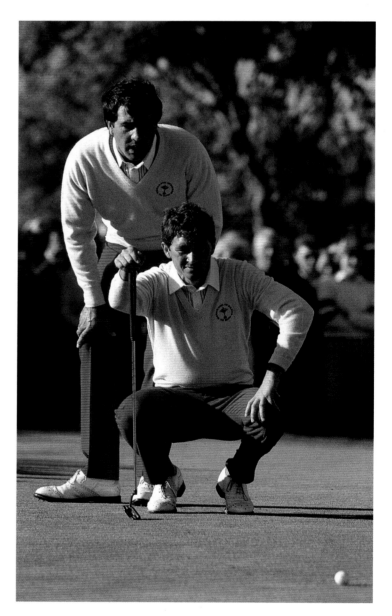

RIGHT: *Europe's Severiano Ballesteros (rear) and Manuel Piñero line up a putt during the second day of the 1985 Ryder Cup at The Belfry.*

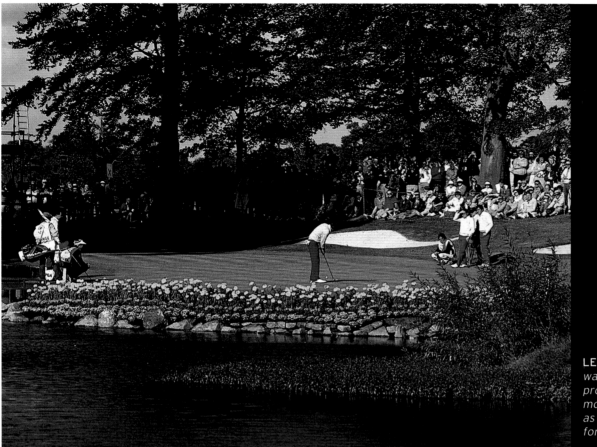

LEFT: *Sunshine, flowers, water and greenery provide a picture-postcard moment at The Belfry as Curtis Strange putts for the USA.*

to the one that came so close to victory at Palm Beach, with Spaniard José Rivero the only real newcomer; the British public were expectant of something special. However, the galleries were made to wait for their moment of glory as the opening day saw Team USA in complete control as they began the defence of their trophy with resolve, claiming three of the four morning Foursomes. Calvin Peete and Tom Kite started the ball rolling with a 3 and 2 victory over the top European pairing of Bernhard Langer and Nick Faldo before the always-steady Wadkins and Floyd beat Lyle/Brown; Stadler/Sutton overcame Clark and Torrance, 3 and 2. For the Europeans, the only highlight was another impressive display from Seve Ballesteros, who drove the par-four 10th as he partnered Piñero to a 2 and 1 victory over Strange/O'Meara.

The afternoon Fourballs were more even, but the USA still ended the day with an important one-point lead, thanks primarily to a narrow victory by Floyd/Wadkins against Torrance/Clark at the last hole. However, Europe were encouraged by the performance of youngster Paul Way, who partnered the more experienced Ian Woosnam to beat Fuzzy Zoeller and Hubert Green by one hole. Meanwhile, another victory for Ballesteros and Piñero, this time against North/Jacobsen by 2 and 1, ensured the home side won the session (there was also a half for Langer and José María Cañizares against Stadler and Hal Sutton) and ended the day within touching distance of the holders – just 4.5-3.5 behind. The new Ryder Cup was starting to catch fire.

DAY ONE

CAPTAINS

Europe: Tony Jacklin   **USA:** Lee Trevino

FRIDAY MORNING FOURSOMES

Ballesteros/Piñero *beat* **Strange/O'Meara,** *2 and 1*

Langer/Faldo *lost to* **Peete/Kite,** *3 and 2*

Lyle/Brown *lost to* **Wadkins/Floyd,** *4 and 3*

Clark/Torrance *lost to* **Stadler/Sutton,** *3 and 2*

Session Score: 1-3

FRIDAY AFTERNOON FOURBALLS

Way/Woosnam *beat* **Zoeller/Green** *by one hole*

Ballesteros/Piñero *beat* **North/Jacobsen,** *2 and 1*

Langer/Cañizares *halved with* **Stadler/Sutton**

Torrance/Clark *lost to* **Floyd/Wadkins** *by one hole*

Session Score: 2.5-1.5

Overall Score: Europe 3.5, USA 4.5

On the second day the pendulum began to swing towards the Europeans as Torrance and Clark opened up with a victory over Kite/North in the morning Foursomes before Way and Woosnam followed suit against Green/Zoeller. But a shock defeat for Ballesteros and Piñero against O'Meara/Wadkins threatened to spoil the party, especially as Langer and Lyle were two-down to the experienced pairing of Stadler/Strange, with only two to play. Lyle won the 17th with a birdie but at the last, Stadler faced only an 18-inch putt for a one-hole win. To cheers from the galleries and gasps from the Americans, the 1982 Master pulled his ball wide. His miss changed the momentum of the Cup, with the scores now tied at 6-6 and Europe on the up.

In fact, Europe went on to take eight of the next 12 points, including an encouraging afternoon Fourballs session – won 3-1,

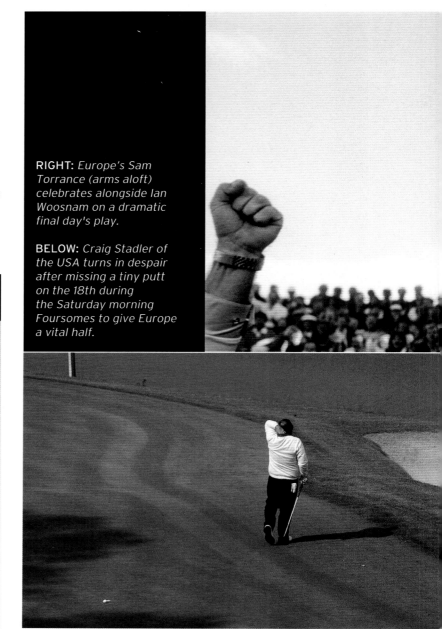

RIGHT: *Europe's Sam Torrance (arms aloft) celebrates alongside Ian Woosnam on a dramatic final day's play.*

BELOW: *Craig Stadler of the USA turns in despair after missing a tiny putt on the 18th during the Saturday morning Foursomes to give Europe a vital half.*

DAYS TWO AND THREE

SATURDAY MORNING FOURSOMES

Torrance/Clark *beat* **Kite/North**, *2 and 1*

Way/Woosnam *beat* **Green/Zoeller**, *4 and 3*

Ballesteros/Piñero *lost to* **O'Meara/Wadkins**, *3 and 2*

Langer/Lyle *halved with* **Stadler/Strange**

Session Score: 2.5-1.5

SATURDAY AFTERNOON FOURBALLS

Cañizares/Rivero *beat* **Kite/Peete**, *4 and 3*

Ballesteros/Piñero *beat* **Stadler/Sutton**, *5 and 4*

Way/Woosnam *lost to* **Strange/Jacobsen**, *4 and 2*

Langer/Brown *beat* **Floyd/Wadkins**, *3 and 2*

Session Score: 3-1

SUNDAY SINGLES

Manuel Piñero *beat* **Lanny Wadkins**, *3 and 2*

Ian Woosnam *lost to* **Craig Stadler**, *2 and 1*

Paul Way *beat* **Ray Floyd** *by two holes*

Severiano Ballesteros *halved with* **Tom Kite**

Sandy Lyle *beat* **Peter Jacobsen**, *3 and 2*

Bernhard Langer *beat* **Hal Sutton**, *5 and 4*

Sam Torrance *beat* **Andy North** *by one hole*

Howard Clark *beat* **Mark O'Meara** *by one hole*

José Rivero *lost to* **Calvin Peete** *by one hole*

Nick Faldo *lost to* **Hubert Green**, *3 and 1*

José María Cañizares *beat* **Fuzzy Zoeller** *by two holes*

Ken Brown *lost to* **Curtis Strange**, *4 and 2*

Session Score: 7.5-4.5

Overall Score: Europe 16.5, USA 11.5

thanks to the ever-increasing influence of the Spanish contingent. Cañizares and Rivero got the ball rolling with a 4 and 3 victory over Kite/Peete before Seve and Pinero won 5 and 4 against a now-deflated Stadler/Sutton, with Langer and Brown adding a further point. It meant that Europe went into the singles with a two-point lead, not enough to be favourites but enough to keep

> **"***I was sure Trevino would put his best players out first. So I put most of my crème in the middle.***"**

Tony Jacklin on his tactics for the singles matches

the home crowd in good voice. This time Jacklin got his tactics right, placing his strongest players in the middle of the field and hoping his inexperienced openers would pull off a surprise or two.

And they did exactly that, starting with an excellent 3 and 2 win for Piñero against Wadkins, thanks to birdies at the 10th, 11th and 15th. The run continued with Paul Way's two-hole triumph against Ray Floyd, sealed when the experienced American sent his bunker shot at the last straight into the lake. Stadler made up for his earlier nightmare by beating Woosnam, but Ballesteros came from three-down to halve with Kite, including two monster putts at the 14th and 15th. Following this, both Lyle and Langer earned crucial points against Jacobsen and Sutton respectively – Lyle's victory coming courtesy of a 25-yard putt at the 16th.

A win for Cañizares piled pressure on the Americans and when the stage was set for a hero, Sam Torrance pipped Howard Clark to the honour after Clark had missed a putt at the 17th against

Mark O'Meara that would have clinched the Cup for the US. The Englishman did go on to win at the last, but in the meantime Torrance took centre stage. Indeed, he reached the par-four final hole all square after mounting an excellent comeback from three-down and hit the tee-shot of his life – long and over trees to the middle of the fairway. It was too much for his opponent Andy North, who sent his own effort straight into the lake, and could only watch in despair as Torrance's second shot took him to within 20 feet of the hole.

The Scot knew he had two putts to win the Ryder Cup for Europe and his walk down the final fairway resembled a victory parade, so loud were the cheers. Once on the green, he needed only one shot to finish. In what has become one of the most iconic shots of the Ryder Cup, he raised both arms aloft in celebration before being engulfed by his team-mates. The trophy belonged to Europe, and history had been made.

Ryder Cup legends

Jack **NICKLAUS** and Tom **WATSON**

Virtually unbeatable as individuals, as a partnership Jack Nicklaus and Tom Watson were truly unstoppable. Together, they played four times in the Ryder Cup, winning all four times. Great friends off the course, the sight of them teaming up proved a dagger to the heart of any European hopes of victory – and their 100 per cent winning record testifies to the champions' potency.

Jack Nicklaus and Tom Watson arrived at the 1981 Ryder Cup determined not just to win but to eviscerate their opponents. The US team included players who had won a combined 37 Majors and the best of them – Nicklaus and Watson, who had won 26 of them – were, quite simply, unbeatable together. They had first partnered four years earlier at Royal Lytham & St Annes and served notice of just how potent a team they could be in beating Tommy Horton and Mark James, winning 5 and 4 in their Foursomes match.

They began in 1981 with a convincing 4 and 3 Foursomes win over Peter Oosterhuis and Nick Faldo before being rested until the second day. That was when America took complete control of the tie, winning the morning Fourballs and afternoon Foursomes 7-1, just half a point short of the all-time Ryder Cup record. Nicklaus and Watson were to the fore. Des Smyth and Jose Maria Cañizares were beaten 3 and 2 in the Fourballs before Bernhard Langer and Manuel Piñero lost by the same scoreline in the Foursomes.

Watson has since said Nicklaus was the reason they won, but that's putting himself down. True, his partner found the green on the four out of five occasions that Watson's drive ended up in the heather, but this was a real team. Nicklaus went on to beat Eamonn Darcy in the singles to complete his perfect Ryder Cup and the final score was 18.5 to 9.5 in America's favour. Nicklaus and Watson's last time playing together was also the last time the USA won the Ryder Cup so convincingly.

The pair also enjoyed enormous success as individuals in the Ryder Cup. Nicklaus' first tournament was in 1969 at Royal Birkdale and is still remembered as one of the greatest acts of sportsmanship in its history. The whole tournament was on a knife-edge and as Nicklaus sunk a four-foot putt on the last, his opponent – Tony Jacklin – was left with a two-footer to tie. Nicklaus conceded the putt, ensuring the Ryder Cup was tied for the first time in history, although America still retained the trophy.

It proved the start of a wonderful story for Nicklaus, playing 15 matches and taking 10 points between 1971 and 1975. Having taken to heart the Ryder Cup concept, he captained the American team

in 1983 and 1987. In both cases it was Nicklaus v Jacklin. In 1983 the score was 1-1 as the USA won by one point. Four years later the USA was beaten on American soil for the first time, losing 15-13.

Tom Watson followed his friend in being both a victorious player and captain. He played under Nicklaus in 1983 and made his final appearance some six years later when his victory over Sam Torrance helped secure a tie at The Belfry. Then, as captain in 1993, his team were a point down after two days at The Belfry, but staged a memorable comeback, winning six singles matches and halving two others to claim victory.

Ultimately, though, Jack Nicklaus and Tom Watson will be remembered for their stunning performances as players. As a pair they were so dominant that they never once had to pla y the 17th hole, let alone an 18th, to win a match. Individually, the two men were astonishing; together, they were completely unstoppable.

RYDER CUP RECORD

Jack NICKLAUS
Ryder Cups: 1969 (tied but USA retains trophy), 1971, 1973, 1975, 1977, 1981, 1983 (non-playing captain), 1987 (non-playing captain). All won, except 1969 tie and 1987.
Total wins: 6 (plus 1 tie to retain the trophy, 1969)
Matches: 28 (won 17, halved 3, lost 8)
Total points: 18.5

Tom WATSON
Ryder Cups: 1977, 1979, 1981, 1983, 1989 (tied but Europe retain trophy), 1993 (non-playing captain). All won, except 1989 tie.
Total wins: 5
Matches: 15 (won 10, halved 1, lost 4)
Total points: 10.5

AS A PAIR:
Matches: 4 (won 4, halved 0, lost 0)
Total points: 4

> **"***Resolve never to quit, never to give up, no matter what the situation.***"**
>
> *Jack Nicklaus on being a winner*

ABOVE: *Unbeatable US pairing Jack Nicklaus (right) and Tom Watson deep in discussion at the 1981 Ryder Cup at Walton Heath Golf Club.*

1987

USA 13
Europe 15

Muirfield Village, Ohio

September 25-27

For the first time in 60 years, and after 13 Ryder Cup matches, the USA were finally beaten on home soil in 1987. Tony Jacklin's Europe retained the trophy with victory at Muirfield Village. The win was all the more noteworthy as the course was designed by US captain Jack Nicklaus, which should have given the USA unassailable home advantage.

WHEN RYDER CUP DEBUTANT José María Olazábal danced the Cha-Cha on the 18th green in Ohio, it summed up everything that made the European team so exciting: a team packed with personality, spirit and exciting golf. And a team that loved winning, too. Considering the USA had never before been beaten on home soil, going back to the very first Ryder Cup of 1927, Olazábal was entitled to a celebratory jig and the American crowd looked on in envy. Why couldn't their players show that same pizzazz?

What a turnaround from just eight years earlier when the USA were simply far too good for their European opponents at Walton Heath and seemed destined to hold onto the trophy for eternity. In those days, with Jack Nicklaus and Tom Watson in action, it was America who boasted the greatest legends in golf and could rightly call themselves the dream team. This time it was the Spaniard Severiano Ballesteros who added to his stature with another Ryder Cup performance to relish, while the likes of Nick

Faldo, Ian Woosnam, Sandy Lyle and Bernhard Langer – not to mention rookie Olazábal – were more than a match for just about anybody. Not that the American team, which included five rookies, lacked fighting spirit. Having been outplayed for the first two days, they won the opening seven singles to make a battle of it in the end. The Europeans seemed to have that little bit extra, however – or just enough, anyway, to produce an historic result.

Despite the strength of the European team the result was still a huge shock. After all, Nicklaus had been deliberately chosen to captain the US side because this was his course – he designed it, he knew it inside out. And it was designed to favour American golfers with super-quick greens and perfect fairways.

Having lost the trophy in England two years earlier, there was an extra determination in the US camp to win it back and media interest was now strong, with ABC Television deciding to cover the matches live for the very first time. There had even been a

LEFT: *Staunch female fans give the USA some serious support at Muirfield as Saturday's play gets underway.*

ABOVE: *Jack Nicklaus, the US captain, gives instructions to his players at Muirfield in 1987.*

proposal – hastily vetoed by Jacklin – that an extra day of singles be added to the competition to make it more TV-friendly but the European captain knew exactly what it would mean for his side (which could boast some of the world's top golfers but could never have the sheer numbers to match the US) and threatened to resign if it was pushed through. Thankfully, Nicklaus encouraged the US PGA to withdraw the proposal because the established format has since ensured a highly competitive Ryder Cup at every venue and it certainly played its part in Ohio as Europe built up a lead on the opening days and then hung on for life at the end.

The Europeans were backed by a 2,000-strong group of highly vocal supporters, mostly from Britain and Ireland, who had flown in anticipating an historic victory, highlighting just how far the Ryder Cup had come. Indeed, they witnessed an astonishing opening day. The morning Foursomes were squared 2-2, with Faldo/Woosnam and then Ballesteros/Olazábal winning matches three and four after Curtis Strange and Tom Kite, as well as Hal Sutton and Dan Pohl, earned early points for the US.

It was a good debut for Olazábal, who went on to form a legendary partnership with his fellow countryman Ballesteros over the next decade, and teamed up with his compatriot to beat Strange/Kite, 2 and 1, in the afternoon. But that was just a taster: Europe, roared on by their supporters, completed an incredible whitewash as they won the Fourballs 4-0. Jacklin ruthlessly dropped those players who lost matches in the morning and his new-look pairings responded with some outstanding performances, starting with a 3 and 2 victory for new boy Gordon Brand Jnr. and José Rivero against Ben Crenshaw and Scott Simpson. Lyle and Langer then beat Andy Bean and Mark Calcavecchia by one hole before Faldo/Woosnam won 2 and 1 against Sutton and Pohl. And so the Spaniards wrapped up a perfect afternoon that owed much to the inspired captaincy of Europe's leader.

DAY ONE

CAPTAINS

USA: Jack Nicklaus   **Europe:** Tony Jacklin

FRIDAY MORNING FOURSOMES

Strange/Kite *beat* **Torrance/Clark,** *4 and 2*

Sutton/Pohl *beat* **Brown/Langer,** *2 and 1*

Wadkins/Mize *lost to* **Faldo/Woosnam** *by two holes*

Nelson/Stewart *lost to* **Ballesteros/Olazábal** *by one hole*

Session Score: 2-2

FRIDAY AFTERNOON FOURBALLS

Crenshaw/Simpson *lost to* **Brand/Rivero,** *3 and 2*

Bean/Calcavecchia *lost to* **Lyle/Langer** *by one hole*

Sutton/Pohl *lost to* **Faldo/Woosnam,** *2 and 1*

Strange/Kite *lost to* **Ballesteros/Olazábal,** *2 and 1*

Session Score: 0-4

Overall Score: USA 2, Europe 6

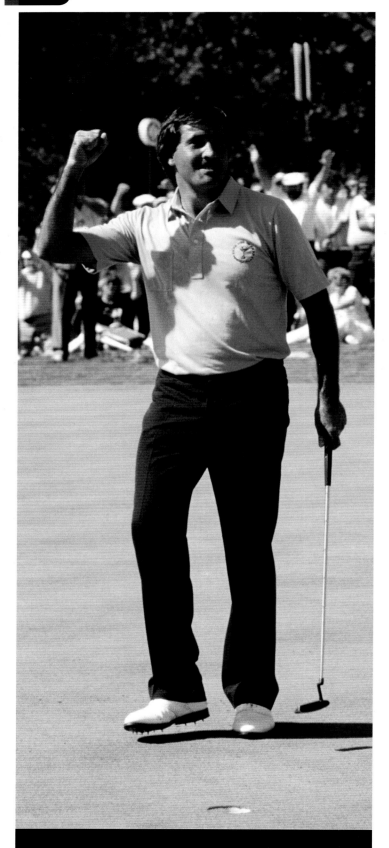

On the Saturday, the USA needed to start well – and did, with Strange/Kite comfortable winners against Rivero and Brand Jnr. in the morning Foursomes and Sutton and Larry Mize denying Faldo/Woosnam their third victory in a row by winning the final hole for a half. But the next two matches set the tone for what was to come: Lyle/Langer won 2 and 1 against Wadkins and Larry Nelson, including an eagle at the 11th, before Ballesteros/Olazábal crept home against Ben Crenshaw and Payne Stewart. The result helped to quieten the home crowd, who had been issued with free Stars and Stripes flags and were asked by Nicklaus to provide more voluble support.

But in the afternoon session (tied 2-2), the Europeans played some outstanding golf. Nick Faldo and Ian Woosnam's performance against Curtis Strange and Tom Kite had to be seen

ABOVE: *Severiano Ballesteros celebrates a winning putt in his singles match against Curtis Strange, his fourth point of the 1987 Ryder Cup.*

DAYS TWO AND THREE

SATURDAY MORNING FOURSOMES

Strange/Kite *beat* **Rivero/Brand**, *3 and 1*

Sutton/Mize *halved with* **Faldo/Woosnam**

Wadkins/Nelson *lost to* **Lyle/Langer**, *2 and 1*

Crenshaw/Stewart *lost to* **Ballesteros/Olazábal** *by one hole*

Session Score: 1.5-2.5

SATURDAY AFTERNOON FOURBALLS

Strange/Kite *lost to* **Faldo/Woosnam**, *5 and 4*

Bean/Stewart *beat* **Darcy/Brand**, *3 and 2*

Sutton/Mize *beat* **Ballesteros/Olazábal**, *2 and 1*

Wadkins/Nelson *lost to* **Lyle/Langer** *by one hole*

Session Score: 2-2

SUNDAY SINGLES

Andy Bean *beat* **Ian Woosnam** *by one hole*

Dan Pohl *lost to* **Howard Clark** *by one hole*

Larry Mize *halved with* **Sam Torrance**

Mark Calcavecchia *beat* **Nick Faldo** *by one hole*

Payne Stewart *beat* **José María Olazábal** *by two holes*

Scott Simpson *beat* **José Rivero**, *2 and 1*

Tom Kite *beat* **Sandy Lyle**, *3 and 2*

Ben Crenshaw *lost to* **Eamonn Darcy** *by one hole*

Larry Nelson *halved with* **Bernhard Langer**

Curtis Strange *lost to* **Severiano Ballesteros**, *2 and 1*

Lanny Wadkins *beat* **Ken Brown**, *3 and 2*

Hal Sutton *halved with* **Gordon Brand**

Session Score: 7.5-4.5

Overall Score: USA 13, Europe 15

RIGHT: *An emotional and ecstatic European captain Tony Jacklin clasps the Ryder Cup after Europe retained the trophy at the Nicklaus-built Muirfield Village, course in Ohio, USA.*

to be believed: Kite and Strange – who was to go on and win the next two US Opens – were a high-quality pairing, but were torn apart, 5 and 4. "I don't think the Americans knew what hit them," Faldo said, when asked to recall the game. "Woosie and I birdied the first five holes – we played some unbelievable golf." Then Sandy Lyle and Bernhard Langer held off a late fight from Lanny Wadkins and Larry Nelson to win
by one hole, with Lyle hitting the shot of the day: a glorious approach to the 18th.

With the Europeans, who were collectively 25-under-par for the afternoon, now five ahead – and needing just four points to retain the trophy – Jack Nicklaus opted for shock tactics on the Sunday. He put his weaker players out first when Europe expected to see the big guns up front. It was a tactic that almost worked because the USA claimed five of the first seven games. Andy Bean stunned Ian Woosnam by winning at the 18th in the opening match – and the scoreboard showed the USA up in five and level in three of the remaining 11 matches. When European talisman Nick Faldo also lost – by one hole to Calcavecchia – Sandy Lyle lost to Tom Kite and José María Olazábal went down to Stewart, what had seemed impossible became more realistic.

But Europe had Howard Clark's early victory over Pohl to hang onto and a surprise hero in the shape of Eamonn Darcy. He was up against golfing legend Crenshaw but it was the American who cracked under the pressure – in spectacular style. Angry at a missed putt on the 6th green, he snapped the blade of his putter while hitting it on the ground in frustration and from then on, was forced to use his irons to putt. Amazingly, he still reached the 18th level, but threw it away with a tee-shot that found water, and when Darcy had a putt to win the match, he calmly holed it for his name to be passed down in Ryder Cup folklore.

With Europe now 13-11 ahead, they needed just one-and-a-half points from five games and a third of these came in surprising fashion when Langer called for a half at the 18th after rolling his putt just inside that of opponent Nelson's with the match squared. To everyone's surprise, Nelson agreed. Fittingly, the match-winning putt came from Ballesteros as he beat World No. 1 Curtis Strange on the 17th green to win 2 and 1 before lifting an arm aloft in triumph. The celebrations, it has to be said, were far less restrained – and as players danced and champagne flowed, Jacklin was almost speechless at what he and his team had achieved. It was a Ryder Cup that would never be forgotten.

❝*It is the greatest week of my life!***❞**

Tony Jacklin hails Europe's victory

Ryder Cup legends
Tony JACKLIN and Bernard GALLACHER

Tony Jacklin and Bernard Gallacher were great Ryder Cup players but even greater captains. In 1985, Jacklin turned a one-sided tournament into the finest competition in golf by beating the USA for the first time in 28 years, then led Europe to its first-ever victory in America, two years later.

LEFT: British legends together: Tony Jacklin (left) and Bernard Gallacher assess the situation at the 1991 Ryder Cup at Kiawah Island.

Tony Jacklin first shot to fame when he won The Open and The US Open in successive years in the late 1960s. With two Majors under his belt by the age of 26, his reputation was further enhanced when he became Ryder Cup captain in 1983, having played in the competition eight times, seven of which were American victories and one a memorable tie.

Jacklin was appointed non-playing captain for the 1983 contest. His first move was to bring Seve Ballesteros in from the cold and although the USA won by a point, Jacklin was about to change things. By 1985 he had a squad of fine players to support Ballesteros, including Ian Woosnam, Sandy Lyle, Bernhard Langer and Nick Faldo. His team at The Belfry in 1985 was better prepared than ever before and triumphed by a massive five-point margin.

Even better was to come when Jacklin took his team to the USA two years later, where they beat captain Jack Nicklaus' side on a course he had designed: Muirfield Village. A Ballesteros win over Curtis Strange completed a 15-13 victory and ensured a first defeat for the USA on home turf - "It was the sweetest moment," he observed. In his final contest as captain, back at The Belfry, Europe retained the trophy with a 14-14 draw. Jacklin had won the Ryder Cup in three of his four captaincies.

Bernard Gallacher followed in Jacklin's wake, having been a successful Ryder Cup player and assistant to his predecessor. He became the youngest Briton in the Ryder Cup when he made his debut in 1969 aged 20, and went on to play eight times. After he beat the legendary Lee Trevino five times, the American admitted: "In the Ryder Cup, Bernard was the only player to get the better of me." But it was not so easy as captain. His first tournament - the 1991 "War on the Shore" at Kiawah Island - ended in defeat. Two years later at The Belfry all of Gallacher's big names - Ballesteros, Faldo, Woosnam and Langer - failed to win on the final day. Gallacher wanted to step down as captain after the defeat, but was persuaded to stay - it turned out to be third time lucky.

His finest moment came in 1995, when Europe regained the Ryder Cup. He said the key to success was an open mind: "Before play at Oak Hill, I never at any time had Sam Torrance playing with Costantino Rocca but they came together because other guys were off-form or tired and they turned out to be a perfect combination." When Gallacher handed over to Seve Ballesteros for the 1997 Cup, it was the last time a European captain would have more than one term - the job was now just too big.

RYDER CUP RECORD

Tony JACKLIN
Ryder Cups: 1967, 1969, 1971, 1973, 1975, 1977, 1979, 1983 (non-playing captain), 1985 (winner, non-playing captain), 1987 (winner, non-playing captain), 1989 (tied but Europe retain trophy, non-playing captain)
Total wins: 2 (plus 1 tie to retain trophy, 1989)
Matches: 35 (won 13, halved 8, lost 14)
Total points: 17

Bernard GALLACHER
Ryder Cups: 1969, 1971, 1973, 1975, 1977, 1979, 1981, 1983, 1991 (non-playing captain), 1993 (non-playing captain), 1995 (winner, non-playing captain)
Total wins: 1
Matches: 31 (won 13, halved 5, lost 13)
Total points: 15.5

> *"The Ryder Cup is more than just golf – it is your country, your team, your tour, your captain that you're playing for. It is the ultimate in golf."*
>
> *Tony Jacklin*

1989

Europe 14
USA 14

The Belfry, Sutton Coldfield

September 22-24

In 1989, US captain Raymond Floyd controversially introduced his team as the "12 greatest players in the world". However, Europe (who by now felt they had plenty of players worthy of inclusion on such a list) matched them all the way in a dramatic contest at The Belfry, which ended in a tie – only the second in Ryder Cup history.

THE COURSE

Brabazon Course
Location: The Belfry, Sutton Coldfield, England
Par: 72
Yards: 7,118

Staging the Ryder Cup for the second time, The Belfry, set in 550 acres of Warwickshire countryside, could describe itself as the spiritual home of the Ryder Cup in England. And it certainly provided some incredible memories.

A QUICK LOOK AROUND The Belfry in the build-up to the 28th Ryder Cup matches showed just how far the competition had come: packed galleries, almost 1,000 accredited journalists, the largest tented village at any sports event in Britain and a crowd whipped up by pre-match hype generated by a headline-hungry media. It would take an incredible contest to live up to all this, but the 1989 Ryder Cup certainly delivered.

With Europe going into the matches as favourites for the first time in living memory, the interest in England was huge but the build-up was given extra fuel by US captain Floyd at the pre-tournament Gala Ball. Perhaps attempting to put his team on the front foot, he introduced his players as the "12 greatest players in the world", partly in deference to the great Ben Hogan, who unveiled his side of 1967 with exactly the same words. But this time it backfired, serving only to infuriate the European team and provide captain Tony Jacklin with a very simple motivational speech on the eve of the opening day.

Tony Jacklin was captaining for the fourth – and final – time in a row. He had endured a difficult time in his personal life following the death of his wife Vivian in a car accident in Spain,

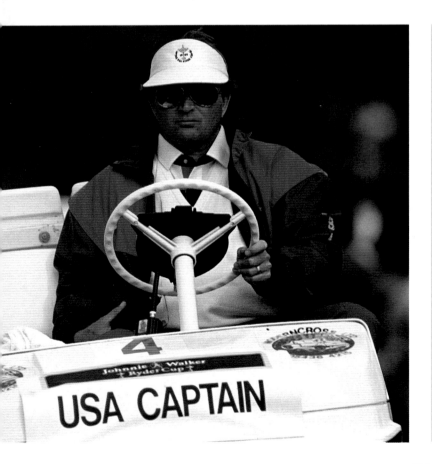

USA CAPTAIN

DAY ONE

CAPTAINS

Europe: Tony Jacklin   **USA:** Raymond Floyd

FRIDAY MORNING FOURSOMES

Faldo/Woosnam *halved with* **Kite/Strange**

Clark/James *lost to* **Wadkins/Stewart** *by one hole*

Ballesteros/Olazábal *halved with* **Watson/Beck**

Langer/Rafferty *lost to* **Calcavecchia/Green,** *2 and 1*

Session Score: 1-3

FRIDAY AFTERNOON FOURBALLS

Torrance/Brand *beat* **Strange/Azinger** *by one hole*

Clark/James *beat* **Couples/Wadkins,** *3 and 2*

Faldo/Woosnam *beat* **Calcavecchia/McCumber** *by two holes*

Ballesteros/Olazábal *beat* **Watson/M. O'Meara,** *6 and 5*

Session Score: 4-0

Overall Score: Europe 5, USA 3

126

RIGHT: *Crowds flock around the greens at The Belfry as the action gets serious in one of the closest Ryder Cups ever.*

OPPOSITE: *US team captain Ray Floyd gets around the course in his buggy during the Ryder Cup matches of 1989.*

but his team was still a powerful one. The Scot Sandy Lyle was missing, following an alarming dip in form, but Bernhard Langer had recovered from the yips to make the squad; Christy O'Connor Jnr. and Howard Clark were the other captain's picks, with Ronan Rafferty the only rookie.

The US, meanwhile, were in a transitional period and included five debutants in Paul Azinger, Chip Beck, Fred Couples, Mark McCumber and Ken Green – perhaps counter-balanced by Floyd's selection of the experienced Lanny Wadkins and Tom Watson as his personal choices. Even so, the Americans began the opening day in impressive fashion as they took a 3-1 lead by the end of the morning Foursomes. Nick Faldo and Ian Woosnam were held to a half in the opening match by Tom Kite and Curtis Strange before Wadkins, who had missed six cuts in his last eight tournaments, proved that the Ryder Cup is different as he partnered Stewart to a vital victory against Howard Clark and Mark James. Even when the incomparable partnership of Severiano Ballesteros and José María Olazábal took a three-hole lead against Beck and Watson the USA refused to crumble, with two birdie putts from Watson eventually helping them halve the match.

Europe's also lost the last Foursomes, where Langer and Rafferty battled back from three-down against Calcavecchia/

Green before going down 2 and 1. Thus, the favourites reached the opening afternoon without having won a single match. The Americans had laid down a serious challenge but it was a situation that would change very quickly indeed, with Europe recovering sufficiently to whitewash their opponents after lunch.

In a high-octane and patriotic atmosphere the home crowd at The Belfry could barely believe their eyes as Tony Jacklin's men won every single Fourballs match to end the day 5-3 ahead, even though the captain made only cursory changes. He kept three of his pairs the same but replaced the out-of-touch Langer and Rafferty with Torrance and Gordon Brand Jnr. Just as at Muirfield Village in Ohio two years earlier, his gamble paid handsome dividends as the new pairing were sent out first and edged to a one-hole victory over Curtis Strange and Azinger.

Further victories for Clark and James against Couples/Wadkins, 3 and 2, and for Faldo and Woosnam against Calcavecchia/ McCumber by two holes put the European team on a high. Ballesteros/Olazábal added the icing to the cake with a hugely convincing 6 and 5 victory over Watson and O'Meara. In the space of a few hours Europe had gone from frustration to elation and, in the process, whipped up an already enthusiastic crowd into a high-pitch whirl of excitement.

The second day of the 1989 Ryder Cup proved far tighter than the first as both sessions were squared 2-2, leaving Europe with a two-point advantage going into the all-important singles. Only Ballesteros and Olazábal were able to register two victories – beating Kite and Strange by one hole (thanks to excellent bunker shots from Olazábal at the 17th and 18th) in the morning, before crushing Calcavecchia/Green, 4 and 2, in the afternoon.

There was a moment when Kite and McCumber beat Langer/Cañizares in the second Fourballs (after Azinger and Beck had already beaten Faldo/Woosnam) when Europe looked like wobbling but victories for Clark and James (by one hole against Stewart/Strange) and then the Spaniards restored morale.

Huge crowds flocked to The Belfry to see the finale and yet again they witnessed a tigerish fight-back from the Americans, who won the opening two matches: Azinger, one-up against Ballesteros, and Beck, 3 and 2, against Langer. There was golf and drama of the highest quality as Ballesteros and Azinger did battle, but also plenty of gamesmanship. First, Ballesteros asked to change his ball on the 2nd green, claiming it was cut, but Azinger disagreed and so did the match referee. That really got the crowd going and when

> ❝*I remember looking up to the sky, with my arms outstretched and tears ran down my face.*❞
>
> *Christy O'Connor Jnr. describes the moment he beat Fred Couples*

SHOT OF THE DAY

No one gave Christy O'Connor Jnr. a chance against Fred Couples but at the 18th, facing a difficult iron shot 235 yards over water to the green and under pressure to win, he produced a formidable shot. The Irishman sent a two-iron to within four feet of the hole before Couples missed a putt, conceding defeat. "It was the greatest and most emotional moment of my professional life," he said.

LEFT: *Europe's Christy O'Connor Jnr. wins his singles match as Fred Couples (right) concedes at the 18th.*

RIGHT: *Celebrations for Europe as José María Cañizares (far right) completes a dramatic victory over Ken Green of the USA to retain the trophy.*

DAYS TWO AND THREE

SATURDAY MORNING FOURSOMES

Woosnam/Faldo beat **Wadkins/Stewart**, *3 and 2*

Brand/Torrance lost to **Beck/Azinger**, *4 and 3*

O'Connor/Rafferty lost to **Calcavecchia/Green**, *3 and 2*

Ballesteros/Olazábal beat **Kite/Strange** *by one hole*

Session Score: 2-2

SATURDAY AFTERNOON FOURBALLS

Faldo/Woosnam lost to **Beck/Azinger**, *2 and 1*

Langer/Cañizares lost to **Kite/McCumber**, *2 and 1*

Clark/James beat **Stewart/Strange** *by one hole*

Ballesteros/Olazábal beat **Calcavecchia/Green**, *4 and 2*

Session Score: 2-2

SUNDAY SINGLES

Severiano Ballesteros lost to **Paul Azinger** *by one hole*

Bernhard Langer lost to **Chip Beck**, *3 and 2*

José María Olazábal beat **Payne Stewart** *by one hole*

Ronan Rafferty beat **Mark Calcavecchia** *by one hole*

Howard Clark lost to **Tom Kite**, *8 and 7*

Mark James beat **Mark O'Meara**, *3 and 2*

Christy O'Connor beat **Fred Couples** *by one hole*

Jose Maria Cañizares beat **Ken Green** *by one hole*

Gordon Brand lost to **Mark McCumber** *by one hole*

Sam Torrance lost to **Tom Watson**, *3 and 1*

Nick Faldo lost to **Lanny Wadkins** *by one hole*

Ian Woosnam lost to **Curtis Strange** *by two holes*

Session Score: 5-7

Overall Score: Europe 14, USA 14

Azinger drove into the lake at the 18th leading by just one hole, there was pandemonium – especially when Ballesteros spotted that Azinger had been allowed a very favourable drop. It put the Spaniard off his stride because he also failed to carry the water and lost the match, which proved a bugbear for the great man for many years to come. "Looking back, I have the feeling something was wrong," he once said.

In the end it didn't prevent Europe from retaining the trophy because they won four of the next five matches despite Kite's mammoth 8 and 7 victory over Clark. Olazábal beat Stewart by one hole while Rafferty earned a point against Calcavecchia (with both Americans finding water at the last), before James beat O'Meara, 3 and 2. With the score now 12-10, Europe needed only two points to retain the trophy and Irishman Christy O'Connor Jnr. was at the 18th, all square with Fred Couples, and hit the approach shot of his life on the way to an emotional and improbable victory.

It was left to José María Cañizares to complete the job against Ken Green and having arrived at the 18th all square, he showed nerves of steel to do exactly that. Both men faced a long putt – Green from below the hole and Cañizares from above – but it was the Spaniard who triumphed as his effort fell only a few feet short. After two misses from his rival, he calmly holed out to spark riotous celebrations.

Dogged resistance from the Americans (who won all four remaining matches), however, somehow denied Europe overall victory – McCumber, Watson, Wadkins and Strange all displayed admirable resolve before Faldo uncharacteristically threw away the final hole against Wadkins when he found water. Woosnam, too, missed one last putt that could have earned an all-important half against Strange. Even so, it had been an incredible match and a remarkable finish – the first tie in the Ryder Cup since "The Concession" of 1969.

CHAPTER SIX
LET BATTLE COMMENCE

With Europe growing in stature in the 1980s, holding the trophy for three contests in a row, it was up to the USA to hit back in the 1990s. The Americans did exactly that, resulting in some fiercely contested - and sometimes controversial - Ryder Cups.

The US team celebrates after their amazing fightback earned them victory by a single point at the 1999 Ryder Cup.

1991

USA 14.5
Europe 13.5

Kiawah Island, South Carolina

September 27-29

THE COURSE

The Ocean Course
Location: Kiawah Island
Golf Resort,
Kiawah Island,
South Carolina, USA
Par: 72
Yards: 7,356

Designed by Pete Dye, the course had only just been completed when the Ryder Cup arrived in town. Naturally, there were still some unfinished parts but with a sea view from every hole The Ocean Course was both scenic and testing.

Before a ball was even struck, the 1991 Ryder Cup at Kiawah Island had been billed "War on the Shore" by an American magazine and it certainly lived up to this tag, proving to be one of the most controversial, yet compelling Ryder Cups of all time. Eventually, it was decided on the last green, in the last match of the last day by a missed putt from Bernhard Langer.

US CAPTAIN DAVE STOCKTON, aware his team needed every advantage, hardly sought to calm the atmosphere. In fact, he infuriated the European team by inviting them to watch a 40-minute film on the History of the Ryder Cup – one edited to feature virtually all American victories and celebrations. Nick Faldo almost walked out in protest and by the time the players teed off, there was no love lost between them.

Matters were hardly helped by a local radio DJ broadcasting a shameful "Wake Up the Enemy" campaign, giving out the phone number of the European hotel and urging US supporters to ring the players in the middle of the night. Indeed, many overly pumped-up fans did exactly that. It seemed the "War on the Shore" tag was being taken too seriously and therefore when Corey Pavin and Steve Pate turned up to play a Fourballs wearing "Operation Desert Storm" forage caps it seemed at the very least tactless and at worst, tasteless. However, no one could say the intense atmosphere wasn't working in America's favour because when Team USA finally got to play golf, they made an impressive start.

ABOVE: Seve Ballesteros tees off at the 4th on Day One, watched by José María Olazábal and the USA's Paul Azinger and Chip Beck.

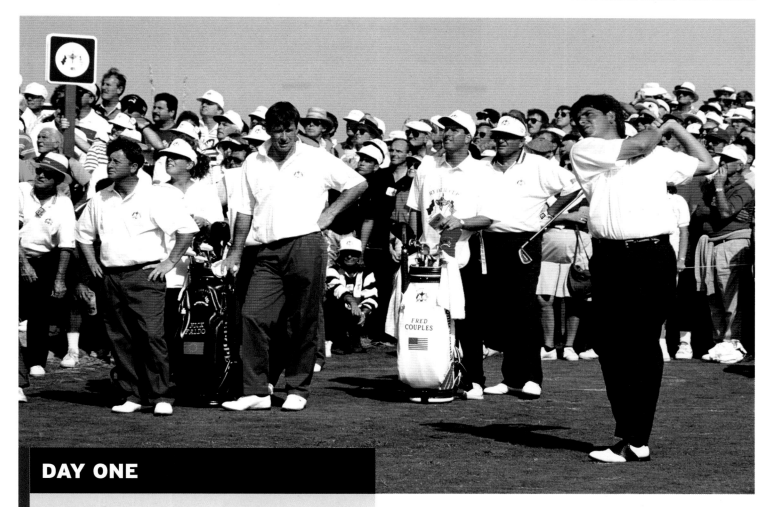

DAY ONE

CAPTAINS

USA: Dave Stockton   **Europe:** Bernard Gallacher

FRIDAY MORNING FOURSOMES

Azinger/Beck *lost to* **Ballesteros/Olazábal**, *2 and 1*

Floyd/Couples *beat* **Langer/James**, *2 and 1*

Wadkins/Irwin *beat* **Gilford/Montgomerie**, *4 and 2*

Stewart/Calcavecchia *beat* **Faldo/Woosnam** *by one hole*

Session Score: 3-1

FRIDAY AFTERNOON FOURBALLS

Wadkins/O'Meara *halved with* **Torrance/Feherty**

Azinger/Beck *lost to* **Ballesteros/Olazábal**, *2 and 1*

Pavin/Calcavecchia *lost to* **Richardson/James**, *5 and 4*

Floyd/Couples *beat* **Faldo/Woosnam**, *5 and 3*

Session Score: 1.5-2.5

Overall Score: USA 4.5 Europe 3.5

ABOVE: Fred Couples hits a tee-shot at Kiawah Island, watched by partner Ray Floyd and Europe's Ian Woosnam and Nick Faldo.

Gallacher's decision to play rookies Colin Montgomerie and David Gilford together in the Foursomes backfired as they were comprehensively beaten, 4 and 2, by Lanny Wadkins and Hale Irwin, while Ray Floyd and Fred Couples eased to a 2-1 victory over Langer and Mark James before Payne Stewart and Mark Calcavecchia beat Nick Faldo and Ian Woosnam. It might have been a clean sweep for the home side, had Seve Ballesteros and José María Olazábal not collected Europe's only point of the morning in a controversial and ill-humoured match against Paul Azinger and Chip Beck that set the tone for the weekend.

Ballesteros was furious when he spotted at the 10th that Azinger had been using a different ball and accused his opponent of cheating (players are required to declare the make and number of the ball they are using at the first tee and inform opponents when changes are made). The match referee ruled in Azinger's favour but Ballesteros continued to complain and both men could barely bring themselves to shake hands when the Europeans clinched victory with a Seve putt at the 17th. "The American team has 11 nice guys and Paul Azinger," a bitter Ballesteros said later.

With the atmosphere intensifying, Europe performed better in the afternoon as the Spaniards, once again faced by Azinger/Beck, won 2 and 1 to close the gap, and when Richardson/James followed up with a convincing 5-4 victory over Pavin/Calcavecchia, the battle was on. Wadkins/O'Meara halved with Torrance/Feherty and it took a surprisingly easy victory by Floyd/Couples against an out-of-touch Faldo/Woosnam to keep the USA ahead by a point.

With his team one point down and his best partnership of Nick Faldo and Ian Woosnam on the back of two consecutive and disappointing defeats, Europe captain Bernard Gallacher knew he must make changes on Day Two to change the situation but his decision could well have lost him the Cup.

Gallacher opted to put Faldo (never the easiest partner for even an experienced player) with rookie David Gilford, a shy and quiet character who appeared nervous in his team-mate's shadow. It's easy to say with hindsight, but at best the choice was a gamble and at worst complete lunacy; quite simply, the chemistry didn't work. Even the most casual observer could see the two weren't talking and barely a word was spoken throughout the entire round (they were comprehensively beaten by Azinger/O'Meara, 7 and 6). Later the British press lambasted Faldo for failing to give Gilford support, although he responded by saying that he should never have been paired with the rookie in the first place. Gallacher has since admitted he made the wrong call.

With Faldo forced to retreat inside his shell to hold his own game together and to keep all thoughts of any outside problems away, he was never going to have the time or patience to babysit a team-mate through such a difficult match. Of course, it was tough on Gilford, who had been playing well in practice. Through a quirk of fate, he never got to pick up his clubs again for his singles opponent Pate was ruled out through injury on the Sunday, forcing him to watch the rest of the Ryder Cup from the sidelines.

Fair or not, the USA were in the mood to take full advantage, especially as Wadkins/Irwin had already beaten Torrance/Feherty 4 and 2 in the opening match of the day. They made it three wins in a row as a slick performance from Stewart/Calcavecchia proved too much for Richardson/James. Europe must have been relieved to see Ballesteros/Olazábal pick up their customary point – 3 and 2 against Couples/Floyd – to keep them in the competition.

Already the home crowd were in good voice, pumped up by a patriotic press as well as the skills of their heroes. The *Charleston News*, for instance, reminded everyone just what was at stake during the Ryder Cup in reporting: "The teams are playing for their countries, their families, their team-mates, Uncle Sam, The Queen, Mom and Dad, the Fatherland and the legends of the leprechaun, all rolled into three days of golf."

With the locals starting to taste blood, Europe realized something must be done to turn the tide and in a bid to quieten them, Gallacher made another gamble in the afternoon Fourballs. After trying out new partnerships in the shape of Langer/Montgomerie and Woosnam/Broadhurst, he was rewarded with improbable victory. Despite playing in his first Ryder Cup (and chosen on the basis of an impressive week during practice sessions), Broadhurst in particular proved sensational, chipping and putting superbly alongside his more experienced team-mate as they beat the more established pairing of Azinger/Irwin, 2 and 1.

Langer/Montgomerie, too, earned a point against Pavin/Pate (the first of many for a young Monty), and when James/Richardson followed suit, winning 3 and 1 against Wadkins/Levi, the scores were level, with Ballesteros/Olazábal still on course. Surely Europe would be unable to go into the singles ahead?

The answer to that question became a simple "no", thanks to some outstanding golf from Payne Stewart and Fred Couples. The Americans were ahead for much of the match and it needed

RIGHT: *Europe's José María Olazábal lines up a putt with Seve Ballesteros during Saturday's play – with the eyes of the world watching.*

BELOW: *Corey Pavin and Steve Pate of the USA in action during Saturday's afternoon Fourballs against Bernhard Langer and Colin Montgomerie.*

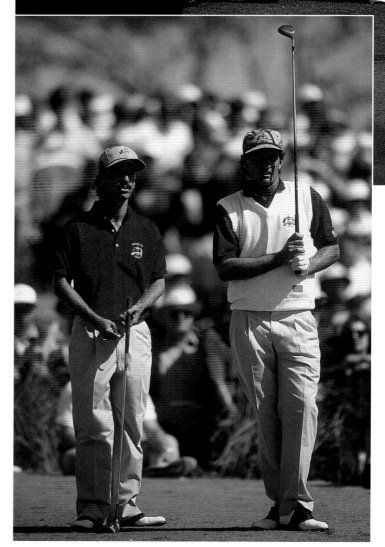

> **DAY TWO**
>
> **SATURDAY MORNING FOURSOMES**
>
> **Irwin/Wadkins** *beat* **Feherty/Torrance,** *4 and 2*
>
> **Calcavecchia/Stewart** *beat* **James/Richardson** *by one hole*
>
> **Azinger/O'Meara** *beat* **Faldo/Gilford,** *7 and 6*
>
> **Couples/Floyd** *lost to* **Ballesteros/Olazábal,** *3 and 2*
>
> **Session Score:** 3-1
>
> **SATURDAY AFTERNOON FOURBALLS**
>
> **Azinger/Irwin** *lost to* **Woosnam/Broadhurst,** *2 and 1*
>
> **Pavin/Pate** *lost to* **Langer/Montgomerie,** *2 and 1*
>
> **Wadkins/Levi** *lost to* **James/Richardson,** *3 and 1*
>
> **Stewart/Couples** *halved with* **Ballesteros/Olazábal**
>
> **Session Score:** 0.5-3.5
>
> **Overall Score:** USA 8, Europe 8

66 *We'd just finished the Gulf War. Patriotism was running high, and I wanted to take advantage of that... I wanted my team to bond.* 99

US captain Dave Stockton tells Golf Digest the secrets of 1991

a nervy six-foot putt from Olazábal on the 18th to deny them a full point. Even so, with four battles already waged, no one knew who would win the war because the final day was to start with both teams locked at eight points all and everything still to play for. The fact that the USA had home advantage and they had only lost the singles four times in the competition's history made them clear favourites, but now the staunchest of their supporters had accepted there was a lot of hard work ahead to make it happen.

As a footnote, the Ryder Cup came at just the right time for South Carolina and was said to completely revitalize the region's economy. Only two years earlier, Hurricane Hugo had devastated the area. Having the celebrated competition in town brought in much-needed revenue and, at the same time, established Kiawah Island as a real golfing retreat. Locally, such was the popularity of the Ryder Cup that 19-and-a-half hours was dedicated daily on the NBA and USA networks.

When the final push of the "War on the Shore" arrived it came as no surprise to anyone, given the events of the previous two days, and controversy arrived with it. US captain Dave Stockton announced one of his key players – Steve Pate – would be unable to take part in the singles but had conveniently forgotten to warn his opposite number. There was always a possibility of Pate being ruled out after he was involved in a car crash shortly before the Ryder Cup matches began, hurting his ribs, but he had played the previous day in the afternoon Foursomes and looked in decent shape. Europe smelled a rat.

The Ryder Cup system is for captains to file a sealed brown envelope containing the name of a player prepared to stand down, should a member of the opposing side become ill or injured. Chosen man David Gilford was already heading for the course when Gallacher saw the draw and quickly realized he would have to reduce his team to 11 players.

Already the psychological war had begun, but what no one expected was for the final day to be so close, for so long. It was eventually sealed by just one missed putt on the 18th green. Gallacher's tactics proved correct as he gave the previously grumpy and distracted Faldo an opportunity to lead his team out and the Englishman responded by beating Raymond Floyd by two holes, but the lead was destined to change hands many times.

Feherty, who had started out so nervously, found his form to beat Stewart before Montgomerie came from four holes down against Calcavecchia, with only four to play, to earn himself an unfeasible half. It wasn't until the Americans won the next two matches – Azinger beating Olazábal by two holes and Pavin eclipsing Richardson, 2 and 1 – that the crowd began to play their part. Whipped up by Azinger and Pavin, the atmosphere was more akin to a football match than a game of golf, with chants of "USA, USA!" ringing round the course.

The score soon moved to 12-12 with four matches to go after Beck beat Woosnam and Ballesteros overcame Levi. A tense finish was assured. Europe's impressive rookie Paul Broadhurst delighted his captain with a 3 and 1 triumph over O'Meara, but two 3 and 2 victories for Couples and Wadkins (over Torrance and James respectively) left the USA 14-13 ahead, with only one last match on course.

All eyes were now on Hale Irwin and Bernhard Langer. Their match had progressed in the shadow of seemingly bigger battles but suddenly everything depended on the result. It was tight, too. Irwin had been two-up at 14, but Langer pulled one back at 15 and

> ## 66 *Telling David he wasn't playing was one of the toughest things I have ever had to do in my career.* 99
>
> *European captain Bernard Gallacher on leaving David Gilford out*

then saw his rival three-putt at 17 – the Ryder Cup would go to the very last match on the final day.

Langer's drive at the 18th was good, but Irwin's veered into the crowd and was expected to be found in the rough; somehow it bounced back to the fringes of the fairway – almost certainly it had been thrown there. Even so, Langer's approach shot made the green and Irwin's didn't. Advantage Europe, or so it seemed – especially when Irwin's next shot (a chip to the green) left him 25 feet short. Gallacher must have thought so as he crouched green-side, dreaming of lifting the famous trophy just as his predecessor Tony Jacklin had done. Still, there was drama to come. Langer's putt from the back of the green was good but sailed just a little further past the hole than anticipated, leaving him an awkward six-footer to finish. Irwin, meanwhile, sent a long putt to within two feet – a shot generously conceded by his opponent. It meant everything, the entire Ryder Cup, depended on Langer's next shot.

The tension as he bent over the ball with his familiar uncomfortable-looking gait was unbearable and when he finally struck, it slithered just wide. Langer collapsed, his face twisted in agony. Meanwhile, the Americans celebrated wildly and the chants of "USA, USA!" were back. One of the greatest Ryder Cups of all time – and one of the most controversial – had been decided on the very last shot of the day.

DAY THREE

FINAL DAY SINGLES

Raymond Floyd *lost to* **Nick Faldo** *by two holes*

Payne Stewart *lost to* **David Feherty,** *2 and 1*

Mark Calcavecchia *halved with* **Colin Montgomerie**

Paul Azinger *beat* **José María Olazábal** *by two holes*

Corey Pavin *beat* **Steven Richardson,** *2 and 1*

Wayne Levi *lost to* **Seve Ballesteros,** *3 and 2*

Chip Beck *beat* **Ian Woosnam,** *3 and 1*

Mark O'Meara *lost to* **Paul Broadhurst,** *3 and 1*

Fred Couples *beat* **Sam Torrance,** *3 and 2*

Lanny Wadkins *beat* **Mark James,** *3 and 2*

Hale Irwin *halved with* **Bernhard Langer**

Steve Pate *halved with* **David Gilford** *(Pate injured, match unplayed)*

Session Score: 6.5-5.5

Overall Score: USA 14.5, Europe 13.5

1993

Europe 13
USA 15

The Belfry, Sutton Coldfield

September 24-26

THE COURSE

Brabazon Course
Location: The Belfry,
Sutton Coldfield,
England
Par: 72
Yards: 7,118

The Brabazon Course had already hosted Ryder Cups in 1985 and as recently as 1989, when its famous 18th hole caused the Americans so many problems as the match was tied. It was opened in 1977 and features water on 13 holes.

Following the controversy of the "War on the Shore", not to mention the conflicts caused by the behaviour of the crowd at Kiawah Island, there was a genuine desire in the golfing world to rein in the Ryder Cup and get back to the principles its founding fathers held so dear. The legendary Tom Watson was the man to bring about a return to sanity - and the Cup with it.

FAIRNESS, GOOD SPORTSMANSHIP AND FRIENDSHIP were meant to be the by-words of a competition played for glory, not cash, and designed to bring people together, not split them apart. And if all this had been forgotten along the way, the organizers of the 30th Ryder Cup matches were determined to get it back. Passionate spectators were all well and good - and the modern trend for chanting and singing was shared by both sets of fans and a regular occurrence - but galleries abusing players, even affecting results by throwing golf balls back towards the fairway? These were issues to be addressed, both practically and philosophically.

The British and American PGAs spent many an hour discussing the situation and eventually agreed a series of proposals aimed at solving some of those issues. When Tom Watson was appointed US captain for 1993, he seemed the perfect man to bring about peace

in our time. One of golf's greatest legends, Watson was almost as popular in Europe as he was back home and had a reputation for respecting the great traditions and history of the game. Indeed, he vowed to stand back from all the mind games, hyperbole and overblown rhetoric that seemed to have set the tone for a controversial Ryder Cup.

Characteristically, Watson immersed himself in the history and tactics of the event, determined to leave no stone unturned in his preparation. He wanted a team of players who could cope with the pressure of winning away from home and selected Ray Floyd and Lanny Wadkins as his captain's picks.

Over in Europe, Bernard Gallacher - who had offered to quit his role after losing in Kiawah Island in 1991 - had been persuaded to stay on as captain and in a tactical blow chose the first Swede in

LEFT: *US captain Tom Watson looks concerned as he keeps up with the action at the 1993 Ryder Cup at The Belfry.*

OPPOSITE: *Joakim Haeggman celebrates an historic moment - he was the first Swede ever to play in the Ryder Cup, and marked it with a singles victory.*

Ryder Cup history for his team: Joakim Haeggman. Other rookies included Peter Baker, Barry Lane and Italian Costantino Rocca.

The teams were in, the date set and everything looked ready for a smooth ride – until the President called. At short notice, the US team were invited to the White House to meet President Bill Clinton, who wanted to wish them well before they flew to England, but many of the players were not impressed. Some perhaps held different political beliefs, while others were angered by Clinton's plans to raise taxes on high earners, which naturally included the golfing fraternity. Their hesitant response was seen as unpatriotic by a shocked US nation and led to a flurry of highly embarrassing headlines. Fortunately, common sense prevailed and Watson did eventually lead his team to the White House, finally allowing the sport of golf to take over the headlines.

It proved to be a tight and tense match, too, and despite the US captain's preparations at the end of the opening day – which was delayed by two hours due to fog – it was Europe holding a slight advantage. Gallacher began battle with his most experienced men but the morning session ended all square in a tense start that featured a shock defeat for the previously unbeatable Ballesteros and Olazábal as they faced Tom Kite and Davis Love, losing by two holes. The turning point came at the 10th when Seve opted to play safe with an iron at the relatively short par-four and the more adventurous Kite made him pay for this by sending a powerful three-wood right to the centre of the green. Torrance/James also lost, 4 and 3, to Wadkins/Pavin, but the excellent new partnership of Faldo/Montgomerie eased to a virtually faultless 4 and 3 victory over Ray Floyd and Fred Couples, while Woosnam/Langer beat Azinger and Payne Stewart by a whopping 7 and 5.

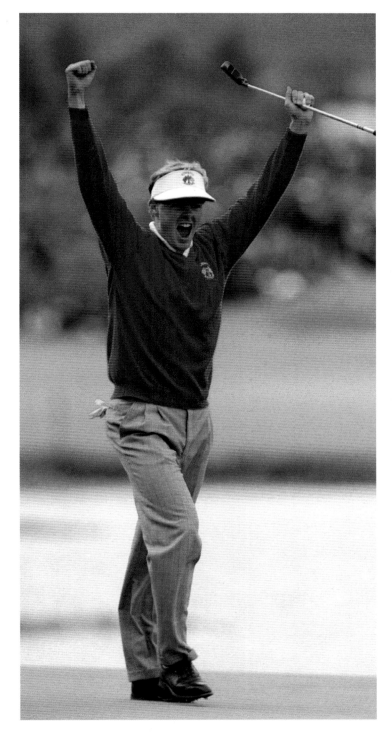

DAY ONE

CAPTAINS

Europe: Bernard Gallacher   **USA:** Tom Watson

FRIDAY MORNING FOURSOMES

Torrance/James *lost to* **Wadkins/Pavin**, *4 and 3*

Woosnam/Langer *beat* **Azinger/Stewart**, *7 and 5*

Ballesteros/Olazábal *lost to* **Kite/Love**, *2 and 1*

Faldo/Montgomerie *beat* **Floyd/Couples**, *4 and 3*

Session Score: 2-2

FRIDAY AFTERNOON FOURBALLS

Woosnam/Baker *beat* **Gallagher/Janzen** *by one hole*

Langer/Lane *lost to* **Wadkins/Pavin**, *4 and 2*

Faldo/Montgomerie *halved with* **Azinger/Couples**

Ballesteros/Olazábal *beat* **Love/Kite**, *4 and 3*

Session Score: 2.5-1.5

Overall Score: Europe 4.5, USA 3.5

> **❝** *This isn't war, this is golf… when it's over, we should be able to go off together, lift a glass and toast one another.* **❞**

Tom Watson before the 1993 Ryder Cup

With the opening day underway, the Ryder Cup organizers could relax in the knowledge that the atmosphere on course was vibrant but friendly, so perhaps their efforts to tone down the excesses of the tournament had been successful. But there had been something of a blip on the eve of the competition when Watson, who handed his players almost minute-by-minute practice schedules and a strict list of rules, inadvertently caused a rumpus.

One of Watson's rules was a week's ban on signing autographs – he wanted his players fully focused – and this included the Wednesday night gala staged at the Metropole Hotel. The formal dinner and speeches night had become something of a Ryder Cup tradition, with players mixing with guests and spending the last part of the evening offering autographs. There was also an unwritten tradition that both teams signed each other's menus as a keepsake. Unfortunately, Watson decided that having turned down autographs all night, he would not be able to assist when the European menu arrived from Sam Torrance for his team to sign.

Torrance was furious and the British tabloids had a field day. With typical relish and jingoistic delight, the *Sun* splashed the story on its front page under the headline "Fork Off". Suddenly,

the bad feeling that Watson had tried so hard to deter had returned and he was subsequently forced to issue a hasty apology. Thankfully the stand-off ended with humour when Gallacher was asked if the European team's evening had been ruined. "Well," he replied mischievously, "Seve did struggle a bit with his fromage."

The problems of the previous night appeared to have been forgotten by lunchtime on the opening day, with the scores level at 2-2. When the afternoon session began Seve Ballesteros and José María Olazábal made amends for their morning slip by firing a string of birdies in a comfortable victory over Tom Kite and Davis Love, which ended on the 15th. Perhaps the highlight for Europe was the performance of local boy Peter Baker on his debut, who partnered Woosnam to a one-hole victory over US rookies Gallagher Jnr./Janzen, holing a spectacular 25-foot putt on the 18th green to seal the point. With light deteriorating towards the end of the evening, Europe were 4-3 ahead, with only Faldo/Montgomerie on course against Azinger/Couples. Faldo's birdie putt at the 17th brought the game level and although the crowd were desperate to see the match finished, it was obvious the light would prevent this from happening.

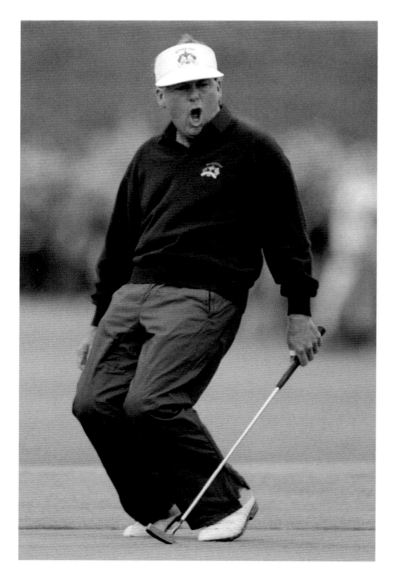

> **❝** *It's gonna be a long night, waiting to play one hole.* **❞**

Paul Azinger after play was called off for the day

DAY TWO

SATURDAY MORNING FOURSOMES

Faldo/Montgomerie *beat* **Wadkins/Pavin,** *3 and 2*

Langer/Woosnam *beat* **Couples/Azinger,** *2 and 1*

Baker/Lane *lost to* **Floyd/Stewart,** *3 and 2*

Ballesteros/Olazábal *beat* **Love/Kite,** *2 and 1*

Session Score: 3-1

SATURDAY AFTERNOON FOURBALLS

Faldo/Montgomerie *lost to* **Cook/Beck** *by two holes*

James/Rocca *lost to* **Pavin/Gallagher,** *5 and 4*

Woosnam/Baker *beat* **Couples/Azinger,** *6 and 5*

Olazábal/Haeggman *lost to* **Floyd/Stewart,** *2 and 1*

Session Score: 1-3

Overall Score: Europe 8.5, USA 7.5

LEFT: *Lanny Wadkins of the USA reacts to his putt during the 30th Ryder Cup Match at The Belfry.*

ABOVE: *Deadly rivals Paul Azinger of the USA (left) and Nick Faldo of Europe do battle in the singles at the 1993 Ryder Cup.*

When play resumed the next day, with crowds already in place at 8 a.m., it came to a shoot-out on the green between Azinger and Faldo – and it was the Englishman who held his nerve to save a half. With his team-mates gathered round the green after completing their practice sessions, Azinger missed from 20 yards and Faldo calmly converted from eight.

"What's for breakfast?" shouted Faldo toward the cheering galleries as he headed for the clubroom, before pretending to faint. But who needs a fry-up breakfast when golf provides all the right sustenance?

With the score 4.5-3.5 and spurred on by Faldo's bravado, Europe won three of the next four matches to move into a healthy lead. Faldo himself set the ball rolling with a 3 and 2 Foursomes victory alongside Montgomerie against Wadkins/Pavin, while

the highlight for the USA was a strong performance from Floyd/Stewart as they beat Baker/Lane, 3 and 2. It needed a brave decision from Watson to turn things around and this came completely out of the blue on the Saturday afternoon. Realizing he must shake things up, he brought in Chip Beck and John Cook, two players who had looked out of touch in previous weeks, and lined them up against Faldo/Montgomerie. His decision might have seemed madness, but it worked.

Cook and Beck matched their opponents every step of the way, with Beck's short game often the key as he chipped and putted from off the green to save par on three holes in a row. By the 18th (where Faldo had begun, more than 10 hours earlier, a hero), he now seemed mentally drained and held out a hand to concede after missing an eight-foot putt to halve the game. Earlier,

Woosnam and Baker had won, 6 and 5, against Couples/Azinger, but it was Team USA's afternoon. Going into the singles, Pavin/Gallagher Jnr. and Floyd/Stewart also posted victories to leave their side just one point behind.

The Americans may have reached the final day trailing by one point but considering their record in Ryder Cup singles, there was reason for optimism. And it proved justified as they stormed to six wins and two halves, inspired by veteran Chip Beck battling back from three holes down to beat Barry Lane.

For Europe, the bad news began on the Saturday night when Sam Torrance reported a toe injury would almost certainly keep him out of action the following day. Just as Gallacher had experienced two years earlier, it meant that Watson was forced to choose a player in his own team to sit out but Lanny Wadkins made it easy for him in generously volunteering to step down. The situation was almost repeated later that night when Europe's Peter Baker rushed to the hospital bed of his 11-month-old daughter following a meningitis scare, only returning the next morning after the doctors had given her the all-clear and confirmed it was nothing more than a bad ear infection.

Had Baker pulled out, the Americans would have been within their rights to claim the match – although in reality, Ray Floyd had offered to stand down, if need be. Thankfully, Baker was able to return and produced an astonishing round under the circumstances, beating Pavin by two holes. Indeed, the day was full of ups and downs, highlighted in the opening match when Woosnam allowed a two-hole lead to slip with six to play and halved against Couples. The indomitable Beck produced an even better result, coming from three behind to win at the last against Lane. Three European wins in a row – for Montgomerie, Baker and Haeggman – then tested the USA to the full, with the words of Watson still ringing in their ears: "If it gets too tough out there for you, remember what Lanny did for you!"

Stewart beat James, while Ballasteros was defeated, somewhat surprisingly, by Jim Gallagher Jnr. to move the score to 12.5-12.5, with three matches on course. With Ray Floyd ahead against Olazábal and Faldo up on Azinger, all eyes were instead on Italian Costantino Rocca – up by just one, with two to play against Davis Love.

A virtual unknown in America, Rocca had played well and looked set for a half at the 17th before buckling under a pressure putt just

SHOT OF THE DAY

Nick Faldo produced one of the most memorable shots of the 1993 Ryder Cup when he aced the 14th during a singles match against Paul Azinger. Already he and Colin Montgomerie had birdied the same hole four times and Faldo wanted to go one better. "I remember walking down the fairway with him on the 14th after he had hit the green again and him saying to me, 'You know, wouldn't it be great to find the hole next time?'" said Monty. "Sure enough, next day, he does it!"

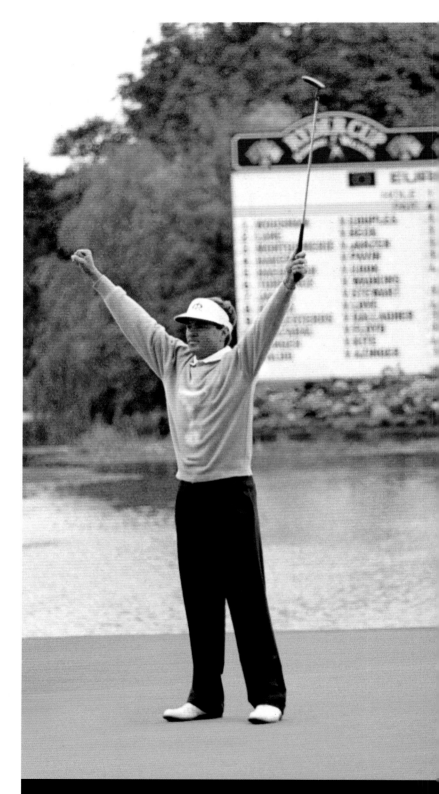

ABOVE: *US hero Davis Love celebrates on the 18th green after defeating European Costantino Rocca at The Belfry.*

RIGHT: *A delighted US captain Tom Watson holds the Ryder Cup trophy aloft following a hard-fought victory that saw his team win by two points.*

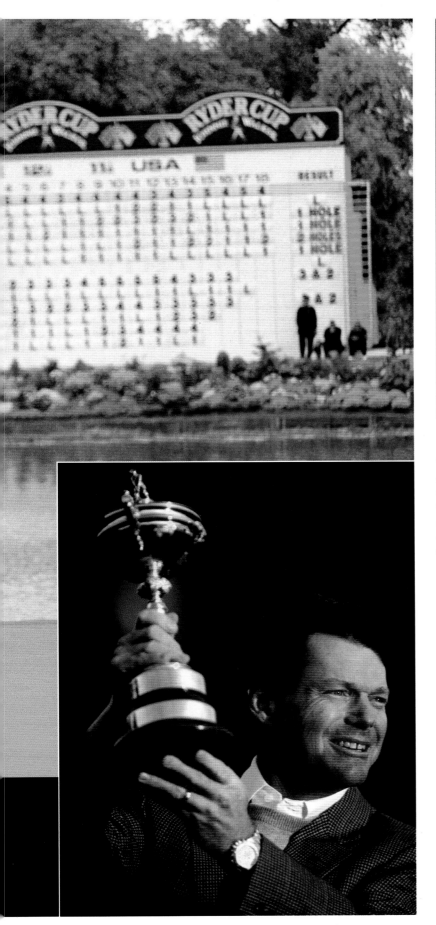

DAY THREE

FINAL DAY SINGLES

Ian Woosnam *halved with* **Fred Couples**

Barry Lane *lost to* **Chip Beck** *by one hole*

Colin Montgomerie *beat* **Lee Janzen** *by one hole*

Paul Baker *beat* **Corey Pavin** *by two holes*

Joakim Haeggman *beat* **John Cook** *by one hole*

Mark James *lost to* **Payne Stewart,** *3 and 2*

Costantino Rocca *lost to* **Davis Love** *by one hole*

Seve Ballesteros *lost to* **Jim Gallagher,** *3 and 2*

José María Olazábal *lost to* **Ray Floyd** *by two holes*

Bernhard Langer *lost to* **Tom Kite,** *5 and 3*

Nick Faldo *halved with* **Paul Azinger**

Sam Torrance *halved with* **Lanny Wadkins** *(Torrance injured, match unplayed)*

Session Score: 4.5-7.5

Overall Score: Europe 13, USA 15

when it mattered. Love knew he had the psychological advantage and his next shot – a huge wood that ripped down the fairway of the 18th – rammed it home. You could almost sense Rocca's fear. Just as he was about to swing his own driver, a huge cheer disturbed his concentration and he was forced to stop mid-swing – Faldo had just aced the 14th and so the pressure doubled. By the time they reached the green, Rocca faced a dangerous downhill putt while Love – determined to leave his shot below the hole – got to within six feet. Inevitably, Rocca missed and the American finished off the job to silence the home crowd.

Team USA players engulfed their hero and when Floyd went three up with three to play against Olazábal, everyone at The Belfry knew the Cup was heading back across the Atlantic. Olazábal did pull two back, but at the 18th hooked his shot into the water and Floyd had no problem in putting-out to clinch victory.

With the trophy long gone, Azinger converted a putt on the same green to earn a battling half against Faldo and wrap up a thrilling 15-13 victory for his team. As he did so, out of sight, Davis Love chased after a disconsolate Rocca. Finding his opponent in tears, he gave him a consolatory embrace. The spirit of the Ryder Cup was back again.

> **66** *This is the best feeling I've ever had in golf!* **99**

Tom Watson on captaining his side to victory

Ryder Cup legends

Severiano **BALLESTEROS** and José María **OLAZÁBAL**

The outpouring of emotion across the globe when Severiano Ballesteros passed away on May 7, 2011 after a long battle against a cancerous brain tumour shows he was not only one of the world's greatest golfers, a colossus with a club, but also one of the sport's most popular and enduring characters. And who can forget so many of his greatest moments came in the Ryder Cup with his great friend, José María Olazábal?

The enigmatic Ballesteros and his close friend Olazábal are by far the most successful partnership in Ryder Cup history, with 11 wins and two halves from their 15 matches together – double the tally of any other. Individually, they were hugely successful, too. Ballesteros won 22.5 points – two more than compatriot Olazábal – and both would captain Europe once their playing days were over. Ballesteros was a fitting captain in 1997 when the Ryder Cup was first hosted in Spain, with Europe winning 14.5-13.5 at Valderrama. In September 2012, Olazábal will follow in his footsteps in leading Europe at the Medinah Country Club.

Ultimately, the statistics only take us so far – the panache, style and attitude that "The Spanish Armada" brought to the Ryder Cup of 1979 were much more than their guarantee of points.

Ballesteros was there in the first year that the British and Irish team included players from Europe, yet he didn't make his mark in 1979, winning only one of five matches as Europe were well and truly beaten. Two years later, he was left out of the team after playing much of his golf in America and declared he would never play in the Ryder Cup again. However, captain Tony Jacklin persuaded him to return in 1983 and following this appearance, he didn't miss a session in the next five tournaments. In 1985, Seve was an integral part of the first side to beat the Americans since 1957 – a victory he celebrated with gusto.

In 1985 he joined forces with José María Olazábal in what became the best-ever Ryder Cup partnership. At Muirfield Village in Columbus, Ohio, the Spanish pair won their first three matches as Europe built up a commanding lead. Ballesteros then beat Curtis Strange and for the first time in history, Europe won on American soil. But the best was still to come. In 1989 and 1991, Ballesteros and Olazábal were truly unbeatable, winning seven points out of eight in the Foursomes and Fourballs.

The pair partnered for the final time in 1993, beating Davis Love and Tom Kite, 2 and 1. In 1997 they were reunited, this time with Ballesteros as captain. With severe rheumatoid polyarthritis in both feet, Olazábal helped Europe to retain the trophy after his friend's captaincy inspired the side. Olazábal declared this team to have the best spirit of any he had been part of.

Sadly, Olazábal will always be remembered for missing the putt that lost the Ryder Cup in 1999 – and for the prior controversy when the US team stormed the green. However, he made a triumphant return in 2006 with Sergio Garcia to win all three of his matches in Europe's record-equalling win at The K Club. All those matches were completed without his dear friend Ballesteros by his side – indeed, Seve's death hit his junior partner hard. The best way to pay tribute, he insists, is to captain Europe to Ryder Cup glory.

> **" The Ryder Cup would not be the match it is today, if not for Seve Ballesteros. "**
>
> *USA Today*

RYDER CUP RECORD

Severiano BALLESTEROS
Ryder Cups: 1979, 1983, 1985 (winner), 1987 (winner), 1989 (tied but Europe retain trophy), 1991, 1993, 1995 (winner), 1997 (winner, non-playing captain)
Total wins: 4 (plus 1 tie to retain trophy, 1989)
Matches: 37 (won 20, halved 5, lost 12)
Total points: 22.5

José María OLAZÁBAL
Ryder Cups: 1987 (winner), 1989 (tied but Europe retain trophy), 1991, 1993, 1997 (winner), 1999, 2006 (winner)
Total wins: 3 (plus 1 tie to retain trophy, 1989)
Matches: 29 (won 18, halved 3, lost 8)
Total points: 20.5

AS A PAIR:
Matches: 15 (won 11, halved 2, lost 2)
Total points: 12

1995

USA 13.5
Europe 14.5

Oak Hill Country Club, New York

September 22-24

Just when it seemed that Team USA were ready to rack up a hat-trick of Ryder Cup victories, they were hit from behind by an ageing European side in New York. In fact, the killer blow came from a player who was someone they had barely heard of, another highly talented Irishman called Philip Walton.

THE COURSE

East Course
Location: Oak Hill,
        Rochester,
        New York, USA

Par: 70
Yards: 7,198

The US PGA chose one of its hardest courses for the 1995 Ryder Cup and set it up for home advantage: the rough was long, the greens were dry and the course was prepared as if for a US Open. But Team USA were unable to take advantage.

NICK FALDO MIGHT HAVE DONE the groundwork and the USA - Curtis Strange, in particular - may have added to their own downfall in throwing victory away when it had seemed almost assured, but it was Walton (only qualifying when José María Olazábal dropped out through injury), who came out of nowhere to make the winning putt and steal back the trophy.

When the American media first saw Walton's name on the team sheet, their reaction had been cynical - who was the man with such a short CV, who had never before played in the USA? In the event, the US fans certainly remembered him as they trooped home

that Sunday evening. "Maybe the Americans know me now," cried Walton, draped in an Irish flag, as he celebrated long into the night. "Tell 'em I'm related to all those Waltons on that TV show!"

In fact, this proved to be a Ryder Cup that still hurts in the States right up to the present day: Oak Hill became Choke Hill and in turn, Heartbreak Hill. For those bedecked in the Stars & Stripes, it was an enormous disappointment after they had started out with such high hopes. Seven players in Bernard Gallacher's side were over the age of 37 and only one (Per-Ulrik Johansson) was under 30. The American media described them as being "over the hill" and

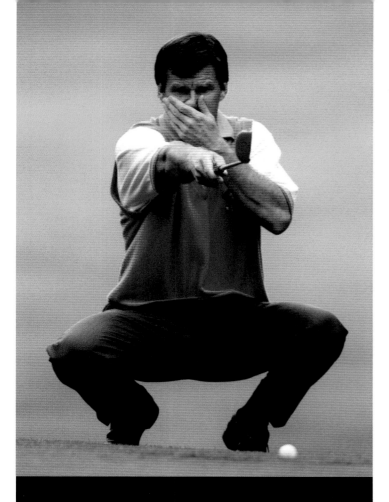

ABOVE: *Nick Faldo lines up a putt during a Foursomes match against Corey Pavin and Tom Lehman at the 1995 Ryder Cup.*

OPPOSITE: *US captain Lanny Wadkins (left) jokes with Curtis Strange on the 8th fairway during practice day at Oak Hill.*

DAY ONE

CAPTAINS

USA: Lanny Wadkins   **Europe:** Bernard Gallacher

FRIDAY MORNING FOURSOMES

Pavin/Lehman *beat* **Faldo/Montgomerie** *by one hole*

Haas/Couples *lost to* **Torrance/Rocca**, *3 and 2*

Love/Maggert *beat* **Clark/James**, *4 and 3*

Crenshaw/Strange *lost to* **Langer/Johansson** *by one hole*

Session Score: 2-2

FRIDAY AFTERNOON FOURBALLS

Faxon/Jacobsen *lost to* **Gilford/Ballesteros**, *4 and 3*

Maggert/Roberts *beat* **Torrance/Rocca**, *6 and 5*

Couples/Love *beat* **Faldo/Montgomerie**, *3 and 2*

Pavin/Mickelson *beat* **Langer/Johansson**, *6 and 4*

Session Score: 3-1

Overall Score: USA 5, Europe 3

> **"***It was a statement that Europe's best team could be beaten.***"**
>
> *Tom Lehman delights in victory over*
> *Faldo and Montgomerie*

predicted not only a comfortable victory for Team USA, but also potentially the end of the Ryder Cup as a seriously competitive tournament. Many of the Europeans were also not on form, with some complaining of injuries. Already Olazábal had pulled out with a toe problem and Nick Faldo was battling a wrist injury; Faldo's preparation was further affected by tabloid news stories that his marriage was under strain.

The story only broke as the European entourage, including Faldo's wife, Gill, boarded Concorde at London's Heathrow. Quite how Faldo, already based in America on the US tour, was able to perform so well is hard to contemplate. The pictures of him greeting his wife at the airport in New York with a formal handshake were painful to see, yet the English golfer was still able to display his usual nerves of steel in what would become one of his career highs. However, it was not until he completed a remarkable comeback from three-down against Curtis Strange in Sunday's singles to all but hand Europe the trophy that his emotions finally got the better of him.

That moment of elation could scarcely have been predicted two days earlier when Faldo first stepped onto the tee at Oak Hill alongside Colin Montgomerie. Two years earlier, the pair had been

impressive playing together at The Belfry but some of the magic appeared to have faded as they lost by one hole to Pavin and Tom Lehman. Faldo was tetchy, attacking Lehman after he tapped home a putt that the European had already conceded. "When I say it's good, it's good," he muttered. Lehman remained stoic, later claiming: "I wasn't going to put up with any crap, especially after he stretches out his arms as if to say 'put the ball in your pocket, you idiot' – I was hot!"

The morning Foursomes ended all square, however. Torrance/Costantino Rocca combined to beat Haas/Couples, 3 and 2, to get Europe on track, and when Love/Maggert cruised past Clark and James, 4 and 3, the scores were levelled by Langer/Johansson following a narrow but crucial win against Crenshaw/Strange at the last. Already Team USA's promise to dominate appeared ambitious but the afternoon Fourballs must have lifted their spirits, with Maggert/Roberts, Couples/Love, Pavin and new boy Phil Mickelson all recording convincing victories.

Surprisingly, Faldo and Monty lost again – 3 and 2 to Couples/Love – and in truth, Europe must have been thankful for a solitary win by Ballesteros/Gilford, 4 and 3 against Faxon/Jacobsen, to at least keep them in the hunt.

For Team USA, taking a two-point overnight lead into Saturday was regarded as nothing more than par for the course, but perhaps the media had overestimated the strength and depth of the American team. The average age of the European team might be high, but the US squad also included several players over the age of 40 (a fact that never seemed to get a mention in the media) and was vastly changed from the side that had done so well to win at The Belfry, two years earlier.

New captain Lanny Wadkins also had to manage five rookies – Brad Faxon, Phil Mickelson, Tom Lehman, Jeff Maggert and Loren Roberts – and received stinging criticism over his choice of captain's picks when he went for Strange/Couples, both personal friends but also players who had hardly been successful on tour that year. Indeed, none of the players in his 12-man squad had won a tournament since June, and the top US player on the PGA Tour money list – Lee Janzen – was not even selected owing to a qualification process that measured points, not dollars. Given the task ahead, were they under- or overachieving in New York?

Wadkins, whose selfless act of volunteering to step down from the singles in 1993 when Sam Torrance was injured had elevated him to Ryder Cup hero status in the eyes of his peers, knew he had a heavy task ahead, no matter what the score or what anyone else said. He was right to be cautious because Europe hit back at the start of the second day, winning three out of the four Foursomes, including a 6 and 5 demolition of Love/Maggert by Torrance/Rocca, with the Italian producing a hole-in-one at the 6th to add further adrenalin to European veins. There was also a welcome win for Faldo/Montgomerie against Strange/Haas and for Langer/Gilford – 4 and 3 against first-day heroes Pavin/Lehman. Team USA's only point came from Roberts/Jacobsen, who won at the last against Woosnam/Walton, and the score moved on to six-all.

Suddenly Europe was in the driving seat, although not for long because this would be a Ryder Cup with more twists and turns than any other in recent memory. In fact, the same afternoon the USA rebounded in winning three out of the four Fourballs to complete another turnaround. European captain Gallacher may have to take some responsibility for the result, completely surprising many experts in changing his line-up despite a successful morning and putting out four completely different pairings after lunch. Maybe he believed fresh legs and clear heads would keep concentration

SHOT OF THE DAY

Costantino Rocca became the toast of Europe when he aced the 6th hole on the Saturday morning, only the third hole-in-one in Ryder Cup history. The Italian took a five-iron to the tee, which proved to be the last club he needed to use. His spectacular shot helped clinch a 6 and 5 victory for himself and Sam Torrance against Davis Love III and Jeff Maggert, sparking a European revival. It must have been a real high for the player who had been criticized for his nervous finale at The Belfry, just two years earlier – "It's hard to lose the hole with a one," he beamed.

levels high but his gamble did not pay off and instead the USA took full advantage.

Faxon/Couples kicked off the home revival in beating Torrance/Montgomerie, 4 and 2. Although Love/Crenshaw lost to Woosnam/Rocca, an impressive victory for Haas/Mickelson against Ballesteros/Gilford, 3 and 2, soon followed. Mickelson in particular made a good impression on debut and would end his Ryder Cup unbeaten – a record he would not be able to repeat until 12 years on.

But the US team saved the best for last. Corey Pavin's astonishing chip-in from above the 18th green earned them an improbable point against Langer/Faldo, having gone into the last all square. The sound of the galleries chanting "Cor-ey! Cor-ey! Cor-ey!" followed the team all the way back to the clubroom and, with the USA 9-7 ahead, there was every reason for the home fans to be thrilled. After all, when had the USA last lost a Ryder Cup after being ahead going into the singles?

"We're still going to win," insisted a defiant Gallacher when he met journalists that evening, but few believed him – even if Wadkins politely refused to crow too loudly and instead urged caution. When asked if the Ryder Cup was already in the bag, he said: "I'm real confident – I have 12 guys playing well but this is golf and a two-point lead is not big enough."

DAY TWO

SATURDAY MORNING FOURSOMES

Strange/Haas *lost to* **Faldo/Montgomerie,** *4 and 2*

Love/Maggert *lost to* **Torrance/Rocca,** *6 and 5*

Roberts/Jacobsen *beat* **Woosnam/Walton** *by one hole*

Pavin/Lehman *lost to* **Langer/Gilford,** *4 and 3*

Session Score: 1-3

SATURDAY AFTERNOON FOURBALLS

Faxon/Couples *beat* **Torrance/Montgomerie,** *4 and 2*

Love/Crenshaw *lost to* **Woosnam/Rocca,** *3 and 2*

Haas/Mickelson *beat* **Ballesteros/Gilford,** *3 and 2*

Pavin/Roberts *beat* **Faldo/Langer** *by one hole*

Session Score: 3-1

Overall Score: USA 9, Europe 7

LEFT: *Oak Hill Country Club in all its glory as a spectacular opening ceremony takes place before the Ryder Cup of 1995 in front of packed galleries.*

RIGHT: *Corey Pavin reacts with delight after chipping in from the edge of the 18th green to win in the Saturday afternoon Fourballs.*

BELOW: *European talisman Nick Faldo plays out of the rough in a tense match with Curtis Strange, which he lost by one hole.*

OPPOSITE: *Philip Walton celebrates a famous win over Jay Haas by jumping into the arms of captain Bernard Gallacher.*

Every final day of a Ryder Cup produces heroes and villains and in 1995, it was almost pantomime time when Europe won the singles, 7.5-4.5 - and the trophy. Curtis Strange threw away victory from three-up against Nick Faldo and then froze when the USA needed only half a point to win. Brad Faxon and Jay Haas also had their chances to secure the win, but failed to do so.

Then there were the heroes - most of them European. Howard Clark had been overlooked all weekend but came out on singles day to provide a hole-in-one and an ensuing victory against Peter Jacobsen. Seve Ballesteros, the magical Spaniard, who despite being a long way past his best put up such a brave show against Tom Lehman that his team was totally inspired, even when he was forced to concede defeat. Then there was Faldo...

With so many distractions in his private life, the Englishman managed just two birdies all week. He hadn't been at his best. Against Strange, however, he played the hero. In truth, all he had to do was stay solid and play par golf while his nerve-shredded opponent staged an incredible collapse, having taken a one-shot lead at the 11th - but then, that's what Faldo does best.

Strange could - and should - have won the point his side needed but three bogeys in the last three holes had destroyed his chances. Instead the pair arrived at the 17th with the American still one-up and the overall match tied. Strange's unimpressive, prodded putt gifted Faldo a chance to draw level - a chance he took. With the tension mounting, it was a similar story at the 18th, although this time Strange had the advantage after a perfect tee-shot to the centre of the fairway, while Faldo found the rough and had already made a mess of a chip to the green. A terrible three-iron shot left Strange short of the green, also chipping out of the rough. Faldo played an exquisite wedge that looped up and landed within six feet of the hole. However, Strange followed suit, sending his ball to eight feet. Everything was down to the last putt.

Unable to watch, Faldo turned his back as Strange sent his effort narrowly past. Faldo strode forward, sent the ball to the middle of the hole and held his arms aloft in victory. "Everything was shaking," he later admitted. "Everything except the putter!" For Europe, there was still one more hero to come: Philip Walton. The man the Americans struggled to recognize was about to become an icon when, with the USA still needing one more half to earn a 14-14 draw and retain the trophy, he held out. Remarkably, Walton put himself three-up by the 16th and survived a nerve-racking finale as his opponent staged a late, fruitless rally. A putt from four feet at the 17th might have secured it, but even after missing to brays from the US crowd, he refused to buckle.

At the 18th Haas made a mess of his drive, sending it into the trees. By the time the pair reached the green both needed bogeys, but a Ryder Cup depended on it. Haas sent his chip six feet past the hole. Thankfully for Walton, his second putt - although eight feet out - was uphill. Finally, his moment of glory arrived.

> **❝** *I can't tell you what this means to me... it's just... I can't!* **❞**

Bernard Gallacher on Europe's comeback

SHOT OF THE DAY

As if to prove all good things come in pairs, Europe's Howard Clark scored a Ryder Cup hole-in-one, just 24 hours after his team-mate Costantino Rocca did the same. Considering only three men had ever aced a Ryder Cup hole before, this was quite an achievement. Clark's moment of glory came with a six-iron at the par-three 11th during a match against Peter Jacobsen.

DAY THREE

FINAL DAY SINGLES

Tom Lehman *beat* **Seve Ballesteros,** *4 and 3*

Paul Jacobsen *lost to* **Howard Clark** *by one hole*

Jeff Maggert *lost to* **Mark James,** *4 and 3*

Fred Couples *halved with* **Ian Woosnam**

Davis Love *beat* **Costantino Rocca,** *3 and 2*

Brad Faxon *lost to* **David Gilford** *by one hole*

Ben Crenshaw *lost to* **Colin Montgomerie,** *3 and 1*

Curtis Strange *lost to* **Nick Faldo** *by one hole*

Loren Roberts *lost to* **Sam Torrance,** *2 and 1*

Corey Pavin *beat* **Bernhard Langer,** *3 and 2*

Jay Haas *lost to* **Philip Walton** *by one hole*

Phil Mickelson *beat* **Per-Ulrik Johansson,** *2 and 1*

Session Score: 4.5-7.5

Overall Score: USA 13.5, Europe 14.5

Ryder Cup legends
Tom KITE

When it came to the Ryder Cup, Tom Kite was the USA's "Mr Reliable" - starring in four American victories and one tied match in his seven appearances. Indeed, his stability and concentration was appreciated by every captain he played for, a fact recognized when he himself was named captain in 1997.

Tom Kite was constantly competing at the cutting edge and while he wasn't always a champion, he was always in the mix - highlighted by the fact that he spent 175 weeks in the Top 10 of the Official World Golf Rankings between 1989 and 1994. Perhaps best known for his unrivalled work ethic, the man from Texas (he was tutored by the same teacher as Ben Crenshaw) was hailed for pushing the boundaries in a glittering and lengthy career. Kite - who with the exception of 1988, won at least one tournament a year from 1981-93 - was the first player to carry a third wedge (as well as pitching and sand wedges), now a more common practice among pros. He also emphasized the role of physical fitness at a time when its contribution to success was debated. No wonder he has since brought out instructional golf books and videos.

Kite was one of the first players to hire a sports psychologist and maybe this is what helped him develop his highly focused, yet relaxed style - especially when it came to his short game. He was a top-class putter, too. His attitude to sport was certainly refreshing and he once said: "Golf has never been work for me - you don't work golf, you play it." Indeed, it's a mantra that for him certainly paid dividends. As a result, Kite - wearing his infamous thick-rimmed glasses - was always at the vanguard of advances in the game. Perhaps in keeping with his forward-thinking attitude, he eventually discarded his spectacles after undergoing then-revolutionary laser eye surgery in 1998.

A year before, he took part in his final Ryder Cup as captain, having resisted the urge to pick himself in a playing capacity at Valderrama. Still, he retained his penchant for innovation even as skipper, showing his players a video titled *Simply the Best* - a compilation of 207 great golfing shots he thought would inspire them. But even this could not prevent Seve Ballesteros' side from inflicting a rare Ryder Cup defeat on Team USA with a narrow 14.5-13.5 victory. The Europeans remembered only too well that as a player, Kite had been involved in four wins, one tie and only two defeats in Ryder Cup competitions. Indeed, his all-round quality in the Ryder Cup is highlighted by two records held by him to this day: back in 1989, he beat Howard Clark, 8 and 7, at The Belfry - a record over 18 holes. Two years earlier, in partnership with Hale Irwin, he beat Ken Brown and Des Smyth, 7 and 6, in the Foursomes - a feat that has also never been bettered.

During his years as a player, the 1992 US Open winner gave much to the Ryder Cup, but always reserved special praise for time spent as part of the excellent US crop. "A lot of the friendships that I have out on the PGA Tour were really fostered and became more significant because of the Ryder Cup matches that I played," said Kite, who was inducted into the World Golf Hall of Fame in 2004, "both friendships with the competition from playing the European players and with my team members. I have a lot of great relationships there that were really improved by the Ryder Cup experience - I loved the competition."

Kite's Ryder Cup points record is also impressive and includes six singles victories in seven matches and a total of 15 points from 28 matches, placing him in the Top 10 of US players of all time.

In recent years, Kite has turned his energies to course design - in collaboration with Bob Cupp, Randy Russell and Roy Bechtol. Completed golf courses include Liberty National (Jersey City, New Jersey), Comanche Trace (Kerrville, Texas), Somersett Country Club (Reno, Nevada), Gaillardia Golf & Country Club (Oklahoma City, Oklahoma) and the Legends on LBJ (Kingsland, Texas). If a Ryder Cup is one day staged at a Kite-designed course, it would seem only fitting - after all, he has given so much to the tournament, both as a player and captain.

> **"** *There's no way of getting used to it. For every eight Major championships, you get one Ryder Cup.* **"**
>
> Tom Kite on the unique nature of the Ryder Cup

RYDER CUP RECORD

Ryder Cups: 1979 (winner), 1981 (winner), 1983 (winner), 1985, 1987, 1989 (tied but Europe retain trophy), 1993 (winner), 1997 (non-playing captain)

Total wins: 4 (plus 1 tie to retain the trophy, 1989)

Matches: 28 (won 15, halved 4, lost 9)

Total points: 17

1997

Europe 14.5
USA 13.5

Valderrama Golf Club, Sotogrande

September 26-28

THE COURSE

Valderrama
Location: Sotogrande,
Spain
Par: 72
Yards: 6,818

Owned by Jaime Ortiz-Patiño and designed by Robert Trent Jones, Valderrama beat off strong competition to become the first course outside Great Britain and America to stage a Ryder Cup. Its narrow fairways and small greens, as well as some 2,000 Cork Oak trees, make this a real test.

The 1997 Ryder Cup was an historic occasion, the first ever to be staged outside of the USA and the British Isles - and there was a sense that the script had been written long in advance. It was Spain's Ryder Cup, also Severiano Ballesteros' Ryder Cup, and he was about to make sure that it belonged to Europe. The moment golf's greatest tournament was pencilled in for Valderrama, there was only one possible candidate to captain Team Europe and Seve got the vote long in advance.

AT 40, HE WAS POSSIBLY TOO OLD and too out of form to qualify as a player, but he put so much enthusiasm and energy into winning the trophy as captain that it was almost as if the Spaniard was out there on the greens, putting Europe to victory. Indeed, many of his players felt if anything, he was perhaps a little too hands-on, while traditionalists believed he stretched etiquette to the limit. The prevailing memory of Valderrama was Seve buzzing around the course in his buggy - always there, closely observing every shot - and inevitably giving his opinion on how it should be played, too. "I knew the Americans were always aware of my presence and I think it made them uncomfortable," he insisted. "It always seemed to me, we won the hole when I was there."

Who knows if this is what that other golfing legend, Jack Nicklaus, had in mind when he suggested that inviting Europe rather than just Great Britain and Ireland to play in the Ryder Cup would make it more competitive, but it certainly underlined the huge strides that the USA's opponents had made since his suggestion was taken up in 1979. Besides, it was only right that Spain should be the first country in continental Europe to get the nod. After all, Seve Ballesteros had made such a huge contribution to Ryder Cup history, as had his compatriots.

Antonio Garrido joined him in 1979 and then there had been Manuel Piñero, José Maria Cañizares, José Rivero and, most significantly of all, Seve's great playing partner, José María Olazábal - who would be European captain in 2012. It was ironic, then, that it was two Spaniards who gave Ballesteros most cause for thought in the build-up to his home Ryder Cup. Miguel Martín narrowly qualified but Olazábal, having recovered from injury, was next on the list and Seve was keen to have him on board. The only problem was that he was permitted just two captain's picks - and Nick Faldo and Sweden's Jesper Parnevik had both not qualified. This could have led to a very tough decision but as fate would have it, Martín injured his wrist shortly before the tournament and it was Olazábal who took his place when the golf began, allowing both Faldo and Parnevik to compete. In fact, it was a major relief for Europe because Faldo proved enormously influential, though not so

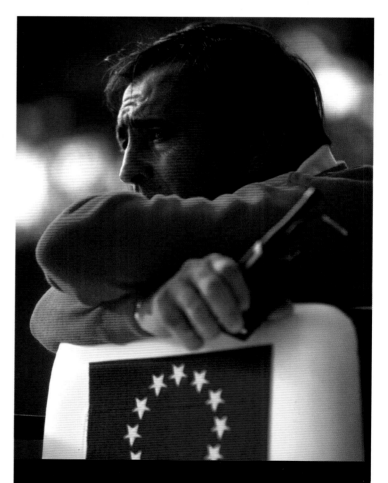

ABOVE: *European captain Seve Ballesteros looks on anxiously during the opening day of the 1997 Ryder Cup.*

OPPOSITE: *Former US President George Bush with José María Olazábal following Europe's famous victory.*

" *Here we were in Spain… losing just wasn't an option – it was Seve and the King of Spain, you felt you were part of an irresistible force.* **"**

Colin Montgomerie on the 1997 Ryder Cup

DAY ONE

CAPTAINS

Europe: Seve Ballesteros   **USA:** Tom Kite

FRIDAY MORNING FOURBALLS

Olazábal/Rocca *beat* **Love/Mickelson** *by one hole*

Faldo/Westwood *lost to* **Couples/Faxon** *by one hole*

Parnevik/Johansson *beat* **Lehman/Furyk** *by one hole*

Montgomerie/Langer *lost to* **Woods/O'Meara**, *3 and 2*

Session Score: 2-2

Overall Score: Europe 2, USA 2

much as the captain himself. Seve even arranged for the Fourballs to be played first in the morning and the Foursomes second for the first time ever because he felt it best suited his team.

Many of the fans, and even some of the players, had not been aware that such a decision was in the home captain's gift. Seve had four rookies in his side, and also knew that the USA would be bringing a strong team, far stronger than the one that had lost at Oak Hill, two years earlier. Open champion Justin Leonard bolstered the side, as did Mark O'Meara, Lee Janzen (who many believed should have also played in 1995) and Jim Furyk. And then there was a certain Tiger Woods making his debut. Spain welcomed them all with open arms – as well as Spanish horses, flamenco dancers and the King of Spain – at a glitzy opening ceremony. The

scene was set for an historic Ryder Cup, or so it would have been, had it not rained for 12 straight hours overnight. In the event, play was delayed until 11.30 a.m., but it was only possible to start so early, thanks to the superb drainage system on the course. When play finally began, Seve sent out Spaniard José María Olazábal and Italian Costantino Rocca first and they responded with a morale-boosting one-hole victory over Davis Love and Phil Mickelson.

Jesper Parnevik and Per-Ulrik Johansson also beat Furyk and Tom Lehman, but Europe's more traditional performers were less successful. Nick Faldo and Lee Westwood lost to Fred Couples and Brad Faxon, while Colin Montgomerie and Bernhard Langer went down to Woods and O'Meara, 3 and 2. Spain's debut Ryder Cup was destined to be a close call.

With play unable to be completed on the opening Friday, the two teams were still playing Foursomes on the Saturday morning and this proved an encouraging session for Europe, their big guns now starting to fire. Langer and Montgomerie responded to early disappointment in crushing O'Meara and Woods, 5 and 3, while Faldo and Westwood also found form as they beat Leonard and Maggert, 3 and 2. Parnevik (whose selection ahead of Padraig Harrington had been controversial) remained unbeaten in partnering Ignacio Garrido to a half against the strong combination of Lehman and Mickelson. Indeed, the only reverse for Europe came in the opening match when Olazábal and Costantino Rocca went down by one hole to Hoch and Janzen.

Seve's men had edged out in front and over the next two sessions, they would build a strong lead when the captain's decisions, even the controversial ones, appeared to reap dividends. On the opening day he had raised eyebrows in leaving Ian Woosnam and Darren Clarke on the bench but once the points started to roll in, the critics were soon quietened. Ballesteros had put so much effort into the build-up to these games, even when it came to the course: he had been personally responsible for re-designing the 17th hole, deliberately narrowing the fairway just at the distance where the big-hitting Americans (particularly players like Woods) would be landing their ball.

BELOW: *US legend Tiger Woods plays from the rough on the 4th hole at Valderrama, but won only half a point over two days.*

RIGHT: *Huge crowds at the 17th green create a vibrant atmosphere at Valderrama as Europe take control of the 1997 Ryder Cup.*

DAY TWO

FRIDAY AFTERNOON FOURSOMES (FROM DAY ONE)

Rocca/Olazábal *lost to* **Hoch/Janzen** *by one hole*

Langer/Montgomerie *beat* **O'Meara/Woods,** *5 and 3*

Faldo/Westwood *beat* **Leonard/Maggert,** *3 and 2*

Parnevik/Garrido *halved with* **Lehman/Mickelson**

Session Score: 2.5-1.5

SATURDAY MORNING FOURBALLS

Montgomerie/Clarke *beat* **Couples/Love** *by one hole*

Woosnam/Bjørn *beat* **Leonard/Faxon,** *2 and 1*

Faldo/Westwood *beat* **Woods/O'Meara,** *2 and 1*

Olazábal/Garrido *halved with* **Mickelson/Lehman**

Session Score: 3.5-0.5

SATURDAY AFTERNOON FOURSOMES

Montgomerie/Langer *beat* **Janzen/Furyk** *by one hole*

Faldo/Westwood *lost to* **Hoch/Maggert,** *2 and 1*

Parnevik/Garrido *halved with* **Leonard/Woods**

Olazábal/Rocca *beat* **Love/Couples,** *5 and 4*

Session Score: 2.5-1.5

Overall Score: Europe 10.5, USA 5.5

The US team certainly didn't appreciate it – there were complaints about the hole from several players before the Cup got underway – and maybe it harmed their game because during the remainder of Saturday (also affected by rain, which meant two matches hung over to the Sunday), Team USA picked up just 3.5 points from a possible 12. With such a strong team on paper, back in the USA there had been predictions that it was almost impossible for Europe to win, but by the Sunday morning Seve's side were 10.5-5.5 ahead, with a massive five-point lead in the bag.

In the Fourballs, Clarke finally made his first appearance, partnering Montgomerie to a narrow victory over an in-form Couples and Love; he was swiftly followed by Woosnam and Bjørn, who added a comfortable 2 and 1 over Leonard and Faxon. Faldo, on his way towards setting a Ryder Cup points record with his eleventh appearance, again joined with Westwood to beat Woods and O'Meara in a match that saw Tiger actually putt into the water on the 17th. For Team USA, the only chink of light was a half for Mickelson/Lehman and Olazábal/Garrido, although even then, a 20-foot putt from Olazábal at the 18th denied them victory.

The afternoon session was almost as convincing – more wins for Montgomerie/Langer and Olazábal/Rocca (in a convincing 5 and 4 triumph over Love/Couples) and a half for the unbeaten Parnevik and his partner Garrido against Leonard/ Woods. It was turning into a disaster for the Americans and only Hoch and Maggert's surprise win against Faldo/Westwood sweetened the pill. As Saturday finally closed, the sight of the scoreboard must have been a daunting one for all Americans, showing a 9-4 lead with matches still in play. Astonishingly, unthinkably, their dream team was taking a battering and only a minor miracle would turn it around.

Looking for exactly that, US captain Tom Kite pulled out all the stops to bring in a motivational speaker on the Saturday night to gee up his players. But this was no run-of-the-mill orator, but former President George Bush, who was staying in Cadiz after being invited to the opening ceremony. Who knows if his speech made a difference but the USA certainly came out fighting the following day and came so close towards achieving a miracle.

ABOVE: *Colin Montgomerie and Ignacio Garrido celebrate under an umbrella after an historic victory for Europe on Spanish soil.*

With no one giving the USA a hope of saving face in Valderrama, let alone winning, captain Tom Kite decided to go for broke in a bid to turn the situation around, packing his team with big-hitters at the front. Considering they were five points behind – the biggest lead Europe had ever taken into the final day – he believed the match might be over before his best players teed off, if he handled it any other way. The result proved how much the American team had underachieved in the opening two days because the quality of golf produced as they won the singles 8-4 was outstanding. It took them to within a point of doing the impossible until their comeback hit a brick wall when Colin Montgomerie, continuing his unbeaten record in Ryder Cup singles, earned a half against Scott Hoch, retaining the Cup for Europe.

In contrast to Kite's tactical team sheet, Seve Ballesteros democratically asked his players where they would like to play – not a scenario relished by his most senior golfers – and some reports suggest it was they who ensured the big four of Olazábal, Langer, Montgomerie and Faldo were placed close to the end in case anything went wrong. Whether or not it was Ballesteros' call proved important because things did go wrong, with the USA rampaging through the card, picking up points at will.

Ian Woosnam, who had seen little play over the weekend, was clearly rusty as he opened the order and was completely out-played by an impressive Fred Couples, losing 8 and 7. The result set the tone for a day of nerves and drama on the European side, during which they were steadied by the Swede Per-Ulrik Johansson beating Davis Love, 3 and 2, to make it four defeats in a row for the US team over the course of a frustrating week. Italian Costantino Rocca went one better in beating Tiger Woods, and now the home side needed just two more victories to retain the Ryder Cup trophy.

Things took a turn for the worse when Team USA suddenly came to life. Lehman crushed a worn-out Garrido, 7 and 6, while Maggert beat Westwood, 3 and 2. Even Faldo missed out, losing 3 and 2 to Furyk. When home-banker Olazábal (who had been two up) lost at the last to Janzen, the Europeans started to worry. With memories of his missed putt in 1991 well behind him, Langer seized one point in beating Brad Faxon – but where would the other come from? Thomas Bjørn might have seized it, but lost the 18th against Justin Leonard and was forced to settle for a half. And so it was all down to Monty at the last – so long as he didn't lose, Europe had overall victory.

" *I don't want to do that again – it wasn't fun out there.* "

Colin Montgomerie on the stress of going last in the Ryder Cup

It was tense, but the result was rarely in doubt. Hoch missed the fairway with his drive and was on the green in three, a good 15 feet from the hole. Montgomerie was on in two, with two putts for victory. But then, under instructions from Ballesteros, Monty conceded Hoch's putt and settled for a gentlemanly half to clinch the Ryder Cup for Europe by a single point. In some ways, this was a strange ending – but "oh so Seve!" And no one could say that Ballesteros – or Spain for that matter – had not delivered. Indeed, the first Ryder Cup to be held in Europe had proved a rip-roaring success. The rain (which returned during the presentation ceremony) made conditions more difficult than expected for spectators and players alike, but the 32nd Ryder Cup yet again provided incredible drama and a close result.

What a debt golf owed that day to Jack Nicklaus and his suggestion, almost 20 years earlier, to bring Europe into the competition – even if it left his beloved America wondering what they had to do to win again.

US captain Tom Kite blamed the weather and the course for his team's defeat in Spain. "It's a golf course that requires as much local knowledge as any I've seen, with the exception of the Augusta National," he insisted. "The only reason we got beat was they knew the golf course and the weather conditions better than us."

DAY THREE

FINAL DAY SINGLES

Ian Woosnam *lost to* **Fred Couples**, *8 and 7*

Per-Ulrik Johansson *beat* **Davis Love**, *3 and 2*

Jesper Parnevik *lost to* **Mark O'Meara**, *5 and 4*

Darren Clarke *lost to* **Phil Mickelson**, *2 and 1*

Costantino Rocca *beat* **Tiger Woods**, *4 and 2*

Thomas Bjørn *halved with* **Justin Leonard**

Ignacio Garrido *lost to* **Tom Lehman**, *7 and 6*

Bernhard Langer *beat* **Brad Faxon**, *2 and 1*

Lee Westwood *lost to* **Jeff Maggert**, *3 and 2*

José María Olazábal *lost to* **Lee Janzen** *by one hole*

Nick Faldo *lost to* **Jim Furyk**, *3 and 2*

Colin Montgomerie *halved with* **Scott Hoch**

Session Score: 4-8

Overall Score: Europe 14.5, USA 13.5

ABOVE: *Proud captain Seve Ballesteros holds the Ryder Cup aloft after a dramatic one-point victory over the USA in his home country.*

Ryder Cup legends
Bernhard **LANGER**

It takes a special kind of character to become a Ryder Cup legend but to follow up those successes by winning the trophy as captain needs something extra. But that's exactly what Europe's Bernhard Langer has achieved over the years and it marks him out as one of the greatest golfers the Ryder Cup has ever seen.

" In 1985... my life was pretty much 95 per cent golf and my wife was the rest. "

Bernhard Langer reveals the life of a golf pro

In an A–Z of the Ryder Cup, L would stand for Langer. The stylish German competed in 10 Ryder Cups and his performances were instrumental in helping Europe to win five, with a tied sixth enough to retain the trophy. The son of a German refugee who escaped from a Russian prisoner-of-war train bound for Siberia, perhaps it comes as no surprise that strength of character and mental agility have proved two of Langer's most important traits.

Legend has it that the young Bernhard – raised in Germany, where golf was not yet popular – was forced to trawl bookstores in his home town of Anhausen, Bavaria, for golfing magazines just to find out the latest Ryder Cup scores. By the time he reached his thirties, the name Langer was inextricably linked with the competition. His superb record of 24 points from 42 games is second only to Mr Ryder Cup himself, Nick Faldo, and his dramatic experience at the 1991 tournament must go down in folklore.

If L is for Langer, K is for Kiawah Island. The 1991 Ryder Cup, or "War on the Shore", went down to the final pairing and Langer was left with a six-foot putt to halve his match with Hale Irwin and retain the trophy for Europe. To everyone's disbelief, his putt shaved the hole, missing by mere millimetres, to hand the trophy to the USA. But there was pride in defeat, for Langer had contributed to quite a stunning spectacle. Indeed, he proved his mettle in winning a tournament in Germany the very next week and went on to compete in four more Ryder Cups.

Away from the Ryder Cup, Langer is a two-time Masters champion and was the world's first official No. 1 when the rankings were introduced in 1986. Famous for his use of the long broom-handle putter during long spells of his career, he also often overcame the "yips" (inexplicable jitters while putting), confirming his mental agility. Maybe for this reason, no one could quite believe that he missed "that putt" in 1991.

His Ryder Cup debut was made alongside Spain's Manuel Piñero in a Foursomes match of 1981, and he also formed excellent partnerships with players such as Sandy Lyle. Then, captaining Europe in 2004 at Oakland Hills, Langer led his team to one of the greatest victories of all – an 18.5-9.5 demolition of Tiger Woods & Co.

RIGHT: *German legend Bernhard Langer stares down the green at The Belfry in 1993.*

RYDER CUP RECORD

Ryder Cups: 1981, 1983, 1985 (winner), 1987 (winner), 1989 (tied but Europe retain trophy), 1991, 1993, 1995 (winner), 1997 (winner), 2002 (winner), 2004 (winner, non-playing captain)
Total wins: 6 (plus 1 tie to retain the trophy, 1989)
Matches: 42 (won 21, halved 6, lost 15)
Total points: 24

Paul AZINGER

If Bernhard Langer (opposite) was famous for his mental fortitude, then Paul Azinger must be made of similar stuff because his achievements as a player were barely interrupted by a personal battle with cancer, which he overcame with the same determination as he displayed on-course.

BELOW: *A typical pose from US star Paul Azinger as he blasts out of a bunker at the 1991 Ryder Cup at Kiawah Island.*

Shortly after the 1993 Ryder Cup, Azinger was diagnosed with non-Hodgkin's lymphoma in his right shoulder but he refused to give in and made an astonishing comeback, culminating in an emotional victory at the 2000 Sony Open in Hawaii. Anyone who witnessed him in action at The Belfry in 1993 could not possibly have guessed how ill he was because his singles battle against old foe Nick Faldo turned out to be one of the most competitive in Ryder Cup history. Even when Faldo holed-in-one, Azinger refused to give in and fought back to earn a half, playing his part in a 15-13 victory for the USA.

In other Ryder Cup appearances, Azinger experienced both highs and lows: tying in 1989, winning in 1991 (when he famously earned a key point against José María Olazábal in the singles) and losing in 2002. But perhaps his greatest moment of all came as captain in 2008. With Team USA desperate for a victory after years of European dominance, he led them to a 16.5-11.5 win in Valhalla. Azinger's style of captaincy, bringing in youthful, experienced players and changing the atmosphere around the US team, played a major part in the victory, confirming him a place in history as a Ryder Cup legend.

Azinger's other golfing achievements have been remarkable, too. He spent almost 300 consecutive weeks in golf's top 10 between 1988 and 1994 and won his first, and so far only, Major in 1993 when he lifted the PGA Championship, beating Greg Norman in a play-off. He also has 12 PGA Tour and two European Tour wins to his name.

But it is the drama of the Ryder Cup that seems to keep drawing him back. And even without a golf club in hand he was at Celtic Manor in 2010, this time as a television commentator.

> **"** *I just want to say the greatest honour you can bestow on a professional golfer is to ask him to captain a Ryder Cup team and I'm awestruck by it.* **"**
>
> *Paul Azinger on being named US captain for 2008*

RYDER CUP RECORD

Ryder Cups: 1989, 1991 (winner), 1993 (winner), 2002, 2008 (winner, non-playing captain)
Total wins: 3
Matches: 15 (won 5, halved 3, lost 7)
Total points: 6.5

1999

USA 14.5
Europe 13.5

The Country Club, Massachusetts

September 24-26

THE COURSE

The Country Club
Location: Brookline,
Massachusetts, USA
Par: 71
Yards: 6, 577

The Country Club is one of the oldest courses in the USA and holds an important place in golf history, being one of the five charter clubs to found the United States Golf Association (USGA). Golf was first played there in 1890.

The 1999 Ryder Cup, which saw Team USA produce the most spectacular comeback the competition had ever seen, will go down in history as the most controversial, dramatic and most talked-about Ryder Cup of all. And it will be forever remembered by all those involved and everyone who saw it as "The Battle of Brookline".

AFTER SO MANY HARD-FOUGHT MATCHES in recent years there was a feeling that the Ryder Cup was coming to a head in 1999 – and it did so in quite thunderous fashion. In Boston, the golf provided more drama than ever but the rivalry spilt over into something far uglier. In sporting terms, it produced the greatest Ryder Cup matches ever, with the USA coming from 10-4 behind to complete an incredible turnaround, but it is impossible to talk about the golf without debating the controversies surrounding it.

Perhaps the PGA should have seen it coming. The jingoism on both sides had been building ever since the "War on the Shore" and what started out as a challenge match had turned into a ferociously patriotic battle. Certainly, it added excitement and made the Ryder Cup even more dramatic, but where would it end? US player Tom Watson reminded everyone it was golf and not war, but no one seemed to take any notice.

With Europe going for a hat-trick of victories and the USA under pressure, Brookline was where it exploded, and afterwards the golfing world had to take a step back and ask what it really wanted from the Ryder Cup. Europe left Boston angered – and not just because they had thrown away victory. What hurt them most was the behaviour of the US team on the 17th green in the very last match when Justin Leonard holed a 45-foot putt that looked set to win the competition. It should have been a moment to savour but with José María Olazábal still facing a putt that could save Europe from defeat, the US entourage invaded the green only to be followed by a cameraman, who ran across the line of his putt in a huge breach of sporting etiquette. Once the ensuing hullabaloo died down, Olazábal missed his putt and the incident then became the focus of European discontent, with captain Mark James insisting, "What happened has left a bad taste in the mouth."

That particular episode, though unsportsmanlike, was not the worst of it. Given the passion of their comeback, combined with six years of waiting, the reaction of the US side might be forgiven, but the behaviour of the crowd, however, was different. Throughout the week, the European players were routinely abused – Colin Montgomerie's 70-year-old father left the course

LEFT: *Mark James, captain of the Europe team, watches on as the action unfolds at Brookline.*

OPPOSITE: *Colin Montgomerie tees off in his Foursomes match. Montgomerie and his partner Paul Lawrie defeated the USA's Phil Mickleson and David Duval.*

midway through on the Sunday, it was so bad; and in a case that disgusted everyone, James' wife, Jane, was spat at.

The British press only served to inflame the situation, with the *Daily Mirror* running a front-page headline "United Slobs of America". And even a public apology from US captain Ben Crenshaw failed to end the debate. "It really was not something that we need to be proud of," he said. "For that, we're truly sorry." The reaction from Europe was terse: Montgomerie replied "No amount of apology can make amends for what they did."

Boorish behaviour was not restricted to the home spectators. Diarists had noted a rise in loutish behaviour, with chanting and drunken abuse from European fans – and Team Europe were not averse to the over-celebration of an important putt, either. But who could have imagined when the players teed off just how much drama lay ahead, especially as it began so badly for the USA with World No. 2 Duval and Mickelson soundly beaten, 3 and 2, in the opening match by the Scottish pairing of Montgomerie/Lawrie? Then Tiger Woods, then ranked No. 1 in the world, continued his losing streak when he and Lehman were beaten by García/Parnevik, 2 and 1. Victory seemed a long way away.

DAY ONE

CAPTAINS

USA: Ben Crenshaw   **Europe:** Mark James

FRIDAY MORNING FOURSOMES

Duval/Mickelson *lost to* **Montgomerie/Lawrie,** *3 and 2*

Lehman/Woods *lost to* **Parnevik/García,** *2 and 1*

Love/Stewart *halved with* **Jiménez/Harrington**

Sutton/Maggert *beat* **Clarke/Westwood,** *3 and 2*

Session Score: 1.5-2.5

FRIDAY AFTERNOON FOURBALLS

Love/Leonard *halved with* **Montgomerie/Lawrie**

Mickelson/Furyk *lost to* **Parnevik/García** *by one hole*

Sutton/Maggert *lost to* **Jiménez/Olazábal,** *2 and 1*

Duval/Woods *lost to* **Clarke/Westwood** *by one hole*

Session Score: 0.5-3.5

Overall Score: USA 2, Europe 6

❝ *...we don't need to be treated like this.* **❞**

European captain Mark James comments on the behaviour of the US team

ABOVE: *US star Payne Stewart in bunker action during a dramatic victory over Europe at Brookline that will never be forgotten.*

The only saving grace for the USA on that opening morning in Boston was an encouraging 3 and 2 win for Sutton/Maggert against the big-name pairing of Clarke and Westwood, who rarely lost when playing together. Love/Stewart also halved against Harrington/Jiménez to save further embarrassment, too. Even so, this was not the start US captain Ben Crenshaw envisaged after reversing Seve Ballesteros' decision of two years earlier and opting to start the opening day with Foursomes, not Fourballs. It was a relief, however, for European captain James, who had already faced criticism back home before a ball was even struck, having caused controversy in selecting Paul Lawrie as a captain's pick and ignoring the claims of Ryder Cup legend Nick Faldo, who had done so much to help Europe win at Valderrama, two years earlier.

James also opted to put his big guns together in partnerships and stick with them throughout the opening four sessions, meaning some of the rookies barely picked up a club before the singles arrived on Sunday. This was a debatable approach - and one criticized by pundits and ex-players on both sides - but it brought dividends in terms of early points because Europe romped through Friday and Saturday to set up a four-point lead. Jesper Parnevik and Sergio García were particularly dominant on the opening day, winning both their first two contests, but the Europeans won five of the eight matches in all to open up an impressive 6-2 lead, which was just what James had been aiming for.

The next day - Saturday - honours were shared between the two sides and that left Europe with a healthy four-point lead to take into the singles, leading 10-6. Indeed, it proved a day of mixed fortunes for Tiger Woods and Steve Pate, who won their morning Foursome match against Jiménez/Harrington at the last, but were then beaten by Montgomerie/Lawrie, 2 and 1, in the afternoon.

Again, all the matches were tight - especially the Fourballs, when every match reached at least the 17th green. In the morning Sutton/Maggert began well for the USA in beating Montgomerie/Lawrie by one hole, with Woods/Pate following suit. But Europe's reply came from Clarke/Westwood, who won 3 and 2 against Furyk/O'Meara, and from Parnevik/García, who won by the same margin against Stewart/Leonard. In the afternoon, Mickelson/Lehman combined to secure a 2 and 1 victory over Clarke/Westwood but this proved to be the USA's only full point. Love/Duval halved with Parnevik/García, as did Leonard/Sutton against Jiménez/Olazábal, before Woods/Pate suffered defeat in the final game, 2 and 1.

Europe's advantage, at 10-6, looked good and captain Mark James was certainly content with his side's display but the only question was, would this be enough? After all, the USA had staged a remarkable comeback from even further behind in Valderrama, and had only just missed out. "It's not too big a hole," US star Hal Sutton boldly told journalists that evening. "We've got 12 great players on this team. We've shown a lot of fight this week and we've got a lot of fight left in us."

Captain Ben Crenshaw also seemed surprisingly upbeat, repeatedly telling anyone who would listen that he had a "good feeling" about the final day's play. Perhaps it was all bluster, perhaps it was blind faith, but it was certainly what his players – and the American public – wanted and needed to hear. Of course, no one knew if he was right, but the scene was set for an incredible final day that would go down in history as the greatest-ever 10 hours of Ryder Cup golf.

If former President George Bush helped to inspire an impressive, if ultimately unsuccessful comeback for the Americans at Valderrama in Spain 1997, it was his son George W. Bush who was credited with going one better in 1999 and helping his country to a famous victory.

US captain Ben Crenshaw asked the then Texas Governor to address his players following a miserable opening two days that saw his side trail Europe, 10-6. Bush responded by reading from the memoirs of a soldier who had been at the Siege of the Alamo – and was delighted to see Team USA invoke that same kind of spirit in storming to victory the very next day.

LEFT: *Tiger Woods reacts to missing a putt during a Fourballs defeat against Colin Montgomerie and Paul Lawrie.*

> **❝** *I'm a big believer in fate – I have a good feeling about tomorrow, that's all I'm gonna say.* **❞**
>
> *US captain Ben Crenshaw considers a final-day comeback*

DAY TWO

SATURDAY MORNING FOURSOMES

Sutton/Maggert *beat* **Montgomerie/Lawrie** *by one hole*

Furyk/O'Meara *lost to* **Clarke/Westwood,** *3 and 2*

Pate/Woods *beat* **Jiménez/Harrington** *by one hole*

Stewart/Leonard *lost to* **Parnevik/García,** *3 and 2*

Session Score: 2-2

SATURDAY AFTERNOON FOURBALLS

Mickelson/Lehman *beat* **Clarke/Westwood,** *2 and 1*

Love/Duval *halved with* **Parnevik/García**

Leonard/Sutton *halved with* **Jiménez/Olazábal**

Pate/Woods *lost to* **Montgomerie/Lawrie,** *2 and 1*

Session Score: 2-2

Overall Score: USA 6, Europe 10

ABOVE: *US players surge onto the 17th green after seeing Justin Leonard hole a massive putt against José María Olazábal.*

OPPOSITE: *Scenes of jubilation at the 17th hole as the US team continued its final day fightback in 1999.*

DAY THREE

FINAL DAY SINGLES

Tom Lehman *beat* **Lee Westwood,** *3 and 2*

Hal Sutton *beat* **Darren Clarke,** *4 and 2*

Phil Mickelson *beat* **Jarmo Sandelin,** *4 and 3*

Davis Love *beat* **Jean van de Velde,** *6 and 5*

Tiger Woods *beat* **Andrew Coltart,** *3 and 2*

David Duval *beat* **Jesper Parnevik,** *5 and 4*

Mark O'Meara *lost to* **Padraig Harrington** *by one hole*

Steve Pate *beat* **Miguel Angel Jiménez,** *2 and 1*

Justin Leonard *halved with* **José María Olazábal**

Payne Stewart *lost to* **Colin Montgomerie** *by one hole*

Jim Furyk *beat* **Sergio García,** *4 and 3*

Jeff Maggert *lost to* **Paul Lawrie,** *4 and 3*

Session Score: 8.5-3.5

Overall Score: USA 14.5, Europe 13.5

No team had ever won the Ryder Cup from more than two points adrift on the final day. But the USA won a stunning 56 holes to 33 to make history at Brookline. Of the pivotal first six matches, all of which were won, not a single one made it as far as the 17th. Europe's finest golfers were not just beaten, but demolished. "It was a mighty display of firepower," said Hal Sutton, who got it all started with a 4 and 2 victory over Darren Clarke.

The crowd were already on a high when Tom Lehman beat World No. 5 Lee Westwood. Lehman had not won on the PGA tour since 1996, while Westwood had won 14 tournaments in the same period, yet the American hit three birdies in a row to be two-up by the 6th and hit every single fairway before winning, 3 and 2. It soon became clear European captain James had made a fatal error of judgement. Having selected his senior players for all of the opening 16 matches, he was left with half a team that was worn-out, and another that hadn't played at all. Andrew Coltart, Jarmo Sandelin and Jean van de Velde had not even picked up a club in fury at this decision, yet they were expected to line up against America's best – and beat them. It just didn't add up.

Mickelson quickly demolished Sandelin, 4 and 3, while Love saw off van de Velde, 6 and 5, and Woods made short shrift of Coltart to make it five points for the USA and for the first time, the lead. The atmosphere at The Country Club was now truly explosive and the crowd, beginning to smell blood, turned up the volume with every putt that was holed – and every European putt missed.

David Duval earned the pivotal point of the day, beating an in-form Parnevik, 5 and 4 – a match that James must have expected to win after deliberately placing the Swede in the middle of the pack. But perhaps weary limbs were costing the Europeans dear... If Duval's display was crucial, the same might be said of Jim Furyk's victory over Sergio Garcia. Furyk had spotted that García – winning matches in tandem with Parnevik – hadn't been striking the ball well, and vowed to hit every fairway to keep his opponent under pressure. It worked, as he won 3 and 2.

Padraig Harrington's narrow victory over Mark O'Meara kept Europe in it, along with Paul Lawrie's confident win against Maggert but with only two matches left, the USA needed just a half to complete a memorable victory. With Leonard v Olazábal and Montgomerie v Stewart, the finale would be breathtaking. With so much at stake on the 17th, Leonard faced a huge 45-foot putt, while Olazábal was 25 feet from the hole. Pandemonium broke loose as Leonard's incredible effort rolled into the back of the cup to set off celebrations only seen once in a lifetime.

What the US players, wives, caddies and camera crew forgot, however, was that the match was still not over: Olazábal still had a putt to halve the hole. As the USA trampled all over the green, including a cameraman who ran across the line of the Spaniard's putt, both European players and management seethed at their opponent's ill-mannered display. We'll never know how much difference the unruly scenes made to Olazábal, but history shows he missed the putt and Team USA completed a remarkable victory.

In a show of sportsmanship, Stewart conceded to Montgomerie at the last, leaving the final score 14.5-13.5 for the second Ryder Cup in a row. In a sad addendum to the story, a few weeks later, Stewart was tragically killed in a plane crash. He did take part in the greatest Ryder Cup of all time, however, which is some legacy.

> **"***They got the momentum early on by holing a load of stuff. We didn't respond with our best play, and then the whole thing got out of hand.***"**
>
> *European captain Mark James explains what went wrong*

The new breed: Europe's Rory McIlroy (left) celebrates holing a putt on the 8th green with team-mate Graeme McDowell during the 2010 Ryder Cup at Celtic Manor.

CHAPTER SEVEN
THE MODERN ERA

Following the Battle of Brookline in 1999, the Ryder Cup was bigger news than ever but needed to rediscover the sporting spirit envisaged by its founder. As the twenty-first century dawned, the competition entered a new era of intense but respectful competition, with Europe in the ascendancy.

2002

Europe 15.5
USA 12.5

The Belfry, Sutton Coldfield

September 27-29

THE COURSE

Brabazon Course
Location: The Belfry,
Sutton Coldfield,
England
Par: 72
Yards: 7,118
Par: 72
Yards: 7,356

Designed by Peter Alliss, The Belfry was hosting its fourth Ryder Cup. On its signature 10th hole, players must decide whether to drive and avoid the water - a part of Ryder Cup folklore.

After the bad feeling that lingered after the Battle of Brookline, the 2002 Ryder Cup was destined to be emotional, dramatic and compelling. Even so, the way Europe gained revenge on the USA, following a remarkable final day at The Belfry, was something truly special, whichever side you happened to be supporting.

THERE CANNOT, IN THE HISTORY of televised golf, have been many more engrossing days than September 29, 2002, when Europe and the USA went into the final day of the Ryder Cup locked at eight points all - and with the world's greatest golfers going head to head.

The 2002 Ryder Cup will be remembered for so many things: Paul McGinley's winning putt, Welsh rookie Phillip Price's amazing victory over World No. 2 Phil Mickelson, European captain Sam Torrance's tactical genius, Colin Montgomerie's consistency and the unfettered celebrations of the home team. But perhaps it should be remembered equally for the way in which the spirit of the Ryder Cup rose from the ashes.

There were still moments of tension - Sergio García kicking his golf bag in frustration at the American celebrations, for example - but after the Battle of Brookline in 1999, it was evident that the players on both teams had resolved to restore the competition's ideals of true sportsmanship and camaraderie. Given that this particular Ryder Cup was also postponed from 2001 due to the horrific 9/11 terrorist attack in New York, just 17 days before it was scheduled to take place - and with both captains agreeing to stick with the players originally selected for that year - golf needed this event to play its particular part in the overall healing process. "I was lucky in that their captain was Curtis Strange," explained Torrance. "We took about three seconds to agree there wasn't going to be a repeat of Brookline."

The drama didn't take long to unfold and by the end of the opening day, it was clear that the 2002 Ryder Cup was going to be something special for the Europeans, who led 4.5-3.5. The opening Fourballs saw Thomas Bjørn steal the limelight as he partnered Darren Clarke against Tiger Woods and Paul Azinger.

LEFT: *US captain Curtis Strange surveys the scene from his buggy during the morning Fourballs on the opening day of the 2002 Ryder Cup.*

OPPOSITE: *Colin Montgomerie (behind) and Bernhard Langer line up a putt during a Foursomes match against Scott Hoch and Jim Furyk.*

DAY ONE

CAPTAINS

Europe: Sam Torrance   **USA:** Curtis Strange

FRIDAY MORNING FOURBALLS

Clarke/Bjørn *beat* **Woods/Azinger** *by one hole*

García/Westwood *beat* **Duval/Love,** *4 and 3*

Montgomerie/Langer *beat* **Hoch/Furyk,** *4 and 3*

Harrington/Fasth *lost to* **Mickelson/Toms** *by one hole*

Session Score: 3-1

FRIDAY AFTERNOON FOURBALLS

Clarke/Bjørn *lost to* **Sutton/Verplank,** *2 and 1*

García/Westwood *beat* **Woods/Calcavecchia,** *2 and 1*

Montgomerie/Langer *halved with* **Mickelson/Toms**

Harrington/McGinley *lost to* **Cink/Furyk,** *3 and 21*

Session Score: 1.5-2.5

Overall Score: Europe 4.5, USA 3.5

> **❝** *The guys were really up for it and the way they performed was incredible. It's the best start we've made to a Ryder Cup for over 30 years.* **❞**
>
> Sam Torrance, Europe's captain

His sensational 20-foot putt on the 18th green halved the final hole, earning Europe the first point of the day. Just a hole earlier, it had seemed that Woods would turn out to be the headline-maker, providing a birdie to take the match to the last. But Bjørn's putt, his seventh birdie of the round, put the first block of blue on the scoreboard and saw Tiger lose for the seventh time in 11 Ryder Cup matches. "I'm so proud of the way Darren and Bjørn led from the front," said captain Sam Torrance.

Lee Westwood and Sergio García, who had never lost a Ryder Cup Fourballs or Foursomes, were next to contribute, beating David Duval and Davis Love, 4 and 3; Westwood's 18-foot putt on the 15th clinching victory. Colin Montgomerie then began what proved to be an almost exemplary weekend in partnering Bernhard Langer to beat Scott Hoch and Jim Furyk by the same score, with the Europeans contributing four birdies including a 20-foot putt from the German on the 14th. Suddenly it was beginning

to look like a European whitewash and so Phil Mickelson and David Toms' hard-fought one-up victory over Padraig Harrington and Niclas Fasth came as a welcome respite for the Americans.

The result must have given Curtis Strange's team renewed vigour for the afternoon Foursomes because Hal Sutton and Scott Verplank began a revival, beating Clarke and Bjørn, 2 and 1, having been two down at the 12th. Garcia and Westwood teamed up to beat Woods and Mark Calcavecchia, largely thanks to an impressive performance on the back nine, but the match was also notable for two terrible missed putts from Woods on consecutive holes. Could it be that the USA were about to capitulate? Not so, because Mickelson/Toms held on to halve with Montgomerie/Langer, clawing their way back from a three-shot deficit, while Cink/Furyk won, 3 and 2, against Harrington/McGinley, controlling the match from start to finish. The result left Europe one point ahead at the end of the day.

With so much to play for and only a point behind, there was a suspicion the Americans would prove highly dangerous on the Saturday and this was certainly the case. After a slow start, the holders were beginning to gain confidence and only the fact that Tiger Woods had failed to win a point seemed to be holding them back. By the end of Saturday, however, he was back on course and the match levelled. Suddenly what had looked to be a miserable defeat had the increasing potential to become a memorable victory.

As the atmosphere began to crackle, Mickelson/Toms continued their excellent form with a 2 and 1 victory over the inexperienced Pierre Fulke and Phillip Price. The European pair were surprisingly ahead after 10, but the match turned when Fulke missed a putt on the 12th that could have doubled their lead; Mickelson and Toms were ruthless as they won three in a row to turn the situation around. Then Mickelson's bunker shot at the 16th helped to secure an unlikely half, which finally broke their opponents' resolve.

Europe's reply saw García/Westwood beat Cink/Furyk, 2 and 1, to maintain their 100 per cent record, although the battling and scrambling nature of the victory summed up just how tight and desperate the match had become. Even veterans Montgomerie and Langer, in outstanding form, had to hold their nerve to beat Verplank/Hoch. In the end, they surrendered a two-hole lead to be level by the 15th and a nerve-jangling putt from Montgomerie on the 17th was needed to regain the lead. The relief on European faces was clear – and for Langer, this was yet another landmark as he secured a record eleventh victory in 18 Ryder Cup Foursomes. The morning was not over yet and when Woods/Love beat Bjørn/Clarke, 4 and 3, Europe were just a point ahead and hanging on.

The afternoon matches proved even more dramatic, during which time nerves and tempers were tested in equal measure, but the big drama came during a match between García/Westwood and Woods/Love, bringing back bitter memories of three years earlier.

RIGHT: *Colin Montgomerie (left) and Padraig Harrington look relaxed on the 14th green during the Saturday afternoon matches.*

BELOW: *Tiger Woods and Davis Love celebrate winning their Fourballs match against Sergio García and Lee Westwood.*

DAY TWO

SATURDAY MORNING FOURSOMES

Fulke/Price *lost to* **Mickelson/Toms,** *2 and 1*

Westwood/García *beat* **Furyk/Cink,** *2 and 1*

Montgomerie/Langer *beat* **Verplank/Hoch** *by one hole*

Clarke/Bjørn *lost to* **Woods/Love,** *4 and 3*

Session Score: 1.5-2.5

SATURDAY AFTERNOON FOURBALLS

Fasth/Parnevik *lost to* **Calcavecchia/Duval** *by one hole*

Montgomerie/Harrington *beat* **Mickelson/Toms,** *2 and 1*

García/Westwood *lost to* **Woods/Love** *by one hole*

Clarke/McGinley *halved with* **Hoch/Furyk**

Session Score: 1.5-2.5

Overall Score: Europe 8, USA 8

García was furious when American team members, as well as a reporter and cameraman, rushed onto the 18th green as he and his partner lost their unbeaten record, with Westwood missing a five-foot putt that would have halved the match. The Spaniard hurled his ball into the lake and stormed off the green, kicking his golf bag as he left.

"It's his bag – he can do bloody well what he likes with it!" declared European captain Torrance as tempers frayed and memories of the way in which the American entourage celebrated Justin Leonard's putt by running onto the green, right in José María Olazábal's putting line in 1999 seeped to the surface. "He just lost a match, he felt he could have won," added Torrance, in explanation. "Good thing I wasn't there, he probably would have kicked me!" Fortunately, that injection of humour and a measured response from the Americans ensured García's moment of frustration had little impact on the overall spirit of the tournament. What the result of that Fourballs meant, however, was the Saturday games were completed with the scores level at 8-8, setting up the possibility of a classic final day's play at The Belfry.

Calcavecchia and Duval began the afternoon with a narrow victory over Fasth/Parnevik despite being three behind at one stage. The match hinged on an outstanding drive from Duval at the 10th, which found the green – something the Europeans were unable to match as both found water while attempting to follow suit. European dreams were reawakened by yet another victory for Montgomerie, this time teaming up with Harrington to beat Mickelson/Toms, 2 and 1. But Woods and Love's victory, together with a half for Hoch/Furyk, meant the day ended with the scores level and the USA feeling on the up. However, that doesn't tell the whole story because there was real drama in the final match, which left the Europeans on a high, too.

McGinley and Clarke showed the kind of battling spirit only the Ryder Cup engenders as they hung on against Hoch/Furyk, despite never being ahead. They were still one-down at the 17th following a Hoch birdie but somehow with the vociferous galleries now frantic, McGinley managed to find the concentration, skill and determination to birdie the 18th and therefore halve the match.

What a crucial putt it was – and there were more to come.

With the scores level and the eyes of the world on The Belfry for the final session of the 2002 Ryder Cup, there was everything to play for and what would follow goes down in history as one of the most engrossing days of sporting drama.

Team USA must have felt confident. As holders, they only needed to draw to retain the trophy and Europe had not secured an overall win in the singles since 1995. But perhaps they hadn't bargained on the tactical gamble that marks out Sam Torrance as one of the Ryder Cup's greatest ever captains. Going against tradition, he front-loaded his team, placing Europe's top eight players in the opening eight singles matches. By contrast, Strange saved his best players, including Woods and Mickelson, for later in the field. The idea, Torrance later revealed, was to whip the crowd into a frenzy by winning early points, a decision that proved inspired.

Montgomerie, so outstanding all weekend, got his team off to the perfect start in annihilating Hoch, 5 and 4, with a performance as fine as any seen at the Ryder Cup. As the crowd roared behind him, he crashed his first drive down the fairway and birdied from 18 feet to take an early lead. Hoch drew level at the 3rd, but Monty was three-up by the end of the first nine and never looked back, eventually admitting: "That's the best I can play. Scott is a great champion and a tough competitor, but I think I was eight-under and there's not much you can do about that."

Quite so, but the Americans were clearly not about to give up – far from it. Toms responded with a narrow victory over García, sealed at the 18th when the Spaniard thundered his tee-shot into the water. Clarke and Duval then halved before Langer, Harrington and Bjørn all won to put Europe 12.5-9.5 ahead and justify their captain's gamble. Only a stunning performance from Verplank, America's wild card rookie, against Westwood kept the USA in contention as he birdied the first and eagled the third to win, 2 and 1.

Paul Azinger, often the USA's most consistent performer, sensed the mood and produced a battling half against Fasth to maintain his unbeaten record in Ryder Cup singles; his remarkable bunker shot at the 18th, which found the hole to save him from defeat, was probably the shot of the day.

SHOT OF THE DAY

It was a huge gamble to place Phillip Price so far down the order in the eleventh tie but what a pay-off Torrance received as the Welshman, ranked 119th in the world, produced the performance of his life against World No. 2 Phil Mickelson. Price was three-down by the 5th, but began a legendary comeback at the 6th when, with his feet almost in the water after driving close to the lake, he produced an inspired shot to the green and subsequently won the hole. That moment changed the whole balance of the game – and perhaps the Ryder Cup, too. An inspired Price was transformed as he won hole after hole, roared on by the home crowd.

> **"** *The most important club used to win the Ryder Cup wasn't a putter or a drive, it was the pencil of European captain Sam Torrance.* **"**

USA Today

OPPOSITE: *Paul McGinley of Ireland leaps in the air after sinking the putt at the 18th green that won the Ryder Cup for Europe.*

RIGHT: *Jubilant Europe captain Sam Torrance celebrates on the 18th after leading his team to victory at The Belfry.*

Perhaps the key for Torrance, though, was what happened in the match between Mickelson and Welsh rookie Phillip Price - a contest that in any context other than the Ryder Cup might have been a foregone conclusion. But Price won with three holes to spare, finishing with a nerveless 25-foot downhill putt at the 16th when the Cup was not yet won and pressure was heavy. "Tell 'em who I beat, go on, tell 'em who I beat!" Price was reported to shout in the post-match celebrations - and who can really blame him for such exuberance?

Remarkable as this performance was, it wasn't enough to clinch overall victory - Azinger's shot from the bunker had seen to that. So it was left to McGinley to complete the job against Furyk. The Irishman needed a half and tension was palpably in the air as he reached the 18th. He had trailed his opponent all the way from the second hole but drew level on the 17th with impeccable timing. Now everything was on McGinley's 10-foot putt after Furyk chipped close from a greenside bunker. Somehow McGinley held his nerve and when the ball finally dropped, it set off wild celebrations in the European camp.

Champagne flowed, Torrance was drenched and McGinley even ended up in the lake as the party began. "I'm very proud," said Torrance. "Apart from my marriage and the birth of my children, this is the proudest moment of my life." This is a common reaction from exhausted but elated captains on either winning team.

DAY THREE

FINAL DAY SINGLES

Colin Montgomerie *beat* **Scott Hoch,** *5 and 4*

Sergio García *lost to* **David Toms** *by one hole*

Darren Clarke *halved with* **David Duval**

Bernhard Langer *beat* **Hal Sutton,** *4 and 3*

Padraig Harrington *beat* **Mark Calcavecchia,** *5 and 4*

Thomas Bjørn *beat* **Stewart Cink,** *2 and 1*

Lee Westwood *lost to* **Scott Verplank,** *2 and 1*

Niclas Fasth *halved with* **Paul Azinger**

Paul McGinley *halved with* **Jim Furyk**

Pierre Fulke *halved with* **Davis Love**

Phillip Price *beat* **Phil Mickelson,** *3 and 2*

Jesper Parnevik *halved with* **Tiger Woods**

Session Score: 7.5-4.5

Overall Score: Europe 15.5, USA 12.5

Ryder Cup legends
Colin MONTGOMERIE

There can hardly be another golfer more immersed in the history of the Ryder Cup, or whose name is woven into the fabric of the contest than Colin Montgomerie. The great Scot has relished the drama of every European putt and every American drive for more than 20 years. His passion for Ryder Cup glory has led to many victories, both as player and captain.

RIGHT: Monty in typical winning pose; this time after holing a birdie putt on the 8th green during the afternoon Fourball matches of the 2002 Ryder Cup.

So, where does one begin with an evaluation of Colin Montgomerie's contribution to golfing history? To put it bluntly, "Monty" is Ryder Cup royalty. Since making his debut in 1991, he has been at the heart of some of the most iconic episodes in the competition's history, not least the moment when he holed the winning putt at Oakland Hills Country Club, Michigan, in 2004 to give Europe a dramatic victory. There are those who will tell you that Ian Poulter's birdie on the 15th just three seconds earlier was mathematically the half-point guaranteeing a European win that day but in the hearts of European fans, it was Monty's day and certainly his face on the back of every British newspaper.

It was Montgomerie, too, who halved the last hole with Scott Hoch to clinch the half-point that secured Europe the Cup in 1997. Remarkably, in eight Ryder Cups he has never lost a singles match. Not everyone loves him - he hasn't always gone down well in the USA, unlike back home, but there is certainly something special about watching Monty play.

At first sight you might not necessarily place him as one of the world's greatest athletes - those rounded, sloping shoulders and a lumbering, almost lethargic gait are in complete contrast to the lean, super-fit youngsters now coming to the fore in world golf. But few can match the accuracy and natural ability of the Scotsman, who was born in Glasgow in 1963, but brought up in Yorkshire, England. Indeed, barely any can match the competitive spirit that has driven him thoughout his 24-year professional career. Monty has scored 23.5 points in eight Ryder Cups as a player, which places him only 1.5 points behind the all-time record holder, Nick Faldo, but perhaps his greatest moment came in 2010 - and without a club in hand.

As captain of the European team at Celtic Manor, Colin Montgomerie gave one of his most convincing performances, displaying true leadership as he inspirationally masterminded yet another remarkable victory for the home team. Later he described the experience as "the greatest moment of my golfing career." What really stood out was not just his meticulous preparation - although in itself impressive - but the big, generous, enthusiastic personality, which makes him such a legend.

There were times in his playing career, particularly in the USA, when he was labelled miserable or even grumpy as frustration with errant cameramen or noisy supporters in the gallery seemed to spill over and affect his concentration. But those who have met the great man will tell you that it's his enthusiasm, zest for life and sense of humour that really stand out - the qualities that made him such a successful captain.

He was willing to set aside differences to count players such as Darren Clarke and José María Olazábal among his vice-captains and employed passionate speeches - and a rallying phone call from Seve Ballesteros (who was fighting a brain tumour) - to prepare his troops for battle. "He was with every player, and every player was with him," explained Ireland's Padraig Harrington after the trophy was won. "We didn't want to let him down - we wanted to deliver for Monty."

What came across in those post-tournament interviews was that Colin Montgomerie trusted his players and they in turn responded to that trust - clearly his passion for the Ryder Cup rubbed off on everyone.

RYDER CUP RECORD

Ryder Cups: 1991, 1993, 1995 (winner), 1997 (winner), 1999, 2002 (winner), 2004 (winner), 2006 (winner), 2010 (winner, non-playing captain)
Total wins: 6
Matches: 36 (won 20, halved 7, lost 9)
Total points: 23.5

He has, of course, stepped down from the captaincy since 2010 and José Maîia Olazábal of Spain will take his place at the Medinah Country Club. Despite this, there's a possibility of seeing Monty somewhere in Chicago, such is his love for the Cup – "It would be nice to be involved in some individual capacity," he admits.

Away from the Ryder Cup, the Scotsman is famously known as probably the best golfer never to have won a Major although as you can see, the label doesn't do justice to an incredible career that includes a record eight Order of Merit titles – and an incredible character, too. Without him, the Ryder Cup just wouldn't be the same.

> " *Personally it means nothing. This is all about a team event.* "
>
> *Colin Montgomerie's teamwork ethic*

2004 Oakland Hills CC, Michigan

Europe 18.5
USA 9.5

September 17-19

THE COURSE

Oakland Hills Country Club
Location: Bloomfield Township, Michigan
Par: 70
Yards: 7,077

The South Course, designed by Donald Ross in 1918, is known by some as "The Monster". Ten Major championships had been held there before the 2004 Ryder Cup. The legendary Ben Hogan described it as "the greatest test of golf I have ever played."

If anyone still regarded Europe as perennial underdogs in the Ryder Cup, they were put firmly in their place in 2004, because that was the day when the Europeans underlined once and for all everything had changed. Not only did they travel to America and win, but they did so by an almost unthinkable record margin in Michigan, producing their best result of the modern era.

HOW COULD ANYONE HAVE PREDICTED what happened at Oakland Hills over a long weekend in September 2004? Suddenly, the US team, which had dominated the Ryder Cup, realized having the better-ranked players was no longer enough to guarantee victory. The Europeans, led by captain Bernhard Langer, took team play to a new level and in scoring 18.5 points, eclipsed every other side in history since the event was changed in 1979 to include players from continental Europe. The result was the USA's worst defeat, even more so than the 16.5-11.5 mauling at The Belfry in 1985, and set down a marker for Ryder Cups to come. As Colin Montgomerie reflected after victory was sealed, the European team would start off favourites for the first time ever in the next one.

Indeed, it was Monty who was destined to hit the winning putt and enhance his reputation as Europe's Mr Ryder Cup, but every team member played their part as Europe took control in the first session, emerging from Friday's morning Fourballs with a 3.5-0.5 lead. After being given the honour of going out first, Montgomerie rewarded his captain with a typically focused and powerful display. He and Padraig Harrington were up against the formidable partnership of Tiger Woods and Phil Mickelson, who brushed aside rumours that the USA's so-called "dream team" didn't get along – and a titanic battle ensued.

Montgomerie set the tone by birdying the opening hole and the European pair picked up a total of seven birdies in the first eight on their way to an impressive 2 and 1 win. By that time, Darren Clarke and Miguel Angel Jiménez had already put Europe ahead after racing to a 5 and 4 victory over Davis Love and Chad Campbell, while Sergío Garcia and Lee Westwood were already on their way

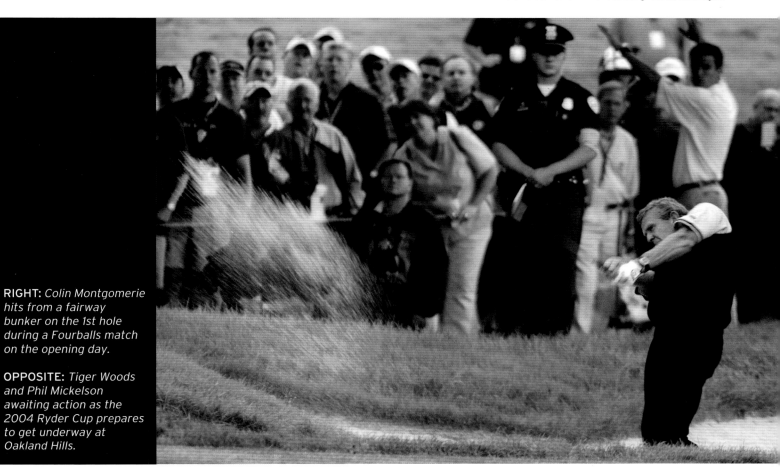

RIGHT: *Colin Montgomerie hits from a fairway bunker on the 1st hole during a Fourballs match on the opening day.*

OPPOSITE: *Tiger Woods and Phil Mickelson awaiting action as the 2004 Ryder Cup prepares to get underway at Oakland Hills.*

to beating David Toms and Jim Furyk, 5 and 3. The USA's only half-point came in a classic tussle between Chris Riley and Stewart Cink against Paul McGinley and rookie Luke Donald, decided at the 18th. With a superb two-iron to the last green, Donald did his best to win it but Riley holed a crucial three-footer to save the USA from losing the session, 4-0. Even so, Langer had a right to be pleased, saying: "I'm thrilled, and so are the players - we wanted to make a fast start and it doesn't get much better than that."

Europe went on to dominate the afternoon Foursomes, too, winning three out of four to finish 6.5-1.5 ahead. Again, Montgomerie and Harrington led the way, making five birdies in the front nine to wipe out Love and Fred Funk, 4 and 2. The Mickelson/Woods partnership continued to be less than the sum of its parts, losing to Clarke/Westwood despite being three-up after five holes. It was all square going into the 18th but a poor tee shot by Mickelson, which veered badly left, resulted in Woods - whose body language revealed his frustration the whole day - having to take a penalty drop. In the end, a bogey five proved enough for Westwood and Clarke to claim their second point of the day, leaving the "dream team" pointless. "Who would have seen that coming?" US captain Sutton later admitted. "And also, who would have seen Davis Love, who played twice today and didn't win a point? You could have owned me today if you'd have wanted to take that bet because I'd bet it all - I'd bet the ranch!"

Everything was going Europe's way. García/Donald beat Perry/Cink, but it wasn't until DiMarco and Haas beat Jiménez/Levet, 3 and 2, that the Americans achieved a full point on the board.

DAY ONE

CAPTAINS

USA: Hal Sutton   **Europe:** Bernhard Langer

FRIDAY MORNING FOURBALLS

Mickelson/Woods *lost to* **Montgomerie/Harrington,** *2 and 1*

Campbell/Love *lost to* **Clarke/Jiménez,** *5 and 4*

Riley/Cink *halved with* **McGinley/Donald**

Toms/Furyk *lost to* **García/Westwood,** *5 and 3*

Session Score: USA 0.5, Europe 3.5

FRIDAY AFTERNOON FOURSOMES

DiMarco/Haas *beat* **Jiménez/Levet,** *3 and 2*

Love/Funk *lost to* **Montgomerie/Harrington,** *4 and 2*

Mickelson/Woods *lost to* **Clarke/Westwood** *by one hole*

Perry/Cink *lost to* **García/Donald,** *2 and 1*

Session Score: 1-3

Overall Score: USA 1.5, Europe 6.5

Europe's Sergio García chips dramatically out of a bunker on Day Two of the 35th Ryder Cup matches at Oakland Hills.

If the USA were to stand any chance of wiping out the bad memories of a miserable Friday, they knew everything must be put right 24 hours later in the second set of Fourballs and Foursomes. After a promising start, this proved a difficult task, though. Certainly, the morning was encouraging, particularly for Tiger Woods, who seemed a different character when partnered with Chris Riley. The pair romped to a convincing 4 and 3 over Darren Clarke and Ian Poulter. Suddenly, there was a glimmer of hope, which the crowd all too readily lapped up with chants of "USA, USA, USA!" reverberating round the course when the possibility of an American comeback looked at least feasible. There were even smiles from Tiger and at one stage it seemed as though a USA whitewash was possible with so much red on the board – especially when Cink and Love III inflicted a rare defeat on Montgomerie, partnered by Harrington.

Europe were not quite done, however for García/Westwood earned a half against Haas/DiMarco and then, crucially, the unheralded partnership of Paul Casey and David Howell came from a hole down, with two to play – and managed to win at the 18th against Furyk/Campbell. No two Europeans playing their first Ryder Cup had ever combined to win a full point since 1979, but that's exactly what Casey and Howell managed to do when the former holed the winning putt on the 18th green.

"Many of you probably thought I'm sacrificing a point when I sent them out, but deep down, I felt that they would be the surprise of the morning," said Langer. "And obviously, I'm very pleased that it happened, especially how it happened. To win the last two holes and gain a huge point for us, that gave us the momentum swing that we were hoping for." Indeed, that late point kept Europe in the driving seat and more importantly, morale was high as Lee Westwood later revealed when he reviewed the day's play. "We all owe David Howell and Paul Casey a beer," he said. "That was the biggest point of the week." US captain Sutton was also pleased with his team's response and at least he knew his players would fight for the trophy – something he may not have been quite so sure of, some 24 hours earlier. He had a quirky way of describing this, too, saying: "The guys played great – I felt their energy. And when I made the telephone call, I didn't get the

SHOT OF THE DAY

Sergio García's putt at the 18th in the morning Fourballs had to be seen to be believed, being all of 45 yards, with 25 feet of break (and a large swale in his line to add to the difficulty). Somehow he timed his shot to perfection as the ball rolled up, down and perfectly into the hole at the end of its momentum for the putt of a lifetime. Even if it was only for a bogey, he sealed a half for the Europeans.

ABOVE: *European players David Howell and Paul Casey look over the 18th green during their morning Fourballs match.*

answering machine: I got them." Unfortunately, when he rang again in the afternoon his players appeared to have gone fishing as Europe won the session, 3-1, to leave themselves 11-5 ahead, requiring only three more points to retain the trophy.

Europe's afternoon haul included three wins, notably a 3 and 2 victory for Irishmen Harrington and McGinley against Woods and Love III. Woods was unrecognizable from the morning, producing a string of errors that included missed putts on the 8th and 9th, as well as a scuffed chip on the 11th. "I basically missed some putts, hit a couple of bad shots and basically put us in a very difficult position to try and win a match," he admitted. "I just didn't have it – it was just not a good time to have that happen." The defeat was crucial because García and Donald won one-up against Furyk and Funk, while Westwood and Clarke cruised to a 5 and 4 victory over DiMarco and Haas. The only American point came from the partnership of Mickelson and Toms, who won 4 and 3 against Jiménez and Levet, but it wasn't enough. Afterwards, Langer again declared himself extremely happy and proud of his team. He also knew the Europeans were on the verge of glory, even if US hero Mickelson refused to admit defeat, insisting: "It would take something exceptional and it's very unlikely, but we won't give up."

DAY TWO

SATURDAY MORNING FOURBALLS

Haas/DiMarco *halved with* **García/Westwood**

Woods/Riley *beat* **Clarke/Poulter,** *4 and 3*

Furyk/Campbell *lost to* **Casey/Howell** *by one hole*

Cink/Love *beat* **Montgomerie/Harrington,** *3 and 2*

Session Score: 2.5-1.5

SATURDAY AFTERNOON FOURSOMES

Haas/DiMarco *lost to* **Clarke/Westwood,** *5 and 4*

Mickelson/Toms *beat* **Jiménez/Levet,** *4 and 3*

Furyk/Funk *lost to* **García/Donald** *by one hole*

Love/Woods *lost to* **Harrington/McGinley,** *4 and 3*

Session Score: 1-3

Overall Score: USA 5, Europe 11

"*We dug our hole deep, but we've got a powerful enough team that we can come out of this hole.*"

Hal Sutton attempts to rally the troops

Considering they were so far behind, it was all the US side could do on the final day at Oakland Hills to come out fighting and they found Bernhard Langer's team ready to do battle. With Tiger Woods scoring an early 3 and 2 victory over Paul Casey and Jim Furyk destroying David Howell, 6 and 4, there was a brief moment of hope for the home team when they gained the momentum. But Europe's team proved strong and ultimately, the talismanic Montgomerie (who had needed a wild card to join the fray after disappointing form in the previous year) was left to execute the winning putt and set up a record victory.

It was 1999 when the 41-year-old Scot last led the European Tour, but something about the Ryder Cup brings out the best in him. As he beat David Toms at the last, he was outstanding and displayed nerves of steel to convert the all-important putt. "Monty, Monty!" chanted the European fans as he strode purposefully up the final fairway in a very different scene to the Brookline of 1999, when a bitter battle with the American galleries left him furious. This time,

however, he had gained the respect – if not the affections, perhaps – of the American public as he proved his mettle just a week after the divorce from his wife Eimear came through and following a year in which his private life had been spread across the English tabloids. But any demons that remained, on or off the course, were swiftly banished as the crowd rose to acclaim him. "It has been a long four months for me personally," he said. "I don't want to talk about it but at the same time, it's quite well known. I have come a long way in those four months – I am proud of myself right now."

This moment of glory was hugely popular in the European ranks, with Paul Casey observing: "For him of all people to hole the putt, it was just perfect and you knew he wouldn't miss." Earlier, the visiting team had at least been made to fight for their victory as US captain Hal Sutton sent out his side in the order in which they had qualified, with Woods giving him a perfect start before former US Open champion Furyk took Howell apart. At one stage the USA were even up in five matches. Slowly but surely, Europe fought

DAY THREE

FINAL DAY SINGLES

Tiger Woods beat **Paul Casey,** 3 and 2

Phil Mickelson lost to **Sergio García,** 3 and 2

Davis Love halved with **Darren Clarke**

Jim Furyk beat **David Howell,** 6 and 4

Kenny Perry lost to **Lee Westwood** by one hole

David Toms lost to **Colin Montgomerie** by one hole

Chad Campbell beat **Luke Donald,** 5 and 3

Chris DiMarco beat **Miguel Angel Jiménez** by one hole

Fred Funk lost to **Thomas Levet** by one hole

Chris Riley lost to **Ian Poulter,** 3 and 2

Jay Haas lost to **Padraig Harrington** by one hole

Stewart Cink lost to **Paul McGinley,** 3 and 2

Session Score: 4.5-7.5

Overall Score: USA 9.5, Europe 18.5

back, with Sergio García providing the inspiration. His 3 and 2 victory over World No. 4 Mickelson was the turning point.

Garcíia, who had never won a singles match in two previous Cups, was two-down after eight holes with a fight on his hands, but the 24-year-old won three holes in a row to completely turn the match around. He won the 13th, too, and clinched an all-important point for his side at the 16th, when Mickelson found the water. "It's important to have that first point for our team," said García. "I was trying not to look at the leaderboards because we didn't start very well, but I really felt I could beat him."

With European spirits back up, the picture quickly transformed. Clarke earned a half against Love and when Westwood beat Perry, coming from two-down to win one-up, Team Europe already knew they would be keeping the trophy – leaving Montgomerie to put the icing on Langer's cake.

Further wins for Levet against Funk, Poulter against Riley, Harrington against Haas and McGinley against Cink made this a record day: the 18.5-9.5 result was the USA's heaviest defeat in the 77-year history of the competition. "We just got outplayed," admitted a disconsolate Sutton. "I made mistakes and I take full responsibility." As for Langer, he was understandably jubilant. "We had so much fun as a team," he said. "I'm so proud of the guys. We were down early and came back strong – they have a lot of heart."

> ❝ *We have beaten one of the strongest American teams ever assembled – a wonderful achievement for everybody involved.* ❞
>
> *Bernhard Langer, European captain*

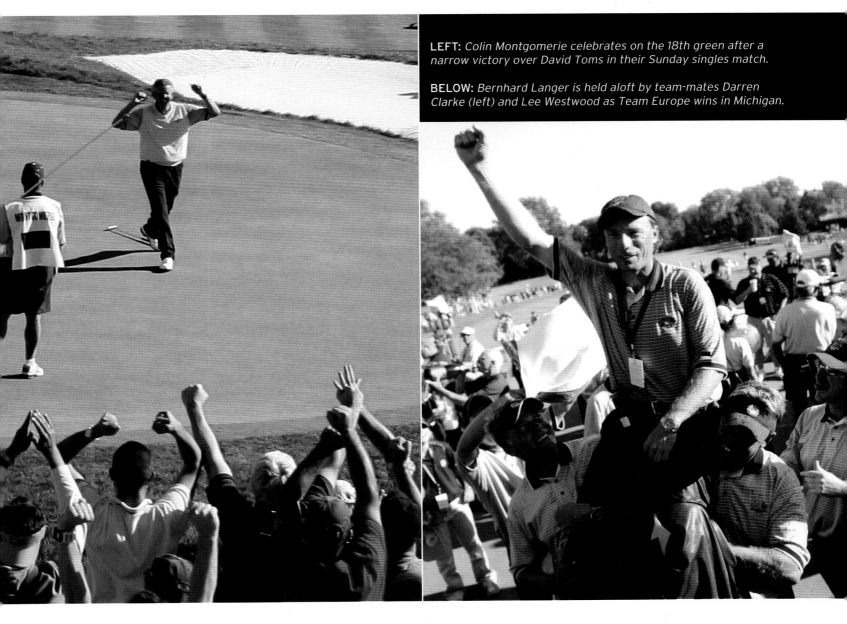

LEFT: *Colin Montgomerie celebrates on the 18th green after a narrow victory over David Toms in their Sunday singles match.*

BELOW: *Bernhard Langer is held aloft by team-mates Darren Clarke (left) and Lee Westwood as Team Europe wins in Michigan.*

Henrik Stenson celebrates holing his putt on the 15th green to beat Vaughn Taylor and win the 2006 Ryder Cup for Europe.

MATCH	HOLE	EUROPE
1		MONTGOMER
2		GARCIA
3		CASEY
4		KARLSSON
5	16	DONALD
6	15	McGINLEY
	15	CLARKE
	14	STENSON
	13	HOWELL
	12	OLAZABAL
	12	WESTWOOD
	10	HARRINGT
	10	

2006

Europe 18.5
USA 9.5

The K Club, County Kildare

September 22-24

THE COURSE

The K Club
Location: County Kildare, Ireland
Par: 72
Yards: 7,335

Owned by Sir Michael Smurfit and designed by Arnold Palmer, the course, 20 miles (32km) southwest of Dublin, only opened in 1991 and having been designed by an American, was expected to suit the US team.

The 36th Ryder Cup has its own place in history after Europe completed a hat-trick of victories by winning at The K Club for the first time in an emotional rollercoaster of a competition. It will be remembered for the vociferous crowds in Ireland, Henrik Stenson's winning putt and for Ian Woosnam's leadership, but most of all this was the story of Darren Clarke.

OVER THE YEARS, there have been many Ryder Cup heroes, both European and American, but few have generated so much empathy and emotion as the man who symbolized the 2006 tournament at The K Club. Northern Irishman Clarke, 38, was a captain's pick for the European team, but arrived in County Kildare little more than a month after the death of his wife Heather from breast cancer, his emotions still raw.

"There was a time when I didn't think I would be able to play," he later admitted in a BBC interview, "but I sat down and deliberated, and weighed up the pros and cons and made my decision to play –

and I'm glad I stuck by it." The European team certainly benefited because Clarke won three out of three before finally breaking down in tears following a 3 and 2 singles victory over US rookie Zach Johnson on the final day, putting Europe 16-8 ahead and on their way to victory.

Right from the start he had been an inspiration to both his team and the crowd – and even his American opponents, who must have sensed his grief. Tiger Woods had lost his father Earl to cancer the same season and must have known just what his rival was going through. Woods had been equally emotional after winning at Hoylake (near Liverpool), nine weeks earlier – his first Major without Earl by his side.

It was clear from the opening day that Clarke would receive tumultuous backing from the Irish crowd. "I'll never forget the reception I was given on the first tee," he said on the opening Friday, having teamed up with Westwood to win against Phil Mickelson and Chris DiMarco in the morning Fourballs. "It was a very, very special moment." He also combined with Westwood – another captain's pick, controversially chosen ahead of Thomas Bjørn – on the Saturday morning to beat Tiger Woods and Jim Furyk, 3 and 2. However, he saved the best until last by triumphing in the singles against Johnson. A birdie at the 5th, a 25-foot birdie putt at the 10th and a remarkable chip from 70 yards at 12 set up a victory to leave him collapsed in tears at the end, falling into the arms of father Godfrey, mother Hetty, sister Andrea and caddie Billy Foster. If it felt like the Darren Clarke Show in that moment, anyone would understand, but it wasn't the Northern Irishman who rolled in the putt to secure the Ryder Cup – that was left to Stenson – and there were plenty of other heroes to celebrate.

On the opening Friday, in a high-octane atmosphere, the action began with old-hand Colin Montgomerie, 43, combining with Harrington to take on Woods and Jim Furyk in a mouthwatering first of the morning Fourballs. But the European pair couldn't quite clinch the early victory they craved, with Woods/Furyk winning one-up to get the Americans off to an encouraging start. The response from the crowd hinted at the emotion and drama to come, however. "That is, without doubt, the noisiest and best reception I've ever had in all the years I've been involved in the Ryder Cup," observed Montgomerie.

In a fiercely and tightly contested opening day, matters improved for the Europeans after this, with Casey/Karlsson halving against Cink/Henry before Spaniards García and Olazábal combined for a hugely impressive 3 and 2 victory over Toms/Wetterich. Clarke and Westwood's narrow win against Mickelson/DiMarco followed to leave the crowd on a high for the afternoon Foursomes, which proved even tighter. The opening three matches were all halved – Irish heroes Harrington/McGinley against Campbell/Johnson; Howell/Stenson v Cink/Toms, with Westwood and Montgomerie against Mickelson/DiMarco. But it took a nerveless putt from Montgomerie – the last of the day – to rescue his pairing from defeat and he was grateful for an outstanding performance from Donald/García, who beat Woods/Furyk by two holes, to keep European spirits high as they ended the day ahead. "To be leading by two points is marvellous and I'm just happy and proud for my guys," said captain Woosnam.

> **" Darren being here was an inspiration in itself and his play was remarkable. "**
>
> *Tiger Woods compliments Darren Clarke's performance, following the recent death of Clarke's wife*

ABOVE: *Sergio García (left) consults with Luke Donald as they play Tiger Woods and Jim Furyk in the opening Foursomes.*

OPPOSITE: *Lee Westwood (right) hugs Darren Clarke after they beat Phil Mickelson and Chris DiMarco (front) in the opening Fourballs.*

DAY ONE

CAPTAINS

Europe: Ian Woosnam   **USA:** Tom Lehman

FRIDAY MORNING FOURBALLS

Harrington/Montgomerie *lost to* **Woods/Furyk** *by one hole*

Casey/Karlsson *halved with* **Cink/Henry**

García/Olazábal *beat* **Toms/Wetterich**, *3 and 2*

Clarke/Westwood *beat* **Mickelson/DiMarco** *by one hole*

Session Score: 2.5-1.5

FRIDAY AFTERNOON FOURSOMES

Harrington/McGinley *halved with* **Campbell/Johnson**

Howell/Stenson *halved with* **Cink/Toms**

Westwood/Montgomerie *halved with* **Mickelson/DiMarco**

Donald/Garcia *beat* **Woods/Furyk** *by two holes*

Session Score: 2.5-1.5

Overall Score: Europe 5, USA 3

> **"He might be a short man, but he's got a huge heart and he's just been awesome."**
>
> *Sergio García assesses captain*
> *Ian Woosnam's contribution*

All the galleries could talk about on Day Two of the 2006 Ryder Cup was Paul Casey's hole-in-one at the 14th but this turned out to be just one highlight in another excellent day's golf for the European side, who won both morning and afternoon sessions to go 10-6 ahead. Sergio García must take a large slice of the credit for having twice won on the opening day and repeated the trick to make it four from four by the end of Saturday.

The action commenced with Cink/Henry holding Casey/Karlsson to a very tight half (although perhaps rookie J.J. Henry deserved to win with an eagle at the par-five 16th). But Garcia's fluent display as he partnered Olazábal to a 3 and 2 victory over Mickelson/DiMarco set Europe on their way in a match that saw World No. 2 Mickelson appear worryingly off-colour. It was the same for World No. 1 Woods, who was particularly wayward as he partnered World No. 3 Furyk in a 3 and 2 defeat against Clarke/Westwood. True to the fairytale, it was Clarke who sealed victory with a chip at the 16th to add to Tiger's problems. The result left the American legend with a record of 13 defeats in 23 Ryder Cup matches and his performance was so disappointing that rumours began to circulate that the great man could even be dropped for the afternoon Foursomes.

In the event he went on to defy the critics in teaming up once more with Furyk to produce an excellent 3 and 2 victory over Harrington/McGinley. Meanwhile, US captain Lehman was adamant that he had never considered leaving his star man out of the team, admitting: "I don't know how you can sit down the best player in the world – that's impossible!" Whatever the truth, he was proved correct in his decision to stick by his man as Woods dramatically improved his driving and short game to post a crucial victory, even if Europe remained four points in the lead by the end

LEFT: *Paul Casey (right) celebrates his hole-in-one on the 14th hole with David Howell during the afternoon Foursomes.*

SHOT OF THE DAY

Paul Casey's sensational hole-in-one at the 14th was an easy pick for Shot of the Day, making its appearance during a 5 and 4 victory over Stewart Cink and Zach Johnson. The 29-year-old Englishman, only recently crowned World Match Play champion, sent his tee-shot 213 yards straight to the pin. To put this achievement into perspective, it was only the fifth hole-in-one in Ryder Cup history and the first since his fellow Englishman, Howard Clark, in 1995. Other Ryder Cup "aces" came from Costantino Rocca (1995), Nick Faldo (1993) and Peter Butler (1973). Twenty-four hours after Casey's effort, Scott Verplank became the first American to complete the same feat.

of play. As Furyk insisted, it was a long way for the side to come back but they had done it before and the point definitely helped.

It didn't look good for the Americans, though, and especially not after García/Donald beat Mickelson/Toms, 2 and 1. Casey – including that hole-in-one – joined forces with Howell to beat Cink/Johnson by a huge 5 and 4. With Montgomerie/Westwood earning a half against Campbell/Taylor, it was once again Europe and Woosnam's afternoon.

It did not go unnoticed, especially by the Americans, that every one of the 12 European players contributed to their points total during the first two days, which perhaps underlines the strength of Woosnam's team. "I'm delighted to have 10 points at this stage," he declared. "I think I played every single player again and as I said yesterday, everybody's added a half a point or a point. We came here playing as a team and we're still playing as a team – and that's what we intend tomorrow."

As far as Lehman was concerned, he knew the writing was on the wall but wasn't about to give up the ghost just yet, with the singles still to come. "There were a lot of tight matches and the difference was we didn't make a lot of putts," he insisted. "But we need to look at the positives because some of the guys played very well today. It's a pretty fine line between zero points, half a point or one point."

DAY TWO

SATURDAY MORNING FOURBALLS

Casey/Karlsson *halved with* **Cink/Henry**

García/Olazábal *beat* **Mickelson/DiMarco,** *3 and 2*

Clarke/Westwood *beat* **Woods/Furyk,** *3 and 2*

Stenson/Harrington *lost to* **Verplank/Johnson,** *2 and 1*

Session Score: 2.5-1.5

SATURDAY AFTERNOON FOURSOMES

García/Donald *beat* **Mickelson/Toms,** *2 and 1*

Montgomerie/Westwood *halved with* **Campbell/Taylor**

Casey/Howell *beat* **Cink/Johnson,** *5 and 4*

Harrington/McGinley *lost to* **Furyk/Woods,** *3 and 2*

Session Score: 2.5-1.5

Overall Score: Europe 10, USA 6

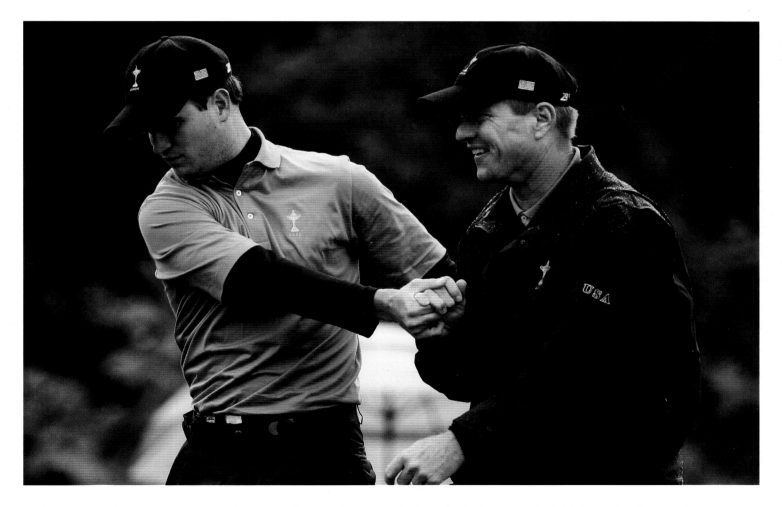

ABOVE: *Zach Johnson is congratulated on his putt on the 15th green by team-mate Scott Verplank (right) during Saturday's Fourballs.*

The final day of the 36th Ryder Cup dawned with Europe in a strong position, four points ahead. With home fans already dreaming of the prize, it came as no surprise when Colin Montgomerie was sent out first to seize the advantage. As so often the Scot did his job to perfection, producing a string of impressive iron shots to win one-up against David Toms. Wonderful approach shots to the 3rd and 4th holes gave him birdies and following this, he sealed victory with a nerve-racking up-and-down bunker shot on the 18th to extend his unbeaten run to eight singles matches. That stoic performance set the tone for Europe, who went on to complete a memorable victory.

The Americans did have a hero in Stewart Cink, however, who made four birdies in the first five against an in-form García – who had won six straight matches in the Ryder Cup. Cink crowned his performance in holing a 50-foot putt at the 12th before winning, 4 and 3, to keep US hopes alive. Woods then beat Robert Karlsson, 3 and 2, in his best display of the tournament, although Karlsson contributed to his own downfall in driving into the lake at the 15th; also sending his second shot in the water at the 16th. While Woods had won three points – his best total in Ryder Cup golf in five attempts – for him, this was no celebration. "I'm not real happy," he declared. "I'm 1-4 in Ryder Cups and it doesn't sit well, nor should it! They just outplayed us." Indeed, his performance was one of few positives for the USA as Europe continued their inexorable drive to glory, with Casey winning 2 and 1 against Furyk, and Howell beating Brett Wetterich, 5 and 4.

In the Singles, Tiger Woods managed to beat Robert Karlsson, 3 and 2, despite seeing his nine-iron dropped in a lake! Woods had asked caddie Steve Williams to clean the club alongside the 7th green, but he stumbled and dropped it in the water. "The

DAY THREE

FINAL DAY SINGLES

Colin Montgomerie *beat* **David Toms** *by one hole*

Sergio García *lost to* **Stewart Cink,** *4 and 3*

Paul Casey *beat* **Jim Furyk,** *2 and 1*

Robert Karlsson *lost to* **Tiger Woods,** *3 and 2*

Luke Donald *beat* **Chad Campbell,** *2 and 1*

Paul McGinley *halved with* **J.J. Henry**

Darren Clarke *beat* **Zach Johnson,** *3 and 2*

Henrik Stenson *beat* **Vaughn Taylor,** *4 and 3*

David Howell *beat* **Brett Wetterich,** *5 and 4*

José María Olazábal *beat* **Phil Mickelson,** *2 and 1*

Lee Westwood *beat* **Chris DiMarco** *by two holes*

Padraig Harrington *lost to* **Scott Verplank,** *4 and 3*

Session Score: 8.5-3.5

Overall Score: Europe 18.5, USA 9.5

ball got muddy," explained Woods. "I handed it to Stevie and he was going to rinse the nine-iron as well. He was dipping the towel and slipped on a rock. It was either him or the nine-iron – and he chose the nine-iron!"

It was England's Luke Donald, in the fifth singles tie, who would ensure the trophy was retained after beating Chad Campbell, 2 and 1, on the 17th green. With so many players still on course, a European victory was assured – and the fairytale was for Clarke to make the winning putt. It nearly came true but as the people's hero played his approach shot on the 16th, Swede Henrik Stenson was holing from seven feet on the 15th against to seize the glory moment for himself. Not that it mattered, of course – the victory was as sweet as it could possibly be for Europe and Clarke still received a thunderous reception after his match ended at the 16th when his putt fell just short. Generously, Johnson lifted his marker to concede, 3 and 2. The celebrations that followed were vivid, frenetic and deafening.

Almost inevitably as the adrenalin seeped away, Clarke broke down in tears and players from both teams rushed in to console him – US captain Lehman and Tiger Woods among them as thousands of fans ran up the fairway to join the party. "Darren, you hurt us so bad, but we're so glad you're on this team!" Lehman told him later. A record-equalling winning margin was completed as McGinley halved with J.J. Henry, Olazábal beat Mickelson, 2 and 1; Westwood, despite complaining of feeling ill, beat DiMarco by two holes.

For the USA, the only consolation was a mesmerizing display from Verplank as he beat Harrington, 4 and 3, including a hole-in-one at the 14th. But the celebrations were all about Europe – and Clarke. Towards the end, Woosnam lifted his hero's arm into the air like a victorious boxer and it must be said, Clarke had fought harder than most for that special moment. As to be expected of a Ryder Cup in Ireland, the post-match celebrations were something to behold, with Clarke downing a pint of Guinness on the balcony. He was swiftly followed – and matched – by Woosnam. US captain Lehman was fulsome in his praise for such impressive opponents, saying: "I don't think there's ever been a European team which has played better."

> **"***Our team came ready, but maybe we weren't quite ready enough.***"**
>
> *US captain Tom Lehman reflects on defeat*

BELOW: *A show of unity as Tiger Woods and Phil Mickelson walk off the 18th green following a match in 2004.*

Ryder Cup legends
Tiger **WOODS** and Phil **MICKELSON**

Quite simply, Tiger Woods is one of the greatest golfers ever to have lived, while Phil Mickelson is the player who has challenged him hardest, yet it is one of sport's great mysteries why neither has been able to dominate the Ryder Cup in the same way as every other competition.

Woods remains one of the biggest draws of the Ryder Cup. But his record in the competition is at best mixed and at worst, hugely disappointing: 14 points from 29. In turn, Mickelson has lost more Ryder Cup matches - 17 out of 34 - than any other American in history. Woods has won 71 times, including 14 Majors, on the PGA Tour and Mickelson has secured four Majors and a total of 39 events on tour, so the pair must be regarded as the heavyweights of Team USA, having spent much of the modern era as the World's No. 1 and 2. So, what happens when they pull on a Ryder Cup shirt?

Perhaps Woods, 10 times PGA Player of the Year, is so driven to concentrate on his own game that when playing in pairs, he loses a little of his edge. And whisper it, but maybe he prefers playing in individual tournaments than for Team USA. He once infuriated team-mates in suggesting he had "a million reasons" (first-prize money) to prefer the WGC-American Express tournament to the Ryder Cup. But one story ahead of the 2010 event suggested Woods took the team's rookie players aside, lecturing them on just how special the Ryder Cup is. It's obvious he cares and as he grows older, his record appears only to improve.

Maybe he has simply been unlucky over the years. In only his second year as a pro, he was part of the US team of 1997. He has played in six tournaments, losing five. Mickelson has had similar difficulties. A veteran of eight Ryder Cups, "Lefty" (a moniker borne out of his distinctive swing) has won the trophy just twice.

In 1997, the pair endured mixed fortunes as Mickelson and Davis Love lost to José María Olazábal and Costantino Rocca in the morning Fourballs, while Mark O'Meara and Woods lost to the indomitable duo of Bernhard Langer and Colin Montgomerie in the afternoon Foursomes. Woods lost again to Rocca in the singles, but Mickelson at least kept the USA in it after beating the dangerous Darren Clarke. Two years later, they enjoyed success when both scored victories in the singles to help the USA win 14.5 to 13.5, but the all-time low must be 2004, when the duo first played together for the USA and were billed a "dream team". It didn't prove that way for they barely talked as they lost in both the Friday Foursomes - Clarke and Westwood reigning supreme - as well as the Fourballs (where they went down, 2 and 1, to Montgomerie/Harrington). Stony faces all round - and they have never since been paired.

Mickelson can at least claim to have played a large part in the victory of 2008, when he became the highest-ranked player in the US side. Playing with Anthony Kim, the pair beat Harrington and McDowell in the Friday afternoon Fourballs, having claimed a half in the Foursomes against Harrington/Karlsson. But he was off-colour at Celtic Manor in 2010, losing the first three matches before sealing his first point in the singles against Peter Hanson. There were signs, though, that Tiger was coming to terms with the format, finishing top points-scorer for the USA and ending with a singles win over Francesco Molinari. Has Woods at last found a way to love the Ryder Cup? Maybe we'll find out in Illinois. One thing is for certain: the crowds will still be chanting his name.

> **"***It's just so neat to be a part of a team and quite frankly, we don't get to do it very often.***"**
>
> *Tiger Woods on the Ryder Cup*

RYDER CUP RECORD

Tiger WOODS
Ryder Cups: 1997, 1999 (winner), 2002, 2004, 2006, 2010
Total wins: 1
Matches: 29 (won 13, halved 2, lost 14)
Total points: 13

Phil MICKELSON
Ryder Cups: 1995, 1997, 1999 (winner), 2002, 2004, 2006, 2008 (winner), 2010
Total wins: 2
Matches: 34 (won 11, halved 6, lost 17)
Total points: 14

AS A PAIR:
Matches: 2 (won 0, halved 0, lost 2)
Points: 0

2008
USA 16.5
Europe 11.5

Valhalla Golf Club, Kentucky

September 19-21

THE COURSE

Valhalla Golf Club
Location: Louisville, Kentucky, USA
Par: 70
Yards: 7,198

Named after the great hall described in Norse mythology, where the souls of Vikings feasted and celebrated with the gods, Valhalla Golf Club became only the third course in the US ever to host a PGA Championship, a Senior PGA Championship and a Ryder Cup.

Valhalla will be remembered - after three successive defeats - as the time when the USA fought back to reassert their authority by recording their biggest victory since 1981. Perhaps just as importantly, under the leadership of captain Paul Azinger and with the introduction of a collection of enthusiastic rookies, it was the moment when America finally rediscovered the joy of the Ryder Cup.

IF THE RYDER CUP WAS BEGINNING to fill some Americans with a sense of foreboding by 2008, then it was perhaps understandable. Three European victories in a row, the last two by record margins, had seen them lose the sense of excitement and child-like enthusiasm that seemed to grip their opponents every two years. But Paul Azinger changed all that in leading his team to a 16.5-11.5 victory during which, for the first time ever, the US led after every session. This was no fluke: it came down to a desire to completely alter the atmosphere surrounding the Team USA.

Azinger wanted his side to enjoy playing Ryder Cup golf and he was also keen for the crowd to get involved. Having campaigned for the right to be given four captain's picks instead of two, he made a point of choosing local boy J.B. Holmes, who joined another Kentucky golfer, Kenny Perry, in the team. Following this, he began his genius "13th man" campaign, even having T-shirts printed up with the slogan.

LEFT: *Rival captains Paul Azinger (left) of the USA and Nick Faldo of Europe pose with the Ryder Cup trophy in Kentucky in 2008.*

OPPOSITE: Justin Leonard celebrates after chipping in to beat Sergio García and Miguel Angel Jiménez on the opening day.

"The fans in Kentucky can be the 13th man," Azinger said. "They're rabid fans, they understand rivalries – they serve alcohol there so anything is possible. But my message really will be simply that I want the crowd to be completely into it." His campaign proved remarkable. The players threw 10,000 lapel pins into the galleries when the team arrived to play practice rounds on Tuesday; they also fired T-shirts out of a cannon in downtown Louisville and attended a Ryder Cup pep rally on the Thursday.

Azinger was unable to pick Tiger Woods, who was still recovering from knee surgery, but he was helped by the high-spirited Boo Weekley, who was adopted by Kentucky fans as one of their own – especially as, at the very first hole he galloped down the fairway using his driver as a toy horse, whipping his butt as he went! The gallery roared their approval and continued to do so from then on.

Kentucky boy Perry, who at 48 had dedicated his season to qualifying for a "home" Ryder Cup, also shone, but the selection of Holmes, ranked 56th in the world, proved an inspiration as he remained unbeaten – winning twice and halving his other match. Despite such focused preparation, it was Europe who started faster, taking the lead in all four matches in Friday's morning Foursomes. Azinger's side, along with the home crowd, however, were not ready to back down and by the end of the morning held a 3-1 lead.

Leonard and Mahan were unplayable in their 3 and 2 victory over Stenson/Casey, while Cink/Campbell clinched the narrowest of victories over Rose/Poulter before Perry/Furyk halved against Westwood/García. But the session was symbolized by the performance of Phil Mickelson and Anthony Kim, a veteran-and-rookie combination typifying the way Azinger wanted the game played. They were three-down against Harrington/Karlsson, but rescued a half at the last. Mickelson's verdict on his new partner was fascinating, saying: "His youthfulness, his excitement, exuberance is infectious and I was very fortunate to be able to spend the day with him. We had a lot of fun playing together."

Fun? Things were certainly looking up for the US side as the afternoon Fourballs proved. Europe might have been ahead in three out of four matches after the first nine, but were unable to hole-out and won just one. And so it was that the Americans took their largest lead on the first day since Europe joined the fray in 1979.

As well as Mickelson/Kim, who won an astonishing match, 2 and 1 against Harrington/McDowell, there were victories for Leonard/Mahan and a half for Holmes/Weekley to leave the score 5.5-2.5 in the home team's favour. This particular Ryder Cup was not going to be like the last three.

> **❝My cheeks are sore from smiling all day. ❞**
>
> *Justin Leonard sums up the spirit in the US camp*

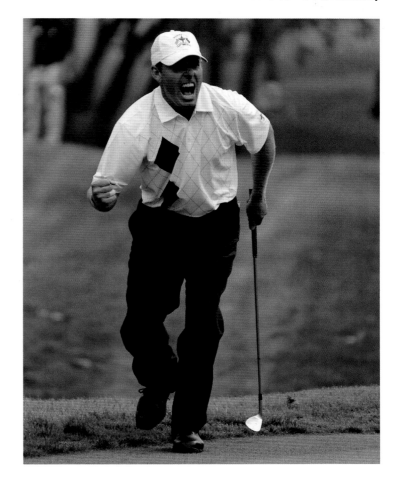

DAY ONE

CAPTAINS

USA: Paul Azinger   **Europe:** Nick Faldo

FRIDAY MORNING FOURSOMES

Mickelson/Kim *halved* **Harrington/Karlsson**

Leonard/Mahan *beat* **Stenson/Casey**, *3 and 2*

Cink/Campbell *beat* **Rose/Poulter** *by one hole*

Perry/Furyk *halved* **Westwood/García**

Session Score: 3-1

FRIDAY AFTERNOON FOURBALLS

Mickelson/Kim *beat* **Harrington/McDowell** *by two holes*

Stricker/Curtis *lost to* **Poulter/Rose**, *4 and 2*

Leonard/Mahan *beat* **García/Jiménez**, *4 and 3*

Holmes/Weekley *halved* **Westwood/Hansen**

Session Score: 2.5-1.5

Overall Score: USA 5.5, Europe 2.5

ABOVE: *Nick Faldo (left) stands behind the USA's Stewart Cink and Chad Campbell (right) during Saturday's Foursomes.*

Europe knew they must do something special on the second day at Valhalla to force their way back into the match – but no one expected captain Nick Faldo to rest his biggest names, Lee Westwood and Sergio García, in order to achieve this. Both men were stood down for the morning Foursomes, raising eyebrows either side of the Atlantic. Westwood (unbeaten in 12 Ryder Cup matches) was said to be suffering from blisters and García (who had previously never lost a Foursomes match) was fatigued, but if Faldo was bracing himself for criticism, then he was saved by the performance of the players he did select. They were led by Ryder Cup debutant Oliver Wilson, who teamed up with Henrik Stenson for a remarkable victory over Mickelson/Kim.

After six holes, the European pairing were four-down but came back to win 2 and 1, going ahead for the first time at the 15th, when Mickelson drove into the trees and Kim fired his approach into the water. And Wilson sealed the point in some style, converting a 20-foot birdie putt at the 17th.

Faldo was further justified when his captain's pick, Ian Poulter – a choice that had caused great controversy back home – shone alongside Justin Rose in a 4 and 3 victory over Cink/Campbell. Meanwhile, Jiménez and Graeme McDowell managed to claim a half against Leonard/Mahan. Kenny Perry and Jim Furyk were the only US pair to win: 3 and 1 victors over the out-of-touch Harrington (subsequently rested for the afternoon Fourballs) and Karlsson. "It was a much better morning," said Faldo. "The United States had their day but we are here in good spirits. This is a physical and mental battle and I believe with what we have seen that you need to give guys a rest. We came off the road a bit and now we're back on it."

The afternoon session would prove even more dramatic and even tighter – in fact, three of the four Fourballs matches went to the 18th as both sides battled to claim two points each, eventually leaving the US just 9-7 ahead. Indeed, the Europeans were so impressive that the fact that Azinger's side were still able to

DAY TWO

SATURDAY MORNING FOURSOMES

Cink/Campbell *lost to* **Poulter/Rose,** *4 and 3*

Leonard/Mahan *halved with* **Jiménez/McDowell**

Mickelson/Kim *lost to* **Stenson/Wilson,** *2 and 1*

Furyk/Perry *beat* **Harrington/Karlsson,** *3 and 1*

Session Score: 1.5-2.5

SATURDAY AFTERNOON FOURBALLS

Weekley/Holmes *beat* **Westwood/Hansen,** *2 and 1*

Curtis/Stricker *halved with* **García/Casey**

Perry/Furyk *lost to* **Poulter/McDowell** *by one hole*

Mickelson/Mahan *halved with* **Stenson/Karlsson**

Session Score: 2-2

Overall Score: USA 9, Europe 7

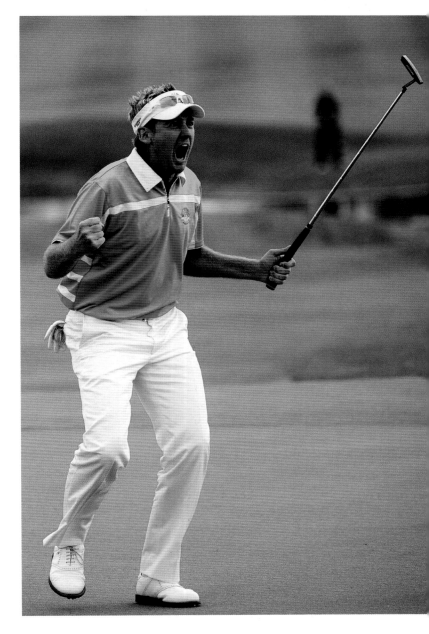

take one-and-a-half points from the session was an achievement, eventually setting up the opportunity for overall victory. Just as in the morning, it was controversial wild card Poulter who led the charge. Paired with debutant Graeme McDowell, he posted a victory at the last over hometown heroes, Perry and Furyk. The European duo were never behind, although McDowell had to sink two pressure putts at 15 and 16 to preserve the lead and when Poulter drained a 14-footer for a birdie at the 17th before knocking in the decisive putt to win the match at the last, he was naturally elated. "Sinking that putt at the last was a special moment," he said. "What a day! G-Mac [Graeme McDowell] played awesome. To play as well as I have played, I'm speechless. I am so proud to be here as one of Nick's picks – I felt I had to do something this week."

He would end the weekend as the top points scorer on either side, which says a lot about his character and determination. However, Poulter's run would not end with a trophy; this was partly down to Boo Weekley and J.B. Holmes edging Westwood and Dane Hansen, 2 and 1 in the opening match of the afternoon. It was a result that kept the US ahead and ended Westwood's long unbeaten record in the Ryder Cup, stretching back 12 matches.

Sweden's Robert Karlsson paired with compatriot Henrik Stenson and hit four birdies in the closing seven holes to secure a half against Phil Mickelson and Hunter Mahan, but perhaps the key result in terms of overall score was Steve Stricker and Ben Curtis battling to halve against Casey/García. The match was so close – 16 out of the 18 holes were halved – and inevitably culminated in dramatic scenes at the last. Europe must have believed they were set for victory when the US found the rough with their approach but Stricker's up-and-down 18-foot birdie putt turned that assumption around – in fact, Casey had to hole a nervy 10-footer to secure a half. "They played really well and never gave us anything," said Casey afterwards. "We would have wanted a full point, but we did well to get a half from a fantastic match."

ABOVE: *Europe's Ian Poulter looks ecstatic after holing a birdie putt on the 18th green during the afternoon Fourballs.*

SHOT OF THE DAY

Boo Weekley conjured up an amazing shot from halfway down the 15th to leave his ball within 2 feet of the pin in an afternoon Fourballs battle against Westwood and Hansen. When later asked if this was his best-ever shot, Weekley replied: "I'd have to say number nine because I've had eight holes-in-one." Team Europe didn't seem quite so impressed, though. Westwood refused to concede the putt, to which Kentucky fans responded with a chorus of boos. That's Ryder Cup rivalry for you.

As if to underline patriotic fervour, the US team - who had worn white on the Friday and blue on the Saturday - announced they would be sporting red on Sunday. Captain Paul Azinger urged their supporters to strengthen the atmosphere as the US attempted to win back the Ryder Cup for the first time since 1999. They certainly responded, although not everyone was pleased by the response, with Lee Westwood saying: "Some people don't know the difference between supporting their team and abusing the opposition - I have been abused from start to finish." But in the end, the US victory was so convincing and so compelling any criticism became lost in the celebrations.

As holders, Europe needed seven points to retain the trophy and the US 5.5 to claim it back. In this, they were helped by a controversial decision from Faldo, who put his star men Harrington, Westwood and Poulter in the final three singles pairings, but found the result was over before they could make an impact. Setting the tone, Anthony Kim thrashed García, 5 and 4, in the first match, and the US won seven of the 12 singles matches on a remarkable day of American celebrations. Perry, Weekley, J.B. Holmes, Furyk, Curtis and Campbell were the other victors, while debutant Mahan halved with Casey. For Europe, the only bright spots were the wins for Karlsson, Rose, McDowell and Poulter.

It was Europe's worse defeat since Walton Heath in 1981, when they were beaten 18.5-9.5, and Faldo was bound to receive criticism although his players were quick to respond, with Westwood saying: "We hold the golf clubs, we hit the shots, not the captain." Rookie Kim, 23, summed up why the Americans had performed so well. Decked in a glitzy, gaudy belt, with USA in red, white and blue letters on the buckle, he displayed confidence bordering on cockiness as he beat García, 5 and 4.

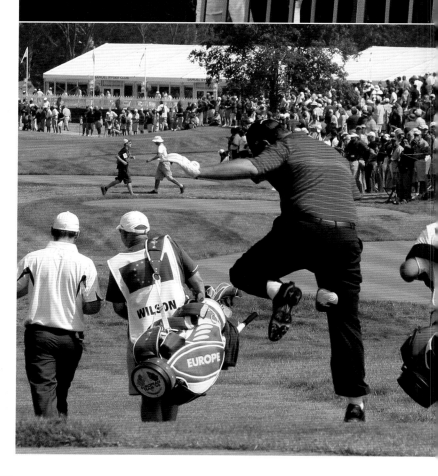

RIGHT: *The entire US team appears on the clubhouse balcony to celebrate a famous victory in 2008.*

BELOW: *Boo Weekley of the USA lives up to his billing as team jester and cheerleader as he "rides" his golf club down the fairway at the 1st tee.*

DAY THREE

FINAL DAY SINGLES

Anthony Kim *beat* **Sergio García,** *5 and 4*

Hunter Mahan *halved with* **Paul Casey**

Justin Leonard *lost to* **Robert Karlsson,** *5 and 3*

Phil Mickelson *lost to* **Justin Rose,** *3 and 2*

Kenny Perry *beat* **Henrik Stenson,** *3 and 2*

Boo Weekley *beat* **Oliver Wilson,** *4 and 2*

J.B. Holmes *beat* **Søren Hansen,** *2 and 1*

Jim Furyk *beat* **Miguel Angel Jiménez,** *2 and 1*

Stewart Cink *lost to* **Graeme McDowell,** *2 and 1*

Steve Stricker *lost to* **Ian Poulter,** *3 and 2*

Ben Curtis *beat* **Lee Westwood,** *2 and 1*

Chad Campbell *beat* **Padraig Harrington,** *2 and 1*

Session Score: 7.5-4.5

Overall Score: USA 16.5, Europe 11.5

With the US three points ahead, Europe needed to make an impact – and quickly. But although they rallied briefly, with Karlsson playing superbly to beat Leonard with four birdies in a 5 and 3 triumph, this wasn't enough. Justin Rose added a comfortable 3 and 2 victory over a surprisingly subdued Mickelson, crowning the win with an 18-foot birdie putt at the 15th and Casey added a battling half against Mahan. The US middle order proved too strong from that point on, though.

Home hero Perry, playing in front of packed galleries full of family and friends, including his 84-year-old grandfather Ken Snr., was an emotional winner on a course where he once blew a two-shot lead on the 18th during the final round of the 1996 PGA Championship. But history was not about to repeat itself for he beat Stenson, 3 and 2 in a round that included seven birdies and an eagle. Afterwards, he excitedly declared: "I said this was going to define my career, but you know what, it made my career!"

The effervescent Boo Weekley revelled in the drama of beating Oliver Wilson, 4 and 2, and when home hero J.B. Holmes again fed off his team-mate's energy, he too produced a result to remember. The captain's pick, selected partly because of his huge hitting on a course that suited his style, won 2 and 1 against Søren Hansen to put the US within touching distance of victory. That honour fell to old-hand Furyk as he recorded a 2 and 1 victory over Spain's Miguel Angel Jiménez to claim the trophy.

With the celebrations in full swing, the US added further wins for Curtis and Campbell. Captain Azinger observed: "It was amazing – the golf was spectacular on both sides and our guys came out on top. I'm just emotional. We had a plan and stuck to it." The USA's unlikely mix of rookies, youngsters and veterans – together with their vociferous 13th man – had done it. And boy, did Kentucky celebrate.

> **"***It is the best day of my golfing life – I wouldn't trade this for $10m.***"**
>
> *Anthony Kim, after beating Sergio García*

Ryder Cup legends
Darren **CLARKE**
and Lee **WESTWOOD**

Sometimes great friends make great partnerships: in business, in life and in golf. And in Ryder Cup terms, there are not many greater friends or better partnerships than Darren Clarke and Lee Westwood, who have shared some incredible moments in the Ryder Cup.

It's clear that Clarke and Westwood are a double act, both on the greens and off them, with so much banter after years of sharing the ups and downs of the golf circuit and an in-depth knowledge of each other's game. When they combined to such great effect in the Foursomes of the 2004 Ryder Cup, Clarke summed it up perfectly, saying: "We know each other's game so well: we play practice rounds with each other, we've got complete trust in each other. It doesn't matter where we hit it, we know the other player and what they're capable of doing."

But Clarke never needed a friend more than in 2006 when he performed so brilliantly at The K Club in Ireland, just six weeks after the untimely death of his wife, Heather. And when he collapsed, triumphant, into the arms of Ian Woosnam on the 16th green on the final day, golf united in mutual respect and admiration for one of its most popular characters. The fact that Clarke even accepted Woosnam's wild card invitation was surprising in itself. Yet it was the way that the Northern Irishman played that truly took everyone's breath away. From the moment he took to the first tee with Westwood in Friday's Fourballs, it was clear that he was at the centre of something special. The applause took minutes to die down, but he was focused and on form while

Phil Mickelson and Chris DiMarco were beaten by one hole. On the Saturday, Tiger Woods and Jim Furyk went down, 3 and 2, as Clarke was simply inspired, winning three out of the four holes he and Westwood claimed during the session. And, finally, of course, he won his singles against Zach Johnson on the Sunday to help Europe to an emotional victory.

Since making his debut in 1997, Clarke had not missed a single Ryder Cup, winning 11.5 points in 20 matches, and much of his success comes down to the strength of his partnership with Westwood. The second most prolific partnership in Ryder Cup history, they won six points from eight matches together - the only two defeats coming in 1999.

Great friends off the course - they even share the same manager - the two men's games complement each other. Yet no one could ever be fooled into thinking they were anything other than fierce competitors, a fact that would not diminish even when Clarke acted as vice-captain in 2010 - if anything, each shot seemed to mean more to him than when he was the one with a club in hand. But he and Westwood know what it means to be victorious in the Ryder Cup arena, with the latter's achievements

RYDER CUP RECORD

Darren CLARKE
Ryder Cups: 1997 (winner), 1999, 2002 (winner), 2004 (winner), 2006 (winner)
Total wins: 4
Matches: 20 (won 10, halved 3, lost 7)
Total points: 11.5

Lee WESTWOOD
Ryder Cups: 1997 (winner), 1999, 2002 (winner), 2004 (winner), 2006 (winner), 2008, 2010 (winner)
Total wins: 5
Matches: 33 (won 16, halved 6, lost 11)
Total points: 19

AS A PAIR:
Matches: 8 (won 6, halved 0, lost 2)
Points: 6

> *"I think it helps if you're really good friends – if you hit a bad shot, you don't feel too bad."*
>
> *Lee Westwood on his partnership with Darren Clarke*

particularly outstanding. He might be only the eighth-highest scoring European of all time, with 19 points, but having ended Tiger Woods' reign as World No. 1, Westwood was always at the forefront of European ambition. He made his debut in 1997, partnering Nick Faldo before being teamed up with Clarke, two years later. The only time they have not been picked together was in 2002, but even then it was a triumph for Westwood, who won three of his four matches alongside Sergio García.

Two years later, the best was yet to come when Westwood was sensational. Twice partnering Clarke and twice playing alongside García, the Englishman took three-and-a-half points going into his singles match against Kenny Perry. It was a tight affair, but Europe were on their way to their biggest-ever win and it was Westwood who sunk the putt to seal victory and take Europe's tally to 14, ensuring they would retain the Ryder Cup. Since then his game has gone from strength to strength. He was unbeaten in 2006, taking four points from his five matches. Now all that's missing in his career is a Major; and when Darren Clarke won the British Open in 2011, aged 42, his first thought was for his great friend. "I hope he's next," he mused. "Of all people, I think Lee Westwood deserves something to be given to him – I'm sure Lee will win Majors."

2010
Europe 14.5
USA 13.5

Celtic Manor Resort, Newport

October 1-4

The sun may have been shining when Graeme McDowell won the trophy for Europe, but the 37th Ryder Cup will be remembered for the rain that lashed down in Wales, forcing the tournament into a "Magic Monday" for the first time and in the process causing it to become one of the most dramatic and close-fought competitions in history. Maybe, just maybe, it was Colin Montgomerie's greatest moment, too.

WHAT A LONG WEEKEND IT WAS – and what a story. In the end, Europe won by just one point, sealed in the very last singles match of the day at the 17th green – and not since 1991 at Kiawah Island had the Ryder Cup seen anything like it.

McDowell showed incredible mettle to birdie a 20-foot putt at the 16th when he knew only a victory there would prevent the US from holding on to their trophy. Then, when his opponent Hunter Mahan conceded after scuffing his putt at the par-three 17th, the crowd of 35,000 celebrated a famous victory. Such moments of drama prove that McDowell, who had clinched his first Major at the US Open earlier in the same year, truly does have nerves of steel. And it showed, too, that Ryder Cup legend Montgomerie, who had led his team to so many glorious triumphs as a player,

was every bit as inspirational and talismanic in the role of captain. Indeed, the sheer enthusiasm, energy and stature of the man seemed to spur Europe on as the famous team spirit that had served them so well in the past once again proved a key factor – especially as Montgomerie chose legends Thomas Bjørn, Darren Clarke, Sergio García, Paul McGinley and José María Olazábal as vice-captains and made good use of them.

Corey Pavin's US team, with Rickie Fowler impressive on debut and Tom Lehman and Davis Love among the vice-captains, put up a good fight. Indeed, there was a glimmer of hope that we were in for a series of close-fought tournaments in the future.

Tiger Woods, who had missed out on the tournament in 2008 through a knee injury, was back and suddenly finding his Ryder

ABOVE: *US star Phil Mickelson braves the rain as a downpour disrupts play on the opening day of the 2010 Ryder Cup at Celtic Manor.*

DAY ONE

CAPTAINS

Europe: Colin Montgomerie   **USA:** Corey Pavin

FRIDAY MORNING FOURBALLS

Westwood/Kaymer *beat* **Mickelson/D. Johnson**, *3 and 2*

McIlroy/McDowell *halved with* **Cink/Kuchar**

Poulter/Fisher *lost to* **Stricker/Woods** *by two holes*

Donald/Harrington *lost to* **Watson/Overton**, *3 and 2*

Session Score: 1.5-2.5

Overall Score: Europe 1.5, USA 2.5

> **"** *Quite simply, Lee Westwood is my top-ranked player and has proved it – simple as that. He's been unbelievable – in the team room, in the locker room, on the range, on the course.* **"**

Colin Montgomerie hails his star man

LEFT: *Martin Kaymer lines up a putt with European team-mate Lee Westwood (right) during the morning Fourballs.*

Cup form as the US won the singles 7-5 in a mammoth effort. But having taken a three-point lead into the final day, this was still enough – just – for Europe to end the Ryder Cup's first-ever Monday session as victors. "This is crazy," declared an exhausted, yet relieved and ecstatic McDowell. "I have never felt as nervous in my life. I was trying to do it for 11 team-mates, for all the fans, for the caddies, for Europe and for Monty – and we were all trying to win it for Seve, too."

He was, of course, referring to Europe's greatest Ryder Cup talisman of all – Severiano Ballesteros, who had missed the drama at Celtic Manor as he recovered from an operation to remove a brain tumour. Tragically, just seven months later, the esteemed Spaniard lost his battle with illness and passed away, although he left his Ryder Cup successors with a message to remember. "The whole team spoke to Seve for about 10 minutes on speakerphone and that was very motivational, very passionate and also very sad to hear him, to hear the way he is," Montgomerie recounted. "It was a real inspiration, especially for the rookies in the team, to speak to Seve and have Seve speak to them."

Not even Seve could have said anything to prepare the players for the conditions greeting them when the action finally got underway, though. Already it was raining when Dustin Johnson hit the first driver of the day and within two hours the downpour was so bad that play was suspended, with Europe up in three out of four matches. Eventually, play was resumed in the late afternoon. "I'm disappointed for everyone connected with the Ryder Cup here at Celtic Manor," said Lee Westwood, who, partnering Martin Kaymer, was two-up after five against Johnson/Mickelson. "Ten years of planning have gone into this."

Play began again at 5 p.m. and perhaps the break did the Americans good because although no Fourballs were completed by the end of the day, the position certainly looked different, with the holders up in two and all square in another. Only Westwood and Kaymer maintained their advantage for Europe, with Stewart Cink and Matt Kuchar leading Rory McIlroy and McDowell, and Bubba Watson and Jeff Overton up on Padraig Harrington and Luke Donald. Meanwhile, Ian Poulter and Ross Fisher tied with Tiger Woods and Steve Stricker.

With so much time lost on the first day, the Ryder Cup organizers had some tough calls to make as to how to proceed on Day Two at Celtic Manor and the decision was made to unveil an altered format. Naturally, this added to the feeling that something new and unusual was taking place in Wales.

The opening Fourballs would be completed in the morning but the second session would consist of six Foursomes, not four, followed by two Foursomes and four Fourballs later that day, with all 12 singles set to be played on the Sunday. At least that was the plan, rain permitting. The marathon of golf began with Westwood and Kaymer winning the first point of the day, beating Mickelson/Johnson, 3 and 2. Following this, McDowell and McIlroy recovered from two-down to earn a half against Cink/Kuchar. But the US were quickly back in the points: Overton/Watson beat Donald/Harrington, 3 and 2, before Woods/Stricker won two-up against Poulter/Fisher. Those victories gave the holders a 2.5-1.5 lead, which became 6-4 after the extended Foursomes.

Zach Johnson and Mahan got the US off to the perfect start in the revised second session with a two-up victory over the Molinari brothers. The Italians did provide a fight-back, though, levelling by the 16th having been behind since the 6th, but Johnson's huge putt on the 17th green broke their resolve and proved to be one of the most important shots of the day. Europe briefly hit back through Ross Fisher and Irishman Harrington, who ended a run of 10 Cup games without a victory to win, 3 and 2,against Mickelson and Dustin Johnson. But an impressive-looking Woods and Stricker – who went out in 32 – extended the US lead with a thumping 4 and 3 win over Miguel Angel Jiménez and Peter Hanson before Westwood and Kaymer halved with Furyk and Fowler.

Once again there was a silver lining for the Americans, who won the 18th to share the spoils, having been behind all match – with rookie Fowler, just 21 years old, calmly putting from four feet after a wonderful chip from his playing partner. "We were down most of the day, so to come back and get a point is big for the team,"

SHOT OF THE DAY

Luke Donald's brilliant tee-shot at the 17th in a second-session Foursomes match against Bubba Watson and Jeff Overton showed a touch of pure class. It landed just three feet from the pin, helping to guarantee a 2 and 1 victory.

RIGHT: *Tiger Woods watches the action on the 13th green after losing his Foursomes match to Lee Westwood and Luke Donald.*

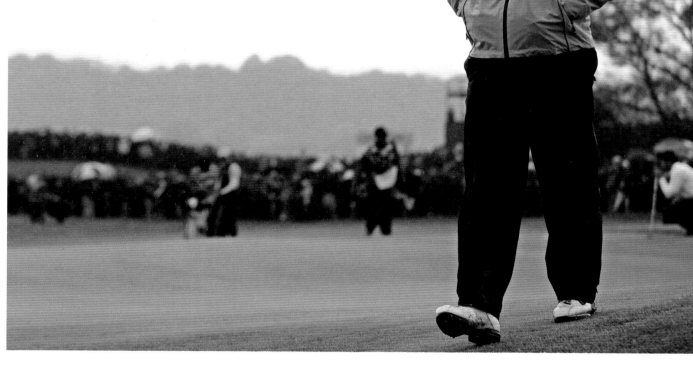

said Furyk. Soon, the action came thick and fast, with Poulter and Donald again on form as they came from behind to win, 2 and 1, against rookies Watson and Overton. However a one-up win for Cink/Kuchar over McIlroy/McDowell put the States firmly in control.

So much golf had already been played but it was clear that the programme would never be completed before the sun went down. It was vital for Europe to at least begin a fight-back and that's exactly what they managed to do after a pep talk from captain Colin Montgomerie (more passionate rant than tactical analysis, he later admitted). Whatever he said, it worked and with two Foursomes and four Fourballs on course at the same time, the scoreboard was completely blue by the end of the day; Europe up in all six matches. Westwood and Donald led the way, storming to four-up against Woods and Stricker, with nine to play and leaving the home crowd in a constant state of fervour.

McDowell and Rory McIlroy, the effervescent Irish rookie lapping up his first Ryder Cup, were also three-up on Zach Johnson and Mahan after seven holes and the sense of elation in the Europe camp was obvious. "It's been a superb session from the moment we set off," said Montgomerie. "It's been a very important two hours of play and we've come through it with flying colours. The job is half done, we've got to keep going and maintain this momentum on Sunday." As for the Americans, they were just glad to see the sun go down.

DAY TWO

SESSION TWO FOURSOMES

Jiménez/Hanson *lost to* **Woods/Stricker,** *4 and 3*

E. Molinari/F. Molinari *lost to* **Z. Johnson/Mahan** *by two holes*

Westwood/Kaymer *halved with* **Furyk/Fowler**

Harrington/Fisher *beat* **Mickelson/D. Johnson,** *3 and 2*

Poulter/Donald *beat* **Watson/Overton,** *2 and 1*

McDowell/McIlroy *lost to* **Cink/Kuchar** *by one hole*

Session Score: 2.5-3.5

SESSION THREE FOURSOMES

Donald/Westwood *beat* **Striker/Woods,** *6 and 5*

McDowell/McIlroy *beat* **Z. Johnson/Mahan,** *3 and 1*

Session Score: 2-0

SESSION THREE FOURBALLS

Harrington/Fisher *beat* **Furyk/D. Johnson,** *2 and 1*

Hanson/Jiménez *beat* **Watson/Overton** *by two holes*

E. Molinari/F. Molinari *halved with* **Cink/Kuchar**

Poulter/Kaymer *beat* **Mickelson/Fowler,** *2 and 1*

Session Score: 3.5-0.5

Overall Score: Europe 9.5, USA 6.5

> **"** *I'd say it wasn't a bad thing that it got dark.* **"**

Corey Pavin comments on the US position

ABOVE: *Rory McIlroy of Europe celebrates after team-mate Graeme McDowell holes a putt on the 15th green.*

Something new for the Ryder Cup: Day Three of the 2010 competition arrived with no singles in sight and rain very much in view. Sunday was meant to be the day when the Cup was won but instead play was delayed until 1.30 p.m. and everyone knew they were heading towards a Monday finale for the first time in the competition's 83-year history. Even so, there was joy for Europe as they completed a storming session to go from 6-4 down overnight to 9.5-6.5 ahead. The Foursomes pairings of Donald/Westwood and McIlroy/McDowell gave Monty the start he had dreamt of before Harrington/Fisher, Jiménez/Hanson and Kamyer/Poulter added victories in the Fourballs. The only blot on a perfect copybook was a halved match between the Molinari brothers against Cink/Kuchar. Even so, it probably felt like a victory after the Italians came from behind, with Francesco Molinari admirably holding his nerve on the 18th to earn a tie.

There were some unwelcome landmarks for the US, including Tiger Woods' heaviest-ever Ryder Cup defeat: he and Stricker were crushed, 6 and 5, by Westwood/Donald. A 35-foot putt by Westwood at the 10th summed up European superiority. Then there was Phil Mickelson, who now has more Ryder Cup defeats than any other American (17 in 34), after he and Fowler were beaten by Poulter/Kaymer.

For Montgomerie, who has never won a Major though he is a true Ryder Cup legend, the events of the afternoon were mind-blowing. "It's incredible what has just happened out there," he said. And things got even better on the Monday when Europe found themselves up in seven of the 12 singles matches by noon. Team USA refused to give up, with Stricker making four birdies in a row against Westwood to begin a stirring comeback. When Westwood found the water with his tee-shot on the 13th, he knew it was over. Dustin Johnson then recorded a crushing 6 and 4 win over Kaymer for his first point before Poulter, Europe's top points scorer, settled European nerves in winning, 5 and 4, against Kuchar. During the tie he produced a wonderful chip-in from the fairway on the 11th. Donald was equally impressive against Furyk, securing victory at the 18th, while Jiménez won his first Ryder Cup singles at the fourth attempt when he beat Bubba Watson, 4 and 3 – including a chip that found the hole direct from a bunker on the 8th. But the Americans somehow found a footing in the match through a combination of old and new: Rookie Overton coming from behind to beat Ross Fisher, 3 and 2, before a revitalized Woods beat Francesco Molinari.

Tiger Woods' performance was one of his best ever in the Ryder Cup, finishing eight under par for his last 10 holes. His round included an eagle on the 12th and a genius 50-foot putt at 13. Such great form must have inspired Phil Mickelson, too, because he finally earned himself a point by beating Peter Hanson, while Zach Johnson cruised past Harrington to leave the score 13-11 to Europe.

The hosts were relying on Edoardo Molinari and McDowell to reach the 14.5 points needed for victory, especially as the Italian was three-up on Fowler, with three to play. Astonishingly, Fowler fought back and stole a half at the 18th, rolling in a 20-foot putt that had the Americans celebrating. All eyes were now on McDowell v Mahan and the shot that effectively secured the Ryder Cup came at the 16th. The Portrush player had just lost the 15th and found himself only one-up, having led by three.

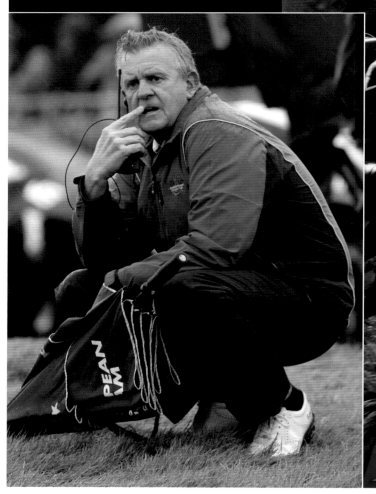

RIGHT: *Graeme McDowell (blue sweater, back to camera) is mobbed by team-mates, caddies and fans at the 17th after winning the trophy for Europe.*

BELOW: *Europe team captain Colin Montgomerie waits nervously as the 2010 Ryder Cup starts to hot up.*

> " *There is nothing like Monty – he is the Ryder Cup for Europe, and to do that for him today was very special.* "

Graeme McDowell on his captain

At this stage the pressure must have been unbearable but he recovered his nerve to land a nail-biting 15-foot birdie putt at the very next hole and extend his lead. That one shot broke Mahan's spirit and when the American conceded at the 17th, he collapsed in tears as Europe celebrated what had turned out to be an exhausting, yet exhilarating victory.

Colin Montgomerie was in dreamland: "It's a very proud moment for us all here in Europe. We all played to a man magnificently, we all gave a 110 per cent, and that's all I could ask." In the end the rain might have teemed down but Europe reigned. Naturally, all eyes would now turn to the Medinah Country Club for the next instalment, with the Americans no doubt hoping for sunshine.

DAYS THREE AND FOUR

FINAL SINGLES

Lee Westwood *lost to* **Steve Stricker,** *2 and 1*

Rory McIlroy *halved with* **Stewart Cink**

Luke Donald *beat* **Jim Furyk** *by one hole*

Martin Kaymer *lost to* **Dustin Johnson,** *6 and 4*

Ian Poulter *beat* **Matt Kuchar,** *5 and 4*

Ross Fisher *lost to* **Jeff Overton,** *3 and 2*

Miguel Angel Jiménez *beat* **Bubba Watson,** *4 and 3*

Francesco Molinari *lost to* **Tiger Woods,** *4 and 3*

Edoardo Molinari *halved with* **Rickie Fowler**

Peter Hanson *lost to* **Phil Mickelson,** *4 and 2*

Padraig Harrington *lost to* **Zach Johnson,** *3 and 2*

Graeme McDowell *beat* **Hunter Mahan,** *3 and 1*

Session Score: 5-7

Overall Score: Europe 14.5, USA 13.5

RIGHT: *Rory McIlroy (left)
and Graeme McDowell talk
tactics as McDowell lines
up a putt during a Fourballs
match at Celtic Manor
in 2010.*

Ryder Cup legends
Rory **McILROY**
and Graeme **McDOWELL**

They might be young in Ryder Cup terms, but the Northern Irish pairing of Graeme McDowell and Rory McIlroy – "G-Mac" and "Little-Mac", as they have become known – has already made its mark on the tournament. Good friends off the course, as well as rivals and occasional partners on it, the pair played a big part in winning the 2010 Ryder Cup for Europe. So, what is it about Irish and Northern Irish golfers when it comes to Ryder Cup drama?

Whenever Europe needs a hero, it seems an Irishman steps up. Darren Clarke's emotional and inspirational performance of 2006 springs to mind, as does the match-winning performances of Eamonn Darcy at Muirfield Village (1987), Christy O'Connor Jnr. at The Belfry (1989), Philip Walton at Oak Hill (1995) and Paul McGinley at The Belfry (2002). Now there are two more heroes on board in the shape of 22-year-old prodigy McIlroy and McDowell, senior of the two by 10 years.

McDowell already had a reputation for being a man with nerves of steel before he linked up with his fellow countryman at Celtic Manor. He had made one previous Ryder Cup appearance (2008), winning 2.5 points, and going into the 2010 tournament, he was the reigning US Open champion. Significantly, he had also won the Welsh Open at Celtic Manor in June, shortly before his US Open win at Pebble Beach, where he became the first Northern Irishman to win the title and the first European to win since Tony Jacklin in 1970. He was also the first UK winner of a Major in 11 years, holding his nerve in difficult conditions to secure the title. Following this, he immediately promised McIlroy that they would make a great Ryder Cup pairing – and he was proved right.

McDowell and McIlroy were chosen by captain Colin Montgomerie as the second of his four Fourball pairings on the opening Friday of the 2010 Ryder Cup when they were up against Stewart Cink and Matt Kuchar. In sodden conditions, play had to be suspended after just four holes and the day ended with the Americans two-up after 11. When the match resumed early the next morning, the Europeans stormed back to salvage a crucial half. Though the friends lost to the same pair in the Foursomes, they returned to beat Zach Johnson and Hunter Mahan later that day, winning the first hole and never looking back as they won, 3 and 1.

The effervescent McIlroy was now revelling in the atmosphere, geeing up the crowd at every opportunity and playing the showman. Indeed, the only shame with Europe three points ahead going into the singles was that he and his friend now had to be split up! McIlroy faced Stewart Cink in the second singles game, while McDowell was given responsibility for closing out the match. This proved a wise decision: already McDowell had shown the composure needed to handle the pressure of winning just a few months earlier, overtaking final-day leader Dustin Johnson to seize the US Open.

Perhaps he was always destined for Ryder Cup action. Having won Ulster schoolboy titles, McDowell went on to a golf scholarship at the University of Alabama, Birmingham, USA. As a teenager, he won numerous college events. He also represented Great Britain and Ireland in the successful 2001 Walker Cup side and when he turned professional in 2002, he divided his time between the US and European tours. With this experience under his belt, he already knew how to beat the Americans and was in control from the start against Mahan.

McIlroy had to settle for a half with Cink but it was still a satisfactory debut for the youngster from Holywood (Ireland, rather than California), who had been tipped for stardom since his father Gerry introduced him to the rudiments of golf as a toddler. In many ways, McIlroy resembled a British Tiger Woods. Schooled from a young age by his father, with his prodigious talent he was soon winning tournaments. He represented Europe in the Junior Ryder Cup and also played against America in the amateur Walker Cup, so he understood what team play was all about. He had also made his mark on the European Tour – starting at 16, turning pro at 17 and winning his first event at 19. By the time he was 20, he was in the world's Top 10 (reaching No. 1 in March 2012 as the reigning US Open champion) and so it came as no surprise that he ended his first Ryder Cup with a commendable two out of four points.

It was McDowell who was to steal the limelight, though, winning the point that secured the Ryder Cup, thanks to a stunning birdie putt at the 16th and Mahan's ultimate concession on the 17th green, leaving Europe to claim a glorious victory. It seems highly likely this will not be the last time that McDowell and McIlroy celebrate together for the Irish legacy appears to be in good hands.

> **"***I'm going to miss him tomorrow.***"**
>
> *Graeme McDowell muses on playing the 2010 singles without his partner Rory McIlroy*

RYDER CUP
OFFICIAL
SOUVENIR PROGRAMME

PRICE 1/-

THE FOURTH INTERNATIONAL GOLF MATCH
GREAT BRITAIN *versus* THE UNITED STATES OF AMERICA
TO BE PLAYED ON THE SOUTHPORT AND AINSDALE COURSE,
SOUTHPORT
ON MONDAY AND TUESDAY, JUNE 26-27, 1933

This Official Programme is published by the Professional Golfers' Association and the proceeds will be devoted
to the British Ryder Cup Fund.

Ryder Cup Records
Complete Ryder Cup Listings

2010, October 1-4
Celtic Manor Resort, Newport, Wales.
Captains: Colin Montgomerie (Europe), Corey Pavin (USA)
Europe 14.5 - USA 13.5

2008, September 19-21
Valhalla Golf Club, Louisville, Kentucky, USA.
Captains: Paul Azinger (USA), Nick Faldo (Europe)
USA 16.5 - Europe 11.5

2006, September 22-24
The K Club, Straffan, County Kildare, Ireland.
Captains: Ian Woosnam (Europe), Tom Lehman (USA)
Europe 18.5 - USA 9.5

2004, September 17-19
Oakland Hills Country Club, Bloomfield Township, Michigan, USA.
Captains: Hal Sutton (USA), Bernhard Langer (Europe)
USA 9.5 - Europe 18.5

2002, September 27-29
The Belfry, Wishaw, Warwickshire, England.
Captains: Sam Torrance (Europe), Curtis Strange (USA)
Europe 15.5 - USA 12.5

1999, September 24-26
The Country Club, Brookline, Massachusetts, USA.
Captains: Ben Crenshaw (USA), Matt James (Europe)
USA 14.5 - Europe 13.5

1997, September 26-28
Valderrama Golf Club, Sotogrande, Spain.
Captains: Severiano Ballesteros (Europe), Tom Kite (USA)
Europe 14.5 - USA 13.5

1995, September 22-24
Oak Hill Country Club, Pittsford, New York, USA.
Captains: Lanny Wadkins (USA), Bernard Gallacher (Europe)
USA 13.5 - Europe 14.5

1993, September 24-26
The Belfry, Wishaw, Warwickshire, England.
Captains: Bernard Gallacher (Europe), Tom Watson (USA)
Europe 13 - USA 15

1991, September 27-29
Kiawah Island Golf Resort, Kiawah Island, South Carolina, USA.
Captains: Dave Stockton (USA), Bernard Gallacher (Europe)
USA 14.5 - Europe 13.5

1989, September 22-24
The Belfry, Wishaw, Warwickshire, England.
Captains: Tony Jacklin (Europe), Raymond Floyd (USA)
Europe 14 - USA 14

1987, September 25-27
Muirfield Village, Dublin, Ohio, USA.
Captains: Jack Nicklaus (USA), Tony Jacklin (Europe)
USA 13 - Europe 15

1985, September 13-15
The Belfry, Wishaw, Warwickshire, England.
Captains: Tony Jacklin (Europe), Lee Trevino (USA)
Europe 16.5 - USA 11.5

1983, October 14-16
PGA National Golf Club, Palm Beach Gardens, Florida, USA.
Captains: Jack Nicklaus (USA), Tony Jacklin (Europe)
USA 14.5 - Europe 13.5

1981, September 18-20
Walton Heath Golf Club, Surrey, England.
Captains: John Jacobs (Europe), Dave Marr (USA)
Europe 9.5 - USA 18.5

1979, September 14-16
The Greenbrier Course, White Sulphur Springs, West Virginia, USA.
Captains: Billy Casper (USA), John Jacobs (Europe)
USA 17 - Europe 11

1977, September 15-17
Royal Lytham & St Annes Golf Club, Lytham St Annes, England.
Captains: Brian Huggett (GB&I), Dow Finsterwald (USA)
Great Britain & Ireland 7.5 - USA 12.5

1975, September 19-21
Laurel Valley Golf Club, Ligonier, Pennsylvania, USA.
Captains: Arnold Palmer (USA), Bernard Hunt (GB&I)
USA 21 - Great Britain & Ireland 11

1973, September 20-22
Muirfield, East Lothian, Scotland.
Captains: Bernard Hunt (GB&I), Jack Burke Jnr. (USA)
Great Britain & Ireland 13 - USA 19

1971, September 16-18
Old Warson Country Club, St. Louis, Missouri, USA.
Captains: Jay Hebert (USA), Eric Brown (Great Britain)
USA 18.5 - Great Britain 13.5

1969, September 18-20
Royal Birkdale Golf Club, Southport, England.
Captains: Eric Brown (Great Britain), Sam Snead (USA)
Great Britain 16 - USA 16

1967, October 20-22
Champions Golf Club, Houston, Texas, USA.
Captains: Ben Hogan (USA), Dai Rees (Great Britain)
USA 23.5 - Great Britain 8.5

Ryder Cup Records

1965, October 7-9
Royal Birkdale Golf Club, Southport, Merseyside, England
Captains: Harry Weetman (Great Britain), Byron Nelson (USA)
Great Britain 12.5 - USA 19.5

1963, October 11-13
Atlanta Athletic Club, Atlanta, Georgia, USA.
Captains: Arnold Palmer (USA), John Fallon (Great Britain)
USA 23 - Great Britain 9

1961, October 13-14
Royal Lytham & St Annes Golf Club, Lytham St Annes, England.
Captains: Dai Rees (Great Britain), Jerry Barber (USA)
Great Britain 9.5 - USA 14.5

1959, November 6-7
Eldorado Golf Club, Indian Wells, California, USA.
Captains: Sam Snead (USA), Dai Rees (Great Britain)
USA 8.5 - Great Britain 3.5

1957, October 4-5
Lindrick Golf Club, Rotherham, South Yorkshire, England.
Captains: Dai Rees (Great Britain), Jack Burke, Jr. (USA)
Great Britain 7.5 - USA 4.5

1955, November 5-6
Thunderbird Country Club, Rancho Mirage, California, USA.
Captains: Chick Harbert (USA), Dai Rees (Great Britain)
USA 8 - Great Britain 4

1953, October 2-3
Wentworth Golf Club, Surrey, England.
Captains: Henry Cotton (Great Britain), Lloyd Mangrum (USA)
Great Britain 5.5 - USA 6.5

1951, November 2-4
Pinehurst Resort, Pinehurst, North Carolina, USA.
Captains: Sam Snead (USA), Arthur Lacey (Great Britain)
USA 9.5 - Great Britain 2.5

1949, September 16-17
Ganton Golf Club, Scarborough, North Yorkshire, England.
Captains: Charles Whitcombe (Great Britain), Ben Hogan (USA)
Great Britain 5 - USA 7

1947, November 1-2
Portland Golf Club, Portland, Oregon, USA.
Captains: Ben Hogan (USA), Henry Cotton (Great Britain)
USA 11 - Great Britain 1

1937, June 29-30
Southport & Ainsdale Golf Club, Southport, England.
Captains: Charleis Whitcombe (Great Britain), Walter Hagen (USA)
Great Britain 4 - USA 8

1935, September 28-29
Ridgewood Country Club, Paramus, New Jersey, USA.
Captains: Walter Hagen (USA), Charles Whitcombe (Great Britain)
USA 9 - Great Britain 3

1933, June 26-27
Southport & Ainsdale Golf Club, Southport, England.
Captains: John Henry Taylor (Great Britain), Walter Hagen (USA)
Great Britain 6.5 - USA 5.5

1931, June 26-27
Scioto Country Club, Columbus, Ohio, USA.
Captains: Walter Hagen (USA), Charles Whitcombe (Great Britain)
USA 9 - Great Britain 3

1929, April 26-27
Moortown Golf Club, Leeds, West Yorkshire, England.
Captains: George Duncan (Great Britain), Walter Hagen (USA)
Great Britain 7 - USA 5

1927, June 3-4
Worcester Country Club, Worcester, Massachusetts, USA.
Captains: Walter Hagen (USA), Ted Ray (Great Britain)
USA 9.5 - Great Britain 2.5

Ryder Cup Points

Total Ryder Cup points (1927-2010) - USA and GB&I/Europe
USA - 489.5
GB&I/Europe - 382.5

Total Ryder Cup points (1927-1977) - USA and GB&I
USA - 268.5
GB&I - 155.5

Total Ryder Cup points (1979-2010) - USA and Europe
USA - 221
Europe - 227

Wins Records

Number of Ryder Cup matches won
USA - 25 wins
Europe - 11 wins (8 as Europe, 3 as GB&I)
Tied - 2

Largest Ryder Cup winning margins
USA
15 -   23.5-8.5 in 1967 (Champions GC, USA)
14 -   23-9 in 1963 (Atlanta Athletic Club, USA)
10 -   11-1 in 1947 (Portland GC, USA);
         21-11 in 1975 (Laurel Valley GC, USA)
GB&I/Europe
 9 -   18.5-9.5 in 2004 (Oakland Hills CC, USA);
         18.5-9.5 in 2006 (The K Club, Ireland)
 5 -   16.5-11.5 in 1985 (The Belfry, England)
 3 -   7.5-4.5 in 1957 (Lindrick GC, England);
         15.5-12.5 in 2002 (The Belfry, England)

Most consecutive Ryder Cup victories
USA - 7 - 1935-1955
Europe - 3 - 2002-2006

Ryder Cup Singles Results 1979-2010

Year	USA	Europe
1979	8.5	3.5
1981	8	4
1983	6.5	5.5
1985	4.5	7.5
1987	7.5	4.5
1989	7	5
1991	6.5	5.5
1993	7.5	4.5
1995	4.5	7.5
1997	8	4
1999	8	3.5
2002	4.5	7.5
2004	4.5	7.5
2006	3.5	8.5
2008	7.5	4.5
2010	7	5

PLAYER STATISTICS

Most appearances

Sir Nick Faldo - 11 (GB&I/Europe)
Bernhard Langer - 10 (GB&I/Europe)
Christy O'Connor Snr. - 10 (GB&I/Europe)
Dai Rees - 9 (GB&I/Europe)
Peter Alliss - 8 (GB&I/Europe)
Severiano Ballesteros - 8 (GB&I/Europe)
Billy Casper - 8 (USA)
Neil Coles - 8 (GB&I/Europe)
Raymond Floyd - 8 (USA)
Bernard Gallacher - 8 (GB&I/Europe)
Bernard Hunt - 8 (GB&I/Europe)
Phil Mickelson - 8 (USA)
Colin Montgomerie - 8 (GB&I/Europe)
Sam Torrance - 8 (GB&I/Europe)
Lanny Wadkins - 8 (USA)
Ian Woosnam - 8 (GB&I/Europe)

Most overall matches played

Sir Nick Faldo - 46 (GB&I/Europe)
Bernhard Langer - 42 (GB&I/Europe)
Neil Coles - 40 (GB&I/Europe)
Severiano Ballesteros - 37 (GB&I/Europe)
Billy Casper - 37 (USA)
Christy O'Connor Snr. - 36 (GB&I/Europe)
Colin Montgomerie - 36 (GB&I/Europe)
Tony Jacklin - 35 (GB&I/Europe)
Lanny Wadkins - 34 (USA)
Phil Mickelson - 34 (USA)

Most overall matches won

Sir Nick Faldo - 23 (GB&I/Europe)
Arnold Palmer - 22 (USA)
Bernhard Langer - 21 (GB&I/Europe)
Severiano Ballesteros - 20 (GB&I/Europe)
Billy Casper - 20 (USA)
Colin Montgomerie - 20 (GB&I/Europe)

Lanny Wadkins - 20 (USA)
José María Olazábal - 18 (GB&I/Europe)
Jack Nicklaus - 17 (USA)
Lee Trevino - 17 (USA)
Lee Westwood - 16 (GB&I/Europe)

Most overall matches halved

Gene Littler - 8 (USA)
Tony Jacklin - 8 (GB&I/Europe)
Billy Casper - 7 (USA)
Stewart Cink - 7 (USA)
Neil Coles - 7 (GB&I/Europe)
Colin Montgomerie - 7 (GB&I/Europe)

Eight players who have halved six matches overall:

Brian Huggett - 6 (GB&I/Europe)
Bernard Hunt - 6 (GB&I/Europe)
Bernhard Langer - 6 (GB&I/Europe)
Justin Leonard - 6 (USA)
Phil Mickelson - 6 (USA)
Sam Torrance - 6 (GB&I/Europe)
Lee Trevino - 6 (USA)
Lee Westwood - 6 (GB&I/Europe)

Most overall points won

Sir Nick Faldo - 25 (GB&I/Europe)
Bernhard Langer - 24 (GB&I/Europe)
Billy Casper - 23.5 (USA)
Colin Montgomerie - 23.5 (GB&I/Europe)
Arnold Palmer - 23 (USA)
Severiano Ballesteros - 22.5 (GB&I/Europe)
Lanny Wadkins - 21.5 (USA)
José María Olazábal - 20.5 (GB&I/Europe)
Lee Trevino - 20 (USA)
Lee Westwood - 19 (GB&I/Europe)

Most Singles matches played

Neil Coles - 15 (GB&I/Europe)
Christy O'Connor - 14 (GB&I/Europe)
Peter Alliss - 12 (GB&I/Europe)
Sir Nick Faldo - 11 (GB&I/Europe)
Bernard Gallacher - 11 (GB&I/Europe)
Arnold Palmer - 11 (USA)
Tony Jacklin - 11 (GB&I/Europe)

Eight players who have played 10 Singles matches:

Brian Barnes - 10 (GB&I/Europe)
Billy Casper - 10 (USA)
Bernard Hunt - 10 (GB&I/Europe)
Bernhard Langer - 10 (GB&I/Europe)
Gene Littler - 10 (USA)
Jack Nicklaus - 10 (USA)
Dai Rees - 10 (GB&I/Europe)
Lee Trevino - 10 (USA)

Most Singles matches won

Billy Casper - 6 (USA)
Sir Nick Faldo - 6 (GB&I/Europe)
Colin Montgomerie - 6 (GB&I/Europe)

Ryder Cup Records

Peter Oosterhuis - 6 (GB&I/Europe)
Arnold Palmer - 6 (USA)
Sam Snead - 6 (USA)
Lee Trevino - 6 (USA)
Peter Alliss - 5 (GB&I/Europe)
Brian Barnes - 5 (GB&I/Europe)
Neil Coles - 5 (GB&I/Europe)
Gene Littler - 5 (USA)
Dai Rees - 5 (GB&I/Europe)
Tom Kite - 5 (USA)

Most Foursomes matches played

Sir Nick Faldo - 18 (GB&I/Europe)
Bernhard Langer - 18 (GB&I/Europe)
Lanny Wadkins - 15 (USA)
Billy Casper - 15 (USA)
Severiano Ballesteros - 14 (GB&I/Europe)
Colin Montgomerie - 14 (GB&I/Europe)
Neil Coles - 13 (GB&I/Europe)
Tony Jacklin - 13 (GB&I/Europe)
Tom Kite - 13 (USA)
Christy O'Connor Snr. - 13 (GB&I/Europe)
Lee Westwood - 13 (GB&I/Europe)

Most Foursomes matches won

Bernhard Langer - 11 (GB&I/Europe)
Severiano Ballesteros - 10 (GB&I/Europe)
Sir Nick Faldo - 10 (GB&I/Europe)
Lanny Wadkins - 9 (USA)
Arnold Palmer - 9 (USA)
Billy Casper - 8 (USA)
Sergio Garcia - 8 (USA)
Colin Montgomerie - 8 (USA)
Jack Nicklaus - 8 (USA)
Tony Jacklin - 8 (USA)

Most Foursomes points won

Bernhard Langer - 11.5 (GB&I/Europe)
Sir Nick Faldo - 11 (GB&I/Europe)
Severiano Ballesteros - 10.5 (GB&I/Europe)
Tony Jacklin - 10 (GB&I/Europe)
Colin Montgomerie - 9.5 (GB&I/Europe)
Billy Casper - 9 (USA)
Arnold Palmer - 9 (USA)
Lanny Wadkins - 9 (USA)
Lee Westwood - 9 (GB&I/Europe)
Sergio García - 8.5 (GB&I/Europe)

Most Fourballs matches played

Sir Nick Faldo - 17 (GB&I/Europe)
Severiano Ballesteros - 15 (GB&I/Europe)
Phil Mickelson - 15 (USA)
Bernhard Langer - 14 (GB&I/Europe)
Colin Montgomerie - 14 (GB&I/Europe)
José María Olazábal - 14 (GB&I/Europe)
Ian Woosnam - 14 (GB&I/Europe)
Lee Westwood - 13 (GB&I/Europe)
Billy Casper - 12 (USA)
Neil Coles - 12 (GB&I/Europe)

Most Fourballs matches won

Ian Woosnam - 10 (GB&I/Europe)
José María Olazábal - 9 (GB&I/Europe)
Severiano Ballesteros - 8 (GB&I/Europe)
Nick Faldo - 7 (GB&I/Europe)
Arnold Palmer - 7 (USA)
Lanny Wadkins - 7 (USA)
Lee Westwood - 7 (GB&I/Europe)
Billy Casper - 6 (USA)
Darren Clarke - 6 (GB&I/Europe)
Bernhard Langer - 6 (GB&I/Europe)
Colin Montgomerie - 6 (GB&I/Europe)
Lee Trevino - 6 (USA)

RYDER CUP STREAKS

Players who have played five matches without losing
Jimmy Demaret (USA) 6-0-0
Bobby Nichols (USA) 4-0-1

Ryder Cup teams winning all points in a series
Foursomes
USA 1947, 4-0
USA 1975 second series, 4-0
USA 1981 second series , 4-0

Fourballs
USA 1967 first series, 4-0
USA 1971 first series, 4-0
Europe 1987 first series, 4-0
Europe 1989 first series, 4-0

Singles
No side has ever won all the singles matches

Players who have played five matches without winning
Alf Padgham (GB&I), 0-7-0
Tom Haliburton (GB& I) 0-6-0
John Panton (GB& I) 0-5-0

MARGINS OF VICTORY

Largest margin of victory - Singles
36-Hole Match
George Duncan, GB&I, def. Walter Hagen, USA, 10 and 8, 1929

18-Hole Match
Tom Kite, USA, def. Howard Clark, Europe, 8 and 7, 1989
Fred Couples, USA, def. Ian Woosnam, Europe, 8 and 7, 1997

Largest margin of victory - Foursomes
36-Hole Match
Hagen/Shute, USA, def. Duncan/Havers, Great Britain, 10 and 9, 1931
Worsham/Oliver, USA, def. Cotton/Lees, Great Britain, 10 and 9, 1947

18-Hole Match
Irwin/Kite, USA, def. Brown/Smyth, Europe, 7 and 6, 1979
Azinger/O'Meara, USA, def. Faldo/Gilford, Europe, 7 and 6, 1991

Largest Margin of Victory – Fourballs
18-Hole Match
Trevino/Pate, USA, def. Faldo/Torrance, Europe, 7 and 5, 1981

POINTS EARNED

Partnerships with most points earned
Severiano Ballesteros/José María Olazábal (Europe) 12 points (11-2-2)
Sir Nick Faldo/Ian Woosnam (Europe) 6 points (5-2-2)
Darren Clarke/Lee Westwood (Europe) 6 points (6-2-0)
Bernhard Langer/Colin Montgomerie (Europe) 5.5 points (5-1-1)
Bernard Gallacher/Brian Barnes (GB&I) 5.5 points (5-4-1)
Peter Alliss/Christy O'Connor Snr. (GB&I) 5.5 points (5-6-1)
Arnold Palmer/Gardner Dickinson (USA) 5 points (5-0-0)
Sergio García/Lee Westwood (Europe) 4.5 points (4-1-1)
Jack Nicklaus/Tom Watson (USA) 4 points (4-0-0)
Larry Nelson/Lanny Wadkins (USA) 4 points (4-2-0)
Peter Oosterhuis/Tony Jacklin (GB&I) 4 points (3-2-2)
Peter Oosterhuis/Nick Faldo (GB&I) 4 points (4-2-0)

Most points earned by one player in a single Ryder Cup
Gardner Dickinson (USA), 1967, 5 points (out of 5)
Arnold Palmer (USA) 1967, 5 points (out of 5)
Larry Nelson (USA), 1979, 5 points (out of 5)
Peter Alliss (GB&I), 1965, 5 points (out of 6)
Tony Jacklin (GB&I) 1969, 5 points (out of 6)

Ryder Cup holes-in-one
1973 (Muirfield) Peter Butler (GB&I) at the 16th hole, Day Two Foursomes Brian Barnes/Butler v Jack Nicklaus/Tom Weiskopf
1993 (The Belfry) Sir Nick Faldo (Europe) at the 14th, Final Day Singles v Paul Azinger
1995 (Oak Hill) Costatino Rocca (Europe) at the 6th, Day Two Foursomes Rocca/Sam Torrance v Davis Love III/Jeff Maggert
1995 (Oak Hill) Howard Clark (Europe) at the 11th, Final Day Singles v Peter Jacobsen
2006 (The K Club) Paul Casey (Europe) at the 14th, Day Two Foursomes Casey/David Howell v Stewart Cink/Zach Johnson
2006 (The K Club) Scott Verplank (USA) at the 14th, Final Day Singles v Padraig Harrington

---

COMEBACKS AND PERCENTAGES

Final Day winning comebacks
1929 Great Britain, from one point behind to win 7-5
1949 USA, from two points behind to win 7-5
1957 Great Britain, from two points behind to win 7.5-4.5
1995 Europe, from two points behind to win 14.5-13.5
1999 USA, from one point behind to win 14.5-13.5

Players with best percentage winning record (minimum 3 matches)
Europe
67 per cent José María Olazábal (P29 W18 L8 H3)
67 per cent Colin Montgomerie (P36 W21 L9 H6)
67 per cent Sergio García (P24 W14 L6 H4)

US
100 per cent Jimmy Demaret (P6 W6 L0 H0)
88 per cent Jack Burke Jnr. (P8 W7 L1 H0)
88 per cent Horton Smith (P4 W3 H1)
83 per cent Walter Hagen (P9 W7 L1 H1)
82 per cent J.C. Snead (P11 W9 L2 H0)
79 per cent Sam Snead (P13 W10 L2 H1)

AGE AND FAMILIES

Youngest and oldest captains
GB & I/Europe
Youngest: Charles Whitcombe 1931, 35 years 9 months, 5 days
Oldest: J.H. Taylor 1933, 62 years, 3 months, 7 days

Family members in the Ryder Cup
Brothers: Charles Whitcombe (1927-1929-1931-1933-1935-1937), Reg Whitcombe (1935) and Ernest Whitcombe (1929-1931-1935)
Bernard Hunt (1953-1957-1959-1961-1963-1965-1967-1969) and Geoffrey Hunt (1963)
Joe Turnesa (1927-1929) and Jim Turnesa (1953)
Jay Hebert (1959-1961) and Lionel Hebert (1957)

Brothers-in-Law: Jerry Pate (1981) and Bruce Lietzke (1981)
Cousins: Jack Burke Jr. (1951-1953-1955-1957-1959) and Dave Marr (1965)

Fathers and Sons: Percy Alliss (1929-1933-1935-1937) and Peter Alliss (1953-1957-1959-1961-1963-1965-1967-1969)
Antonio Garrido (1979) and Ignacio Garrido (1997)

Father-in-Law and Son-in-Law: Max Faulkner (1947-1949-1951-1953-1957) and Brian Barnes (1969-1971-1973-1975-1977-1979)

Uncles and Nephews: Christy O'Connor Snr. (1955-1957-1959-1961-1963-1965-1967-1969) and Christy O'Connor Jnr. (1975-1989)
Sam Snead (1937-1947-1949-1951-1953-1955-1959) and J.C. Snead (1971-1973-1975)
Bob Goalby (1963) and Jay Haas (1983-1995-2004)

Future Ryder Cup venues
2012 Medinah Country Club (Medinah, Illinois)
2014 Gleneagles Hotel (Auchterarder, Perth & Kinross, Scotland)
2016 Hazeltine National Golf Club (Chaska, Minnesota)
2018 Le Golf National (Saint-Quentin-en-Yvelines, France)
2020 Whistling Straits (Haven, Wisconsin)

Index

Credits

The publishers would like to thank the following sources for their kind permission to reproduce the pictures in this book.

Action Images: /Trevor Jones/Sporting Pictures: 105, 154-155

Colorsport: 92-93, 104; /Stewart Fraser: 106-107

Corbis: /Bettmann: 28, 29, 46-47, 61, 78

Getty Images: /Allsport: 8 right; /Jim Bourg: 3; /Simon Bruty: 122, 137, 152; /David Cannon: 6, 96-97, 114, 115, 116, 124-125, 126, 132, 142, 143, 146-147, 149, 164, 166, 200, 209; /Central Press: 20-21; /Central Press/Hulton Archive: 33; /Timothy A. Clary/AFP: 9 right, 185 right, 197; /Chris Cole: 141, 145; /J.D. Cuban: 148; /Adrian Dennis/AFP: 173, 176, 177, 189, 206; /Terry Disney/Central Press/Hulton Archive: 57; /Tony Duffy: 118-119; /Jacqueline Duvoisin/Sports Illustrated: 135; /Graham Finlayson/ Sports Illustrated: 102; /Fox Photos: 38; /Fox Photos/Hulton Archive: 44; /Stuart Franklin: 4-5; /J. Gaiger/Topical Press Agency: 16-17; /Sam Greenwood: 199, 207; /Haynes Archive/Popperfoto: 30-31; /Jeff Haynes/AFP: 165, 167; /Harry How: 190, 191; /Hulton Archive: 26, 36-37; /Rusty Jarrett: 136; /Craig Jones: 178-179; /Ross Kinnaird: 205; /Andy Lyons: 170-171; /Bob Martin: 103, 127; /Bob Martin/ Sports Illustrated: 169; /Edward Miller/Keystone/Hulton Archive: 58-59; /Donald Miralle: 184-185; / Brian Morgan: 99, 101, 108, 112-113; /Don Morley: 70-71, 87; /Stephen Munday: 130-131, 134, 138-139, 144, 159, 202-203; /Sven Nackstrand/AFP: 188, 193; /Dennis Oulds/Central Press/Hulton Archive: 81; / Popperfoto: 35, 64-65, 86, 150, 157, 158, 160, 168; /Andrew Redington: 175, 210-211; /Tim Sloan/AFP: 198; /Jamie Squire: 156, 172, 174, 180, 183, 186-187, 192, 194-195, 208; /Bob Thomas: 56, 63, 68, 75, 84, 88-89, 94, 121, 123, 128, 133, 140, 163; /Tony Tomsic/Sports Illustrated: 120; /Topical Press Agency: 42

Old Golf Images: 8 left, 9 left, 10-11, 12, 13, 14, 15, 18, 19, 22, 23, 24-25, 27, 32, 34, 39, 40, 41, 45, 50, 51, 52-53, 55, 62, 67, 69, 72, 95, 98, 100, 109, 110, 117, 129, 153, 161, 182, 196, 201, 204, 212

Press Association Images: 60, 74, 80, 82-83; /AP: 43, 48, 54, 73, 76-77, 79, 90, 91; /Elisa Amendola/ AP: 151; /Morry Gash/AP: 181; /Ross Kinnaird: 162; /S&G and Barratts: 85; /David F. Smith/AP: 66; / Kathy Willens/AP: 111

Topfoto.co.uk: 49

Every effort has been made to acknowledge correctly and contact the source and/or copyright holder of each picture and Carlton Books Limited apologises for any unintentional errors or omissions that will be corrected in future editions of this book.